BIRDS' NESTING

IN

INDIA.

BIRDS' NESTING

IN

INDIA.

A CALENDAR OF THE BREEDING SEASONS, AND A POPULAR GUIDE TO THE HABITS AND HAUNTS OF BIRDS.

CAPTAIN G. F. L. MARSHALL, R.E., F.Z.S

GYAN

Published by

Gyan Publishing House
5, Ansari Road
Daryaganj, New Delhi-110002
Phone: 011-47034999, 9811692060
E-mail: books@gyanbooks.com

Distribution Network
gyanbooks.com
India, USA, Canada, UK, Australia, France

ISBN: 978-81-212-8911-5 (PB)
First Published, 1877

2nd Impression 2023

Printed at: Gyan Press, Delhi.

BIRDS' NESTING IN INDIA

AUTHOR: CAPTAIN G. F. L. MARSHAL

BIRDS' NESTING

IN

INDIA.

A CALENDAR OF THE BREEDING SEASONS, AND A POPULAR GUIDE TO THE HABITS AND HAUNTS OF BIRDS.

ILLUSTRATED.

BY CAPTAIN G. F. L. MARSHALL, R.E., F.Z.S.,

AND MEMBER OF THE BRITISH & INDIAN ORNITHOLOGICAL UNIONS.

Calcutta:

PUBLISHED BY THE CALCUTTA CENTRAL PRESS CO.,

5, COUNCIL HOUSE STREET.

1877.

CONTENTS.

LIST OF ILLUSTRATIONS.

PREFACE.

Ten years ago when beginning to make a collection of birds' eggs in this country, I was struck by the diversity in the breeding seasons, and the want of any guide to assist the beginner in his researches. Since then I have kept a continuous record of my observations, and, with the intention of eventually publishing them, I have endeavoured to gather together, as far as possible, the recorded experiences of others; and this little book is the result. Many friends have kindly placed their collections at my disposal, and for a great deal of the information regarding the rarer birds, I am indebted to the courtesy of Mr. A. O. Hume, in permitting the use of extracts from a draft of his book on "Indian Birds' Nests and Eggs," which has as yet only been printed for private circulation: to this source are due the valuable observations from Sikkim by Mr. Gammie; from Hansi (Punjab), the Central Provinces, and Bundelkhund by Mr. Blewitt; from the Nilgiris by Miss Cockburn and Messrs. Davidson and Wait, and by many others from various parts of India, while the information from Bengal is chiefly due to Mr. Parker. Of private collections from which notes have been taken those of Captains Cock and C. H. T. Marshall, and of Mr. W. E. Brooks, were the most important, and to all these gentlemen my thanks are due.

The notes from upper India are comparatively full and complete, but as regards Eastern and Peninsular India they are as yet very meagre, more especially from the latter. A good deal of new information has been collected since the manuscript of this book was put in hand, and more is being accumulated month by month; but the knowledge already gained is valuable as far as it goes, and believing that it is better that what is known should be made at once available to the public, rather than that indefinite delay should be made for fuller detail, I offer no further apology for the incompleteness of the record.

This book will not in any way supplant the carefully detailed work which Mr. Hume is compiling on the nidification of Indian birds, but it will supplement it by abstracting, in a convenient form, certain points of information, and so facilitate the direction of research into the proper channels. Mr. Hume's work, when published, and, it is to be hoped, it soon will be, should be in the hands of every lover of Natural History in this country.

No details are here given as to the materials and apparatus necessary in forming a collection and in preparing and preserving specimens: those who wish to commence collections of eggs or of skins of birds, will find all information as to details in Mr. Hume's "INDIAN ORNITHOLOGICAL COLLECTOR'S VADE-MECUM," a most useful little book published by the Calcutta Central Press Company (5, Council House Street, Calcutta), and priced one rupee: but with reference to collections of eggs, it is necessary to repeat here that eggs are *scientifically* worthless as specimens, unless the species of bird to which they belong has been *accurately ascertained;* and to do this effectually it is necessary for all except the most practised observers that the skin of the parent bird should be in all cases obtained and preserved.

If egg collectors, into whose hands this book may come, would kindly communicate to me any notes they may make from their own experience in correction or extension of the information now recorded, it would confer a great obligation on me, and enable me, in case a second edition may be required, to render it more complete and satisfactory than I am able to do in the present case.

The list of birds in Part II serves as an index, the order of arrangement followed by Jerdon is adopted, and having ascertained from this list the months in which any particular bird breeds, the further details required will be found on reference to the lists for those months.

MARSHALL DEL

TAKING THE BROADBILLS NEST,

BIRDS' NESTING IN INDIA.

CHAPTER I.

INTRODUCTORY; BREEDING SEASONS AND HINTS ON BIRDS' NESTING.

Birds' nesting has gained in civilised countries a very evil reputation, in many cases unfortunately only too well deserved, by the wanton cruelty with which it is attended; and it must be stated clearly to begin with, that the publication of this book is not intended in any way to encourage the idle and foolish destruction of birds, nor to countenance the wholesale robbing of young and eggs from nests, which has brought the very name of birds' nester into discredit, and has changed what should be, and is, if properly carried on, a healthy and instructive pursuit into a deserved reproach.

That the collecting of birds' eggs may be done without cruelty is not to be doubted by any one who has devoted time and thought to the question. Few birds attach any importance to fresh eggs, it is only as the process of incubation progresses, and the maternal instincts are developed, that any grave anxiety is shown by the parent birds when the eggs are approached; even at this stage many birds will forsake the nest at once if the eggs are touched; and when the eggs are quite fresh, the simple fact of the nest being touched, or even the detection by the parent bird that the nest has been discovered, is sometimes enough to lead to its desertion: in such cases the taking of the eggs is clearly not followed by any distress to the parent birds. Not many years ago I used to feel very much more strongly on this point than I do now; the pain at robbing a nest used quite to embitter the joy of discovering a prize; but it happened on one occasion, during a march through the Bolandshahr district, that

I found a nest of a kind I had long sought in vain, the whistling teal (*Dendrocygna arcuata*). These curious little ducks perch in trees and lay their eggs in nests made of sticks and twigs in trees. The nest was in a babul tree, at the edge of a large swamp, about ten feet from the ground; and standing on a bank close by, I could see both parent birds seated side by side on the nest, with their little heads laid lovingly together, and their soft eyes watching me with no signs of dread. A severe mental struggle followed. My desire to get the eggs turned the scale, and I determined on shooting both the parent birds so as to leave no desolate mourner. I startled them from the nest, and as they flew off, fired right and left, killed the drake, but alas missed the duck. The deed was done, and there was nothing left but to take the egg which I did with a saddened heart and walked on to my camp three miles distant. All that day the memory of the poor little solitary duck haunted me. I could not get it out of my mind, and the next morning I determined to return to the spot, though it took me six miles out of my way, and put an end to the misery of the unhappy survivor by shooting her. On reaching the place, there I found her, seated on her empty nest, the scene of the previous day's calamity, seated indeed, but not alone, she was accompanied, and no doubt successfully cheered by another drake that had already aspired to the place in her affections vacated by her unfortunate partner only the day before. In this case the nest contained only a single egg which was quite fresh, the usual number laid for hatching being from seven to ten.

The behaviour is, however, very different when the little family arrangements are further developed. I once found the nest of a golden-crested wren, with eight eggs in it. The eggs were new to me at the time, and as I was anxious to find out accurately to what bird they belonged, I set a snare by the nest, and in a few minutes caught and killed the hen bird, and then taking the nest I sat down to pack it, and the eggs and the little bird to convey them safely away. While I was engaged on this, the cock bird appeared and soon perceived the disaster that had happened to his home, his plaintive chirping was most piteous to hear, and I hurriedly moved away, but there was no escaping, the poor little thing followed me incessantly, keeping pace with me and flitting from tree to tree, till passing out of the pine wood I got into open treeless ground, and there, unable to trust his frail little wings to the long flight, and fearing to alight on the open common, he fell back, and to my great relief his cries of woe were soon lost to hearing. The eggs were so hard set in this case that I was unable to preserve even one of them, and that day's work I have ever regretted. It cannot of course be known how long the little bird mourned his loss, or what his end was, but on the other hand no one can doubt that the sorrow for the time was real and deep.

When the eggs are hatched, and the helpless young lie in the nest dependant solely on the parent birds for food and life, the maternal instincts are of course quicker and more deep-seated, and many anecdotes could be told of the devotion of birds to their young, and of their courage and ingenuity in defending them. I will only mention one instance which occurred to a friend of mine. A nest of the golden oriole, often known as the mango bird (*Oriolus kundoo*), had been found in the garden containing young, and was taken and brought into the house with the intention of rearing the young for the cage. The nest was placed by an open window, and there was discovered by the parent birds. They took charge of it as if nothing had happened, coming fearlessly into the verandah and feeding the young all day long. After a few days the nest was removed to another house more than half a mile distant, and still the parent birds followed it, tended it in the new situation, and eventually I believe reared up the young and carried them off as soon as they were able to fly. The golden oriole is a shy retiring bird, and for it to overcome so far its dread of man shows a very high order of parental affection.

One more instance, perhaps the most curious of all, I must give before passing on to resume my subject. The heroine this time being a kite (*Milvus govinda*). Kites are not attractive birds, except for the wonderful grace of their flight, and it is hard to imagine a tender heart beneath their fierce but treacherous and withal cowardly exteriors. In the month of January in lower Bengal when with the kites the breeding season is at its height, a solitary female, over whom the instincts of the season evidently had their sway, but who from some cause or other was unprovided with a nest or eggs, appropriated an empty pill-box that had been thrown on to the roof of a portico, and gathering some sticks and straws round it in the corner of the roof to serve as a nest, she commenced and carried on with admirable perseverance a forlorn attempt to hatch it. When approached and driven from her place she would return to defend the beloved treasure dashing fiercely at the intruder. How long it would have taken before her hopes of welcoming a young kite out of the pill-box would have been finally abandoned was not proved, for a heavy storm of rain reduced it to a pulp, and in its place the egg of a domestic fowl was put down, and on that the kite now joined by a male kite who keeps careful guard over her, is still sitting. The eggs will be hatched in a few days, and the life of the young chick, which will probably be short and adventurous, will commence.*

It is not *essential* to the pursuit of natural historythat collections of eggs or skins should be made; but the act of collecting is the simplest and readiest if not the only certain way of rendering the eye sufficiently familiar with the appearance of birds to enable any one to recognise and distinguish at a distance the various kinds one from another, and for this reason the making of a collection is very advisable. The interest in the subject so far from ceasing would even increase when the collection was formed and the knowledge gained in the act of collecting remains. Experience proves that, after the acquisition of specimens is no longer desired, there is a pleasure in intelligently watching and noting the habits of birds and animals in life, the intensity of which grows in the minds of all true lovers of nature, just in proportion as its gratification is no longer encumbered with the necessity for taking the lives of harmless and beautiful creatures.

The duties of an Englishman in India frequently entail a great deal of out-of-door life, much of which is in many instances solitary. To such, the need of a pursuit to interest the mind and divert it in leisure hours from the groove of official routine is very great, and to this end the study of natural history is pre-eminently adapted. Few countries offer greater inducements or better opportunities for it than India does, and its pursuit not only affords occupation and interest both in-doors and out-of-doors, but it is also accessible to all and necessitates no more costly apparatus than is within the means of every official Englishman. The habits of close observation which it fosters are especially useful; and the careful record of personal observations supplies the much-needed data, without which general laws cannot be discussed or deduced. As to the healthy interest it developes in life, those who have experienced it will testify. A country which to others may seem a dreary waste is often to the naturalist a very mine of wealth, a ride across it, or a march through it, becomes replete with interest and enjoyment; and it is earnestly hoped that, on perusing these pages, some of the many Englishmen scattered over India in solitary places may be induced to take up the study of ornithology, and find in it a new and growing interest which will while away many a pleasant hour.

* This curious instance of aberrant instinct was pointed out to me by Col. Tucker, R.E., on whose house the event occurred and indeed is still occurring.

A knowledge of the habits and seasons of birds is especially useful to sportsmen who seldom have the time for ascertaining the breeding seasons of game birds by personal observation, and in consequence of the want of this information many of our Indian game birds are slaughtered while they have eggs or young chicks, even by men who would be the first to condemn the deed if it were done wittingly. In England long experience has rendered every one familiar with such things, but in this country the seasons are known only to a few. At present no means exist for others of readily ascertaining them, and sportsmen are helpless in the matter. A case in point quite recently came under my observation. A large bag of the likh florikin (*Sypheotides auritus*) had been made in the very height of the breeding season, but no idea that such was the case had ever entered the head of the man (a true sportsman) who had shot them, and he was quite ignorant of the extent of the damage unconsciously inflicted. I feel sure that the publication of any facts that will aid in preventing this misdirection of sport will be welcomed by all, and if each will supplement the existing knowledge of the subject by carefully recording his own personal experiences, we should in a few years have sufficient materials accumulated for a complete record of the breeding seasons, and the way would be paved at all events for an unwritten law, known and honoured by all sportsmen for the observation of close seasons, and then, but not till then, India will become, as it ought to be, equal to the best country in the world for a day's small game shooting. The occasional holiday with a gun, so looked forward to by many, would no longer result in a weary trudge with a nearly empty bag at the end, as is now not unfrequently the case; and partridge-shooting would then afford as good sport as snipe-shooting does at present, but which is in the latter case entirely owing to the fact that the snipe by removing themselves *en masse* to other countries inaccessible to sportsmen, when the breeding season comes round, are able to carry on their domestic arrangements in peace and security.

But to return to the birds' nesting, the real reason why the difficulties arise out here, is the irregularity in season of breeding in tropical climates as compared with temperate climates. In the latter, breeding among birds is almost universally confined to the spring and early summer months. On coming out to India, people naturally assume that the rule holds good out here, which is only very partially the case, and the first difficulty that besets a beginner in collecting birds' eggs in this country is the absence of any information on this point. At first, search for nests is only made in the spring and summer months, but in the course of time eggs are found incidentally in other months, both earlier and later, and it gradually becomes evident that hours of fruitless search and watching of birds, to trace from their movements where their nests are concealed have been thrown away, which a little experience would have saved by teaching that the breeding season were either already over or had not yet begun, or in some instances even never would begin in that part of the country. It is to answer at all events partially this question, when do the birds breed? that these notes are published. The question is now being answered in full detail for each bird by Mr. Hume's book already referred to in the preface, and this little book will give a review of the year month by month, indicating the direction in which search can at any given time be profitably carried on.

In dealing with a limited area, either tropical or temperate, it would be comparatively easy to furnish a complete guide on this point in a small compass; but with a large country like India, including every variety of climate from the eternal snows of the alpine Himalayas to the unvarying round of heat in the southern peninsular on the one hand, and from the arid deserts of Sind to the humid forests of Assam on the other hand. It is a task of much difficulty to afford full details in a single book. The area dealt with is bounded by the main ridge of the Himalayas on the north; the Suliman range and the Arabian sea on the west; by the Indian ocean on the south; and by the bay of Bengal and Assam on the east. Climate has by far the largest influence in determining the breeding period with birds, and thus over so large an area it is clear that great variations must occur at different points. Speaking generally, it may be assumed that the colder the climate, the more uniformly will the breeding season be confined to the warmer months; and the hotter and less variable the climate, the more irregularly will the breeding season be spread throughout the year. Among hot climates the drier the climate, the more the breeding season inclines to the summer and monsoon months; while in damp tropical climates the winter months are more prolific in proportion; but in India, excluding the Himalayas, there is no place where eggs of some species may not be obtained in every month of the year.

The fewest number of kinds of birds known to breed in this country in any one month is twenty-eight, and that month is November; and further research will probably show that this number is under the mark. In May four hundred kinds of birds are known to breed, and the number is probably little short of five hundred. Of the twelve hundred or so species found in this country, the breeding of about six hundred has already been ascertained, of the remainder many are migratory and do not breed in this country at all, but there still remains a wide field for discovery, the great bar to further progress being the deadly character of some parts of the country at certain seasons of the year. The great majority of the birds, the breeding of which is yet unknown, frequent swamps or dense forests, and probably breed at seasons of the year when exploration is not only attended with extreme discomfort, but with serious risk of life. Some few kinds, such as hawk owls *(Ninox)* and some of the goat suckers (*Caprimulgidæ*) and others, though they breed in accessible and healthy localities, escape observation by their shy and retiring habits.

In every part of India the vultures and many of the large eagles breed during the cold season, the most notable exception is the breeding of the Indian tawny eagle (*A. vindhyana*), the spotted eagle (*A. nævia*), and the long-legged eagle (*A. hastata)* in the height of the hot weather in moist localities, such as Saharunpoor, the Terais, and Calcutta, but in other parts these species too conform to the general rule. Many of the owls, especially the large ones, breed in the winter, and almost all the others breed in the early spring. The water birds breed during the rainy season. In July and August, in the country affected by the south-west monsoon, and in December in those parts of the south-east coast which are under the influence of the north-east monsoon. In some places the herons are known to breed in the spring, this has been ascertained in Oudh and also at Saugor, but it is unusual. The small warblers also of all kinds breed chiefly, though not without exception, during the rainy season. For the rest the season varies with locality.

In the Himalayas the chief season is April, May, and June, but many eggs may be found in February and March; and also in July. All the finches breed late, chiefly in July in the higher ranges. From August to November birds' nesting does not repay the labor and fatigue of walking in the hills, few, if any, eggs are to be found, and only definite search after particular kinds, which there may be good reason to believe are then breeding, should be made. In December and January the big vultures and eagles have eggs, and their eyries should be sought for.

The seasons for any particular kinds that may be spread throughout the whole range of the Himalayas are usually somewhat earlier in the eastern, and later in the western portion.

In the hills of south India the season is much the same as in the Himalayas, but it begins earlier, and ends later. There too a second or autumn brood is frequently hatched, while in the Himalayas, with birds that have two broods, the first is usually in March, and the second in June. In the southern hills, the ranges being less lofty and easily accessible to and from the plains, birds' nesting may be carried on with more or less success over a much longer period by extending the rambles to the forests at the foot of the hills from time to time.

In the plains, where the tropical extremes of temperature occur, the season never ends, every month of the year yields a fair harvest. Some individual species breed all the year round, and where some leave off, others begin, so that the birds' nester may be always fully employed. In the dry parts of the plains, more especially towards the north and west, the autumn months are comparatively barren seasons, the end of the cold weather, and throughout the hot weather and rains being the most prolific periods.

In searching for birds' nests the great secret of success after all is patience and perseverance, and when this is backed by keen eyesight and a knowledge of the habits of birds, success is certain. When the time of breeding is known, the way is cleared to a great extent; but when the time for any particular species is only to be found out by observation, search may be guided by noting the breeding times of closely allied kinds of birds. If the breeding of one species is known, it may generally be inferred, though it is not always the case, that other species of that genus will breed about the same time in that locality. An exception to this is found among the crows, the common crow (*Corvus impudicus*) breeding in the upper provinces in June, while the raven (*C. corax*) and the corby (*C. culmenatus*) both breed in those parts during the winter. Other exceptions will occur to all who have collected eggs in this country, but the rule generally offers a fair guide.

When this method leads to no results, the simplest way with common species is to shoot a specimen from time to time and ascertain by dissection whether breeding is in progress or not. Of course, if the birds are rare, this method cannot be carried out; for it defeats its own object, and watching must be resorted to. With birds in which the sexes differ in plumage, the disappearance of the hen birds, while the cocks are still to be seen about, leads to the inference that the former are in all probability sitting on eggs somewhere close by, and if watched, the male bird may be seen to carry food to the female, and thus lead to the discovery of the nest. Some birds put on handsome plumes or tufts of feathers as the breeding season approaches, which indicates when search for the eggs should be made. If watched closely, many kinds of birds may be detected pairing; or, in the case of such as build nests, they may be seen carrying bits of stick or straw, or wool or feathers in their bills to the tree or hole where they are preparing their little home. This latter of course leads not only to the knowledge of the breeding season, but also what is more to the point to the discovery of the nest. Some birds that are widely spread over the country breed in one locality or another nearly throughout the year. Some again breed nearly throughout the year in the same locality. Among these latter may be mentioned the striated bush babbler (*Chattarhœa caudata*), the pin-tailed munia (*Munia malabarica*), the black-bellied finch lark (*Pyrrhalauda grisea*), the common sandgrouse (*Pterocles exustus*), and all the commonest doves in the plains.

To ensure success in discovering nests to any extent, it must be repeated that close and persevering search is necessary, many nests and sometimes those of the rarest birds are found accidentally, but even in these cases the finding generally results from a habit of keeping a watch on the movements of birds, and without labor and perseverance no great results can be looked for in this or in any other pursuit. With birds that sit close the nest itself must be searched for; and likely spots must be beaten, or otherwise disturbed, to cause the bird to fly off; but in many cases this is not necessary, as birds often quit their nests on the first signs of the approach of man. In forest country if the trees are too numerous, or the underwood is too thick to allow of complete search, it is best to keep a sharp look-out some thirty yards ahead of where you are walking to catch sight of the birds as they rapidly and often silently flit from the nest and reveal its situation. In this manner I found in one morning nests of the small billed mountain thrush (*Oreocincla dauma*), the dusky bush thrush (*Geocichla unicolor*), the black-throated jay (*Garrulus lanceolatus*), and several others in the course of a quick ride through a secluded forest. It is sometimes advantageous to sit quite still for a time and watch, but as a rule moving about gives the best chance. One morning in the hot weather I had sat down to light my pipe at the foot of a tall clump of surkerry grass, when a little wren warbler (*Prinia stewarti*) flew up with a straw in its mouth, suddenly caught sight of me and alighting on a twig close by, looked at me in evident astonishment without moving for two or three seconds, then opening its bill and dropping the straw it gave a most melancholy *chee-e-ep*. I looked round, and just at my back, fortunately uninjured, was the nest neatly woven in among the stalks of the grass about a foot above the ground; it was unfinished, and I left it in peace and moved away. Tapping the trunks of trees with a stick in passing is a good plan, as it will generally put a bird up off a nest that would otherwise sit close and escape observation; but even with those species that lay in deep holes in trees, a sound of approaching footsteps is often enough to rouse the bird. I once found the nest of a speckled piculet (*Vivia innominata*), in this way, seating myself on a bank to rest for a few moments under a tree, and looking up among the branches, a head of a little bird protruded from a tiny hole caught my eye. The bird had been roused by the sound of my approaching footsteps, and was looking out to see the cause. The hole which was pierced in the wood of an old trunk at some distance from the ground was so small that I could only put one finger into the entrance, and was almost invisible until the eye was guided to it. To find nests of this description, such as woodpeckers and barbets, the easiest way is by listening carefully in the woods in the early part of the breeding season when the tapping noise made by the birds in digging out the holes with their bills guides the eye to their position.

To find nests in bushes and trees when the birds are close sitters, it is sometimes a good plan to disturb the birds by beating the foliage; but by far the best way is to select the most likely localities where birds are most numerous and carefully search every bush. In open country, with scanty jungle and few trees, every bush and tree should be searched, especially where birds are abundant. Large isolated trees which are so marked a feature in the plains are very favorite resorts, and most of them are more or less tenanted in the season. If the country is quite open, or if the jungle is like the common "beri" thorn jungle, too low and thick to search systematically, better results will be got on horseback than on foot, and in such situations many nests may be found while cantering about on a sure-footed pony. When the country is quite bare of vegetation, as in some plains and fallow lands, or even low stubble, a look-out should be kept well ahead for plovers or sandgrouse and other birds which creep quietly away from their eggs long before you can get near them. If little bushes or tufts of grass are scattered about here and there, the pony should be guided to pass close by them; and if a lark or pipit or other bird of similar habits should happen to have a nest under the shelter of one of them, the bird will rise sometimes almost at the horse's feet. For thick low jungle where the riding plan fails, the place should be beaten or dragged with a rope, which latter will make even quail, which are exceedingly close sitters, rise from their eggs. The object of the rapid approach on horseback is to startle the bird and make it rise hurriedly, as otherwise it would creep quietly away unobserved to the other side of the bush.

With gregarious birds the matter is more simple, the breeding haunts may easily be found in most cases, except when the powers of flight are very great as with the spinetails and swiftlets, by noting where they tend to congregate when the proper season arrives. When once the breeding ground is known, it is easy to find the individual nests.

A plan tried by Captain Cock of nailing up a sheepskin to a tree, and watching with binoculars the birds that came to take the wool, was found very successful with tits and some small birds, but experience is the best guide in all cases; and with these general remarks I must have the reader to arrange his own course of action in each case.

CHAPTER II.

HABITS AND HAUNTS OF BIRDS, WITH GENERAL DESCRIPTION OF TYPES OF EGGS.

Vultures, *(Otogyps, Gyps, Percnopteron, Gypaetus).*—Build a large conspicuous nest of sticks; sometimes many feet in width and depth; generally a huge solitary tree is chosen for the purpose, and the nest is difficult to reach, indeed often nearly inaccessible. The usual number of eggs laid in each nest is one; two is the greatest number ever laid, and that only by a few species; so that a good collection of the eggs of these birds requires a great deal of difficult climbing and perseverance. Some kinds, the king vulture and the "roc," lay pure white eggs. Of other kinds the eggs are more or less spotted, those of the "scavenger" and bearded vulture being often very richly coloured. The great brown vulture *(Vultur monachus)* only occurs here in the cold weather, all the other vultures are permanent residents, some breeding wherever they are found, others congregating at particular spots when the time for nest building arrives.

Falcons, (*Falco.*)—Of the eight species of true falcons which are found in India, only three are known to breed here; the rest are cold weather visitants migrating to north and west in the summer. Of the three which remain, one, the laggar falcon (*F. juggur*) is found in dry plains; the two others, the "shahin" (*F. perigrinator*) and the black cap falcon (*F. atriceps*) affect wooded and rugged country. The nest, though large, is generally well concealed. From three to six eggs are laid, which are always well marked, sometimes very richly coloured.

Hobbies, (*Hypotriorchis*).—Nothing is known of their breeding in this country. The European hobby (*H. subbuteo*) is a rather rare winter visitant. The Indian hobby (*H. severus*) is a permanent resident in the eastern Himalayas, where its nest will probably be found in high trees in forest tracts.

Merlins, *(Lithofalco)*.—The merlin of Europe (*L. esalon*) is a rare cold weather visitant. The red-headed merlin (*L. chicquera*) is very common, it is a permanent resident, and chiefly found in mango groves. The nests are well concealed in thick foliage, and the eggs are of the same type as those of the true falcons.

Kestrils, (*Tinnunculus, Erythropus.*)—The common kestril (*T. alaudarius*) is found all over the country in the cold weather, but retires to the mountain ranges to breed. Of the breeding of the other two kestrils (*E. cenchris* and *E. vespertinus*) very little is known. The former is said to breed in the Nilgiris, and the latter may probably breed in the Himalayas. The eggs are richly coloured.

Pigmy falcons, (*Hierax*).—Of these beautiful little birds very little is known. Only one kind is found in India, in the extreme north-east. They feed on insects and frequent forests. They do not appear to be migratory.

Hawks, (*Astur, Lophospiza, Micronisus, Accipiter*).—The six species known in India are all permanent residents, though in the cold weather some of them wander far from their breeding haunts. Of the besra sparrow hawk (*A. virgatus*), nothing is known as to its breeding. They affect wooded localities and often fly high. The eggs of *Astur* and *Micronisus* are pale blue or grey unspotted. The sparrow hawks lay boldly blotched eggs. One only (*M. badius*) breeds in the plains; the others all breed in mountain ranges and temperate climates.

Eagles, (*Aquila, Neopus*).—The golden eagle (*A. chrysaetus*) is said to breed in the alpine Himalayas, making its nest on cliffs; but no eggs have been taken as yet. The black eagle (*N. malaiensis*) also breeds on cliffs, the other resident eagles breed on trees. All the true eagles are more or less migratory. The great tawny eagle (*A. fulvescens* vera or *A. nævioides*) and the barred imperial eagle (*A. bifasciata*) leave the country altogether in the breeding season. Eagles frequent open or wooded places, perching on high trees and soaring in search of prey. The nests are conspicuous, and they lay two or sometimes one egg; white with a few spots or blotches.

Hawk eagles, (*Nisaetus, Limnaetus, Spizaetus*).—Bonelli's eagle (*N. bonellii*) frequents open plains as well as wooded hills. The other hawk eagles are confined to forest tracts, and from the unhealthiness of the woods at the breeding time, but few of their nests are taken. They perch in trees with thick foliage and keep a good deal out of sight. They have a loud rather musical call which often leads to their detection. Their eggs generally two in number are sparingly spotted or streaked. They are partially migratory, but probably all breed within Indian limits.

Serpent eagles, (*Circaetus, Spilornis*).—The short-toed eagle (*C. gallicus*) is a permanent resident and frequents dry open plains, perching on isolated trees. It lays a single white egg. The crested serpent eagles (*Spilornis*) are found in forests and well-watered tracts. *S. cheela* breeds in the warm sub-Himalayan valleys. The nest is placed about half way up a tree near water, and the eggs two in number are slightly spotted. They migrate to the well-watered plains in the cold weather. The others are probably permanent residents were found.

Fishing eagles, (*Pandion, Polioætus, Haliætus*).—These are always found in the neighbourhood of water. They build enormous nests of sticks on high trees. The osprey (*P. haliætus*) probably breeds in this country, but the eggs have not as yet been taken. They are very handsomely blotched. The other fishing eagles are permanent residents where they occur, and lay unspotted white eggs.

Buzzards, (*Buteo, Archibuteo, Poliornis*).—Of the true buzzards (*Buteo*) only one, the long-legged buzzard (*B. canescens*) is known to breed in India. It breeds in the far north-west. The others are confined to the mountains of India and affect well-wooded slopes. Their eggs are boldly blotched. Of the genus *Archibuteo* nothing is known. The two species that occur in India (*A. hemiptolopus and A. strophiatus*) are some of the rarest birds in collections. The white-eyed buzzard (*P. teesa*), the only representative of the genus *Poliornis* in India proper, is very common throughout the plains, and a permanent resident everywhere. Its eggs, three in number, are unspotted as a rule.

Harriers, (*Circus*).—Are cold weather visitants to India, retiring north and west to breed. One the marsh harrier (*Cœruginosus*) may prossibly breed in a few localities, but the majority of them leave the country. They breed on the ground in marshy tracts and lay bluish unspotted eggs.

Kites, (*Haliastur, Milvus, Baza, Elanus*).—The brahminy kite (*H. indus*) is found in all well-watered districts, and is a permanent resident where found. Of the breeding of the crested kite (*Baza lophotes*) nothing is known. It is wide spread in its distribution, but rare everywhere. The black-winged kite, (*E. melanopterus*) is common in well-wooded districts. All the kites, except the larger Indian kite (*M. major*) which migrates to the plains in the cold weather, appear to be stationary in their habits. They all build on trees and lay handsomely blotched eggs.

Owls, (*Strix, Scelostrix, Phodilus, Bulacca, Otus, Ascalaphia, Huhua, Bubo, Nyctea, Ketupa, Ephialtes, Athene, Heteroglaux,*

Glaucidium.)—A great number of owls are found in India, most of them are permanent residents. The short-eared owls (*Otus*) are the only truly migratory ones. They all lay pure white eggs of a rounded shape. The grass owl (*Scelostrix candida*) lays on the ground in grass. The rock-horned owl (*Ascalaphia bengalensis*) lays on shady ledges of banks. Some of the wood owls (*Bulacca*) lay occasionally on ledges of rocks. The screech owl (*Strix indica*) and the spotted owlet (*Athene brama*) lay sometimes in buildings or deserted wells, but the place *par excellence* for finding owls' eggs is in natural hollows in decayed trees. Some of the larger owls which would find holes in any ordinary tree rather tight quarters lay in hollows at the bifurcations of the trunks of large trees. Owls are seldom seen, owing to their nocturnal habits, but some species or other is to be found in every part of India. Some of them live in houses inhabited by man, but the great bulk of them frequent well-wooded districts away from human habitations.

Hawk owls, (*Ninox*).—Nothing is known of the nidification of these curious birds. They affect wooded localties, and are more widely spread than is usually thought. They appear at twilight, perching on conspicuous dead boughs.

Swallows, (*Hirundo*).—Are very widely spread. They are often gregarious and generally found near water over the surface of which they feed. They occur throughout India, and breed much near human habitations. Their nests, of whatever shape, are all made of pellets of clay, fixed against a building or rock generally with a soft lining. The eggs are pure white in some, but spotted in others. The common swallow (*H. rustica*) is migratory. A few pairs only remain to breed in the Himalayas. All the others are permanent residents where found, except perhaps *H. daurica* which breeds in the Himalayas only, but is found in the plains in winter.

Martins, (*Cotyle, Chelidon*).—Are very locally spread through India. the sand martins (*Cotyle*) are found near large rivers. The crag martins (*Cotyle*) and the house martins (*Chelidon*) chiefly affect rocky country, and of the breeding of these latter very little is known. They are all more or less gregarious. The crag martins lay spotted eggs. The sand martins lay pure white eggs. They are partially migratory.

Spine tails, (*Acanthylis*).—Of the breeding of the spine tails nothing is known, their amazing powers of flight, and the great distances they traverse in a day, render observation of their habits almost impossible. They probably breed in company against precipitous rocks.

Swifts, *(Cypselus.)*—The breeding of the larger swifts is difficult to ascertain from the same reason as in the case of the spine tails. They fly with great ease and swiftness, and though not, as far as is known, migratory; in the true sense of the word, they wander far and come and go irregularly. The palm swifts are much more local and do not wander far from their breeding haunts. The eggs of all swifts are pure white and very elongated. They are all more or less gregarious breeders.

Swiftlets, *(Collocalia.)*—Three kinds of swiftlets breed in India. They are gregarious, with great powers of flight, and wander far. They breed on rocks. Some of the species make the "edible nests" so highly valued by the Chinese. Their eggs like those of the swifts are pure white and very elongated.

Tree swifts, *(Dendrocheledon).*—Only one species is found in India, and that confined to forests and very local. The egg (only one is laid) is pure white and elongated.

Frogmouths, *(Otothrix, Batrachostomus).*—Are confined to forests and very local, little is known of them. They probably breed in holes or on stumps and lay white eggs.

Goatsuckers, *(Caprimulgus.)*—These birds are widely spread, but each species is comparatively local. They are crepuscular in their habits, and frequent wooded or waste jungly land. They are permanent residents wherever found, and lay two elongated eggs, beautifully marked with pink or brown and salmon colour, on the bare ground or on a few dead leaves. They lie exceedingly close, not rising till they catch your eye. The beds of shady nullahs, ravines, at roots of trees, or in dense underwood, are the spots where they usually deposit their eggs, but they are sometimes laid by a sprig in an open field; and to find them careful and persevering search is necessary. Of *C. macrourus* and *C. mahrattensis,* the eggs have not yet been found. Though not gregarious, one or two nests may sometimes be found very near each other.

Trogons, *(Harpactes).*—Are not migratory. They frequent dense forests and lay pure white eggs in holes in decayed trees. Only two kinds are found in India, and they are very local.

Beeeaters, *(Merops, Nyctiornis).*—Are found all over India.

Some frequent forests, and some open plains, but as a rule they are seldom found far from water, except the common bee eater (*M. viridis*), which is found everywhere in the plains. They make no nest, and lay very round pure white eggs in deep holes in banks or in level ground. Sometimes old rat holes are used, but often they excavate for themselves. They are permanent residents, and the breeding of all, except the blue-ruffed bee eater (*N. athertoni*), is well known. They are generally, though not always, gregarious and breed in colonies.

Rollers, (*Coracias, Eurystomus*).—Lay round white eggs in holes in decayed trees. They are not migratory as a rule, though they sometimes wander in the cold season far from their breeding haunts. The common roller (*C. indica*), the "jay" of Englishmen in India, often breeds about houses. It is a well-known and conspicuous bird.

Kingfishers, (*Pelargopsis, Halcyon, Ceyx, Todiramphus, Alcedo, Ceryle*).—Are essentially non-migratory. Wherever they are found they breed. They lay round white eggs in deep holes in banks, making no nest. Many species are found in India, but most of them are very local; and partly owing to their rarity, partly owing to the unhealthiness of the localities, they affect during the breeding season. The nests of only a few species have as yet been discovered in this country. The kingfishers in India all belong to genera, which keep near water and breed in holes in banks. Some genera belonging to other countries inhabit forests, and lay their eggs in holes in decayed trees. Here, though banks of rivers or canals are by far the most approved localities, instances have occurred of eggs being found in holes in the sides of wells, in banks of ponds, and even in mud walls in a village.

Broadbills, (*Psarisomus, Serilophus.*)—The nidification of these birds is little known. They appear generally to build a globular or pear-shaped nest,* hanging from the tips of boughs, and lay white eggs. Only two species occur (*P. dalhousiæ* and *C. rubropygia*), both confined to the Eastern Himalayas, and both rather rare, though permanent residents. They affect oak forests and keep to the tops of trees.

Hornbills, (*Homraius, Rhyticeros, Hydrocissa, Meniceros, Tockus, Aceros*).—These are the "toucans" of Englishmen in India. They inhabit forests or wooded country; and where they occur are permanent residents. They all nestle in holes in decayed trees generally at a considerable height from the ground. The entrance to the hole is

---

* See frontispiece.

more or less plastered up after the female has entered, and the eggs are white.

Parrots, *(Palæornis, Loriculus).*—These occur throughout India some local, some widely spread, but all where they occur are permanent residents. They lay pure white eggs in holes in trees, generally they use a natural hollow, but sometimes they cut the entrance hole themselves, always choosing a tree decayed internally. The nest holes are often at a considerable height from the ground. They are gregarious when not breeding, and often a number of nests may be found in the same tree. They affect cultivation and open wooded country.

Woodpeckers, *(Picus, Hypopicus, Yungipicus, Hemicircus, Chrysocolaptes, Muelleripicus, Gecinus, Chrysophlegma, Venilia, Gecinulus, Micropternus, Brachypternus, Chrysonotus).*—There are a great number of species in India. Only two species are widely spread, the yellow-fronted woodpecker *(Picus mahrattensis)* and the common gold-back woodpecker *(Brachypternus aurantius).* The rest are local and confined to particular parts of India. They are as a rule only found in well-wooded districts. They all lay pure white eggs, and deposit them in holes in trees which they cut for themselves with a neat circular orifice.* The nest holes are always on the under-sides of boughs, or in perpendicular trunks to keep out rainwater. Woodpeckers are not migratory. They breed wherever they are found.

Piculets, *(Vivia, Sacia).*—Only two species occur in India, and these are confined to the Himalayas. In habits they exactly resemble woodpeckers, and lay white eggs in artificial holes in trees. They are not migatory.

Wrynecks, *(Yunx).*—One species, the common wryneck *(Y. torquila)* is common in the plains in the cold weather, but it migrates in the spring. It is said to breed in Kashmir, but no details are recorded. They nestle in holes in decayed trees and lay pure white eggs.

Honey guides, *(Indicator).*—One species is found though extremely rarely, and nothing is known of its habits.

Barbets, *(Megalæma, Xantholæma).*—Many species occur in India. They closely resemble woodpeckers in their habits, but they feed on fruit. They are non-migratory, breeding wherever they are found. They usually inhabit forests or well-wooded country, lay pure white eggs, and de-

* Mr. Gammie has recently discovered that in Sikkim the bay woodpeckers (*Micropternus*) make their nest holes in black ants' nests attached to trees, a most remarkable fact.

posit them in holes which they cut fort hemselves in trees. They usually select a decayed tree, and the circular orifice pierced, they occupy the natural cavity in the centre of the trunk or bough.

Cuckoos, *(Cuculus, Hierococcyx, Polyphasia, Surniculus, Chrysococcyx, Coccystes, Eudynamis).*—All these birds are migratory more or less, and parasitic in their habits. They appear for breeding purposes in the spring in the hills, and in the rains in the plains, and lay their eggs in other birds' nests, selecting, according to circumstances, the bird most likely to prove useful in rearing their young for them. One of the hawk cuckoos *(H. sparverioides)* is said to build its own nest in the Nilgiris, but this requires confirmation.

Ground cuckoos, *(Zanclostomus, Centropus, Taccocua).*—These birds are somewhat locally distributed; they chiefly inhabit dense jungle and thickets, and where they occur are permanent residents. They build massive stick nests often domed over, in thick cover, and lay white eggs, rather chalky in texture.

Spider-hunters, *(Arachnothera).*—These are a Malayan form, only two species extending to India. The nest of the big spider-hunter *(A. magna)* is a very neat massive deep cup, sewn to a leaf of the plantain tree, and the eggs are deep greyish brown.

Honeysuckers, *(Œthopyga, Leptocoma, Arachnechthra.)*—One species, the purple honeysucker *(A. asiatica)*, is spread throughout India. The other species, and there are many, are very local. The greater number confined to the Himalayas. They build a beautiful little pear-shaped hanging nest, with a side entrance, overhung by a fringe, and lay two much speckled eggs. They are partially migratory and frequent warm valleys and jungles.

Flower-peckers, *(Dicæum, Piprisoma, Myzanthe, Pachyglossa).*—These birds are generally local and are not migratory. The nest is a beautiful little purse-shaped structure of a delicate felt-like substance hung not by a point but by an edge from a bough. The eggs are white in some species and spotted in others. They affect well-wooded localities, and often keep to the tops of high trees for feeding; though the nests are as often as not quite low down. The last two genera are only found in the eastern Himalayas.

Tree-creepers, *(Certhia, Salpornis.)*—The true tree-creepers *(Certhia)* are confined to the Himalayas where they are permanent residents. The nests are high up in trees behind crevices in bark and exceedingly difficult to find. The eggs are spotted. Of the spotted grey creeper *(Salpornis spilonota)* nothing is known. It is found in many localities, but nowhere common.

Wall-creepers, *(Tichodroma)*.—Only one species occurs in India. It breeds in the Himalayas at 3,000 to 5,000 feet altitude, descending to the foot of the hills in the cold weather. The nest is slight, placed in a crevice in a rock.

Nuthatches, *(Sitta, Dendrophila.)*—These are all permanent residents where they occur. They are found in forests or well-wooded tracts. They make their nests in hollows in decayed trees, lining the hole with feathers, wool, or moss, and closing up the entrance with a stiff gummy substance, till only a tiny circular orifice is left. The holes are often near the ground, but sometimes very high up in large trees. The eggs are spotted rather boldly.

Hoopoes, *(Upupa.)*—The common hoopoe *(U. epops)* migrates to the plains in the cold weather, but breeds only in the north-west Himalayas. The Indian hoopoe *(U. nigripennis)* is a permanent resident throughout the country. They nestle in holes in trees or buildings, lining the hole with a few feathers and leaves. They are domestic in their habits, often breeding about human dwellings. The eggs are greenish or brownish grey.

Shrikes, *(Lanius)*.—Butcher birds or shrikes are permanent residents where they occur. They usually place their nest in the fork of a thick bush, but sometimes they wedge it up against the trunk of a tree, or even place it on a dead stump. The eggs are typically whitish, with a thick ring of spots near the larger end; but sometimes the whole egg is more or less spotted. Shrikes generally frequent open country and avoid forests. The brown shrikes are migratory and leave upper India in the spring.

Wood shrikes, *(Tephrodornis)*.—The nests of the woodshrikes are small and very neatly made, usually placed in forks high up in trees and difficult to detect. The birds are not migratory, but the breeding of only one species, the common woodshrike *(T. ponticeriana)*, is known. Its eggs are very much like miniatures of the true shrikes.

Pied shrikes, *(Hemipus.)*—These birds are local and frequent hilly country. Very little is known as to their habits.

Cuckoo shrikes, *(Volvocivora, Graucalus.)*—These, like the woodshrikes, are permanent residents where they occur; but the nests are very difficult to find. They are small, neatly made, placed high up, and the outside is assimilated in appearance to the bark of the tree they are on. The eggs are boldly streaked and very handsome.

Minivets, *(Pericrocotus).*—Are almost always found in forests or well-wooded districts. They are gregarious during the cold weather, and some of them are migratory, but all the kinds that occur in India breed in this country. The nest is beautifully built, almost like a tumbler, with perpendicular sides, and placed on a horizontal branch high up. They are very difficult to find. The eggs are well spotted.

Drongo shrikes, *(Dicrurus, Buchanga, Chaptia, Bhringa, Edolius, Dissemurus, Chibia).*—Are almost entirely confined to forest tracts, with the exception of the common drongo shrike or "king crow" *(D. albirictus)*, which is found every where. They are not migratory, though some of the hills species ascend to higher elevations as the weather gets warmer; and the white-bellied king crow *(D. cœrulescens)* seem to disappear from the plains in the breeding season, but of its habits very little is known. They all make a loose basket work saucer-shaped nest of roots wedged into a horizontal fork at the end of a bough often at a considerable height from the ground. The common king crow (*D. albirictus*) sometimes lays pure white eggs, but the typical colour in this family is white, with a few claret or brown spots.

Swallow shrikes, *(Artamus).*—Are very local and little is known of their habits. They are generally found in clearings in forests, and are probably permanent residents.

Flycatchers, (*Tchitria, Myiagra, Leucocerca, Chelidorhynx, Cryptolopha, Hemichelidon, Alseonax, Ochromela, Eumyias, Cyornis, Muscicapula, Nitidula, Niltava, Anthipes, Siphia, Erythrosterna*).—The habits of this group show many variations. As a rule, flycatchers are to be found in forests and retired glens; but they also sometimes frequent gardens and orchards. Probably, all the Indian species breed within the limits of this country. The only doubtful ones being the robin flycatchers (*Erythrosterna*). Most of the flycatchers migrate to the plains in greater or less numbers during the cold weather. Out in the open plains the white-browed fan-tail (*L. aureola)* is the only widely distributed permanent resident. The paradise flycatcher (*T. paradisii),* the black-naped azure flycatcher (*M. azurea*), and the white-throated fan-tail *(L. fuscoventris)* breed in some of the moister and better wooded districts. Some of the blue red-breasts (*Cyornis*) breed in the plains of south India. All the others breed in the hills, and the greatest number breed in the Himalayas. Their nests are all ingenious. Some of them most beautiful little structures, seldom at any great height from the ground, and often resting on it. The eggs are in all cases prettily marked and spotted.

Wrens, (*Tesia, Pnœpyga, Troglodytes, Rimator*).—Are only found in the Himalayas within the Indian limits. They frequent moist forests and live in thick undergrowth. They are not migratory. Very little is known of their breeding, but they probably all make domed nests in thick creepers against trunks of trees.

Shortwings, (*Brachypteryx, Callene, Hodgsonius*).—Are found only in mountainous countries and like the wrens frequent dense underwood in forests. Very little is known of them, but they do not appear to be migratory.

Whistling thrushes, (*Myiophonus*).—Are hill birds, though they extend especially in the cold weather into the forests below. They are seldom found far from water or in open country, and they breed in retired places exclusively in the hills. The eggs are long, pointed, and freckled all over with minute spots.

Ground thrushes, (*Hydrornis, Pitta*).—Are birds of very retiring habits, keeping on or near the ground in tangled brushwood or dense cover. They appear to be very local in their distribution, and some of them migrate, but their shyness prevents much observation of their habits. The eggs are white, more or less spotted and streaked.

Water ouzels, (*Hydrobata*).—Are only found in the Himalayas frequenting streams of running water. The eggs are pure white.

Long-billed thrushes, (*Zoothera*).—Only one species is found in India. It is confined to the Himalayas, and frequents tangled brushwood by streams in dense forest. Nothing is known of its nidification or migrations. The eggs of *Zoothera*, as far as they are known, resemble those of *Pitta*.

Rock thrushes, (*Petrocossyphus*).—Are migratory birds frequenting rocky plains. They are only known to breed in India in the far north-west. The eggs are blue, slightly speckled.

Chat thrushes, (*Orocœtes*).—Are found commonly on wooded hills. They breed only in the Himalayas, but in the winter descend to the warm valleys and even to the plains. They all build their nests on the ground; and their eggs are clouded somewhat similarly to the eggs of the English robin.

Bush thrushes, (*Geocichla*).—Are migratory, breeding only in the hills, but extending far into the plains in the cold weather. They frequent open forests and glades. The position and shape of nest and the colour of the eggs are exact miniatures of those of the blackbirds to which these birds are very closely allied.

Blackbirds, (*Turdulus, Merula*).—Breed only in the hills and wander less in the cold weather than the bush thrushes or true thrushes. In habits and nidification, and also in the colour of their eggs, they closely resemble the English blackbird.

Thrushes, (*Turdus, Planesticus, Oreocincla*).—The true thrushes are rare in India. The Nilgiri thrush (*O. nilgiriensis*) is found in the hills of south India as a permanent resident. The black-throated thrush (*P. atrogularis*) is a cold weather visitant to the plains of upper India. The small-billed mountain thrush (*O. dauma*), which breeds in the Himalayas, also visits the plains in the winter, but the remainder of the thrushes are only found in the Himalayas. Many of them being extremely rare. Of the breeding of the genus *Planesticus*, nothing is known in this country. The eggs of *Oreocincla* are like miniatures of the whistling thrushes; being long, pointed, and freckled all over with minute pale spots. The breeding of the genus *Turdus* out here is similar to that of the missel thrush at home.

Finch thrushes, (*Paradoxornis, Heteromorpha*).—Nothing is known of their nidification. They are shy birds and rare, frequenting thick cover. They are only found in the eastern Himalayas and Khasia hills, where they are probably permanent residents, at 3,000 to 10,000 feet above the sea.

Tit thrushes, (*Chleuasicus, Suthora*).—Are also rare and confined to the eastern Himalayas and Khasia hills. Of their nidification nothing is known. They frequent brushwood and grass jungle.

Jay thrushes, (*Conostoma, Grammatoptila*).—Are shy, forest-loving birds, only found in the higher ranges of the eastern Himalayas. The red-billed jay thrush (*C. æmodium*) is only found near the snows. They do not appear to migrate. They build in thick brushwood or forest. The egg of *Conostoma* is white, with blotches and streaks. That of *Grammatoptila* is pale blue unspotted.

Shrike thrushes, (*Thamnocataphus, Gampsorhynchus*).—Are also confined to the eastern Himalayas, and their nidification is unknown. They occur at low elevations and frequent brushwood. Of one kind, the white-winged shrike thrush (*T. picatus*), only one specimen has ever been procured.

Tit babblers, (*Pyctorhis, Trichastoma*).—Only one of these, the yellow-eyed babbler (*P. sinensis*) is common. The other species are only found in north-east India. They frequent low jungle and brushwood, and are not migratory, breeding wherever they are found. The egg of the only species of which the breeding is known is beautifully marked with spots, clouds, and streaks.

Quaker thrushes, (*Alcippe*).—Are small birds frequenting dense forests and chiefly hilly countries. They are not migratory nor gregarious to any extent. The eggs are profusely spotted, and sometimes lined or blotched.

Wren babblers, (*Stachyris, Mixornis, Timalia, Dumetia, Pellorneum*).—Are a Malayan family, and the greater number of the species are confined to the north-east corner of India. The genus *Stachyris* is confined to the Himalayas, and is a strictly arboreal genus. All the others frequent brushwood and low thick jungle, and are generally gregarious. *Mixornis* and *Timalia* are eastern Himalayan forms. *Dumetia* is found in all India, but not very common anywhere. *Pellorneum* has an equally wide distribution, but is more common in hilly than level countries. They do not migrate. They build on or near the ground in brushwood. The eggs of some are pure white, of others more or less thickly speckled, and in one case, that of the rufous-bellied wren babbler (*D. hyperythra*), the eggs are streaked as well as spotted.

Scimitar babblers, (*Pomatorhinus, Xiphoramphus.*)—This is purely a hill genus. They are found at low elevations haunting under wood in open forest country. They do not migrate. One species is found in the Nilgiris. All the others are confined to the Himalayas and hill ranges of north-east India. They build on or very near the ground making a domed nest and laying very fragile elongated eggs. These are always, as far as is known, pure white, unspotted.

Laughing thrushes, (*Garrulax, Trochalopteron.*)—A group of richly-coloured, noisy, and generally gregarious birds which do not migrate and are confined to hilly countries. The nests are solitary, but the birds even in the breeding season keep usually in small parties. They are never found far from forests and love densely wooded tracts.

One species of *Garrulax* and three species of *Trochalopteron* are found in the hills of south India. The rest are all from the northern mountains. The nests are always in small trees or bushes in thick woods, never in open country. The eggs of one or two species are pure white; but the general colour of eggs of the various kinds of *Garrulax* is unspotted blue, sometimes pale, sometimes a very deep rich shade. In *Trochalopteron* the eggs are blue, sometimes unspotted. In one case (*T. phæniceum*) they are scrawled and streaked; but the usual type is that of the English song thrush (*T. musicus*) blue, with a few conspicuous dark spots.

Bar wings, (*Actinodura*).—Are confined to the eastern Himalayas and Khasia hills. They frequent forests, and though they breed on the ground, they are very arboreal in their habits. They occur usually from 3,000 to 10,000 feet elevations, and do not migrate. Their eggs are very little known.

Sibias, (*Sibia*).—Are only found in the Himalayas and Khasia hills. They are noisy, do not migrate, and are strictly arboreal in their habits. The eggs are clouded aud somewhat streaked on an ashy ground.

Babblers, (*Acanthoptila, Malacocercus, Layardia, Chattarhæa*).—Are some of the commonest and most widely spread birds in India. The genus *Acanthoptila* is confined to the Himalayas and is very little known. The others are plains birds, only one (*M. malabaricus*) being confined to the hilly portions of south India. They are to be found everywhere feeding chiefly on the ground and flitting about in brushwood in small parties, being of gregarious habits; though the nests are always solitary. They lay unspotted blue eggs. One species (*C. earlii*) is almost a reed-babbler, and is seldom found far from water. It frequents reeds and long grass among which its nest is placed.

Reed babblers, (*Megalurus, Chætornis, Schænicola, Eurycercus*).—Are very local; partly gregarious and only found in marshy tracts. Some of them appear to migrate, but their habits are not well known. The eggs are usually spotted on a white ground, but more information is required.

Bulbuls, (*Hypsepetes, Hemixos, Alcurus, Criniger, Ixos, Kelaartia, Rubigula, Brachypodius, Otocompsa, Pycnonotus, Phyllornis, Iora*).—The Malayan region is the head-quarters of the bulbul family, but no less than twenty-seven different kinds are found in India. They are found everywhere, and where found are permanent residents. Some kinds occur in the plains only and some in the hills. They are arboreal in their habits. Most of them prefer forest country, more or less dense, but some are found in open slightly wooded country. They build small neat cup-shaped nests, often very slight in structure; generally fixed in forks where two or three shoots divide near the ends of boughs; but sometimes hung from a horizontal fork like a tiny basket. The eggs are typically pinkish white, thickly spotted, and blotched with claret or purple. Of the green bulbuls (*Phyllornis*), the eggs are white, with a few brownish marks, and in the genus *Iora* the ground colour is greyish white, and the markings are very curious, jagged irregular streaks of greyish, reddish, or purplish brown.

Blue birds, (*Irena*).—Only one species is found in India, and that only in the Malabar forests. They are strictly arboreal in their habits and do not migrate. They keep in small parties near the tops of high trees. The nest is rough and untidy, not the least like an oriole. The eggs are pale greenish, streaked and spotted with dusky.

Orioles, (*Oriolus*).—Are permanent residents in India, but they wander much in the cold weather. They are quite arboreal in their habits, and build in trees a beautitul neat basket-shaped nest. They are not gregarious. The eggs are glossy white, with a few dark spots. They are found all over India, both in hills and plains.

Robins, (*Copsychus, Kittacincla, Myiomela, Grandala, Thamnobia*).—This group comprises many widely differing forms. The magpie robin (*Copsychus saularis*) is found throughout India in wooded tracts and gardens. The shama (*Kittacincla macroura*) is very local, and inhabits only dense thickets in forests. The long-winged blue chat (*Grandala cœlicolor*) is a most anomalous form, approaching in some points very near the starlings. It is only found near the snow in the alpine Himalayas. The white-tailed blue chat (*Myiomela leucura*) is also confined to the Himalayas, and is found at rather high altitudes. The true robins of India (*Thamnobia*) are found in the open plains throughout the country. All the robins build on or very near the ground often in banks or clefts of rocks. They do not migrate; are solitary, and lay spotted or more often clouded eggs.

Bush chats, (*Pratincola, Oreiocola*).—A group of small birds found throughout the plains, especially in dry open country in the cold weather, but retiring, as a rule, to the hills to breed. Only a very few nestle in the plains. Their habits are very much those of the robins, and their nests and eggs are also very similar. The genus *Oreiocola* differs from *Pratincola*, in that the only species which occurs here (*O. Jerdoni*) is a shy, retiring bird, frequenting dense thickets and long grass jungle. Its breeding habits are unknown.

Stone chats, (*Saxicola*).—Are only cold weather visitants to this country, and are found in dry open plains; feeding on the ground and perching on stones, rocks, and occasionally on bushes. None of them are known to breed in India; but where they do breed, their nests are on the ground near shelter, and the eggs are blue, with a few faint spots.

Rock chats, (*Cercomela*).—Are very similar in their habits to stone chats, and are found in similar localities. One (*C. fusca*) is a permanent resident in India, and breeds where it is found. Of the other very little is known. It is extremely rare. Their eggs are like those of stone chats.

Redstarts, (*Rutacilla, Chæmorrornis*).—The redstarts are all migratory, only one (*R. rufiventris*) wanders throughout India in the cold weather, but many species are found in the Himalayas. They are generally to be met with by water in open country. One species (*C. leucocephala*) breeds in the alpine Himalayas, and the plumbous water robin (*R. fuliginosa*) breeds throughout the Himalayas. These two latter lay spotted eggs. The others, as far as has been ascertained, lay unspotted blue eggs, rather elongated in shape; but they are not known to breed in this country.

Wood chats, (*Larvivora, Ianthia, Tarsiger, Calliope, Cyanecula*).—The wood chats are migratory birds. A few are found in the plains in the cold weather. A few breed in the hills, and others leave the country altogether for breeding purposes. They frequent open forests, perching low and feeding near the ground. The blue throat wood chat (*Cyanecula suecica*) is generally found near water, often in the weeds at margins of tanks. Their nests are very little known, but the eggs appear to vary much in character. Of *Larvivora* the eggs are mottled and streaked. Of *Ianthia* they are faintly zoned. Of *Tarsiger* they are unspotted blue. Of *Calliope* unspotted pale buff.

Reed warblers, (*Acrocephalus, Arundinax, Dumeticola, Locustella, Tribura*).—The reed warblers are generally migratory. The three species of *Acrocephalus* are found throughout India in the cold weather and retire to the Himalayas to breed. They lay white eggs thickly spotted. The other genera are very little known. They inhabit dense swamps and marshy tracts, and are very difficult to flush, and consequently rare in collections. None of them are known to breed in the plains.

Hill warblers, (*Horornis, Horeites.*)—A group of small plain coloured birds found at high elevations in the eastern Himalayas, and some on the Khasia hills. They frequent brush-wood and thick grass and shun observation. The eggs vary a good deal, but typically appear to be richly coloured, chocolate brown, or dull purple. The nests are near the ground in thick brush-wood.

Tailor birds, (*Orthotomus*).—Are found throughout India, shunning the dry open plains, and creeping about in trees or brush-wood. They are non-migratory, and the eggs are spotted.

Wren warblers, (*Prinia, Drymoipus, Burnesia, Franklinia*).—A large group of tiny birds which are spread throughout India, not however ascending the Himalayas to any height. They affect open plains or gardens creeping about in grass or bushes. They make purse-like nests, deep with an opening near the top, or a little cup sewn in leaves like a tailor bird's nest. They do not migrate, but breed wherever they are found. The eggs of the *Prinias*, with ten tail feathers, are brick red. Those of the *Prinias*, with twelve tail feathers, are blue, with small spots. The smaller species of *Drymoipus* lay blue eggs, richly streaked and blotched, while the larger species lay dull-coloured clouded eggs. Of *Burnesia* and *Franklinia* the eggs are profusely speckled.

Grass warblers, (*Cisticola, Gramminicola*).—Are spread locally throughout the plains in marshy spots, frequenting thick grass and shunning observation. The eggs are spotted.

Scrub warblers, (*Drymœca*).—One species only is found, and that in the trans-Indus hills in low scrub jungle, where it is a permanent resident. The eggs are profusely spotted.

Tailed hill warblers, (*Suya*).—These birds are found only in the Himalayas where they take the place of the *Drymoipi*, which they much resemble in appearance and habits. They are not migratory in the true sense of the word, but descend to the warm valleys in the winter. The eggs are zoned.

Tree warblers, (*Neornis, Hyppolais, Phylloscopus, Reguloides, Culicepeta, Abrornis, Tickellia*).—A large group of very small birds, many of which are brightly coloured. They are migratory as a rule. Only one (*Hyppolais rama*) is known to breed in the plains, and that very rarely, the majority migrating north and west. The genus *Neornis* build cup-shaped nests, and lay deep dull purple red eggs, with a tendency to a zone at the large end. They are permanent residents in the eastern Himalayas. Of the breeding of the *Phylloscopi* very little is known, but some of them certainly breed in the Himalayas. The *Reguloides*, *Culicepeta*, and *Abrornis* also breed in the Himalayas to a great extent; typically they make domed nests on the ground in mossy or grassy banks; but some build high up in trees (as *R. proregulus*), and others (as *R. occipitalis*) breed often in holes in decayed trees. The eggs of *Culicepeta*, *Abrornis*, and at least one of the *Reguloides* (*R. occipitalis*) are pure white, with some of the *Reguloides*, they are spotted, but the breeding of these birds is comparatively little known. Of *Tickellia* the breeding is unknown, but it appears to be a permanent resident in the Himalayas.

Golden-crested wrens, (*Regulus*).—Only one species is known, and that is a permanent resident in the Himalayas at high elevations. In habits it closely resembles the English golden-crested wren, and its nest is similar, but the eggs have not as yet been taken.

Whitethroats, (*Sylvia*).—Are migratory birds, appearing in the plains of India in the cold weather. One species only (*S. affinis*) is known to breed in the north-west Himalayas, and this in its habits is identical with the English whitethroat.

Fork tails, (*Henicurus*).—Are an Indo-Malayan family of birds. They occur in India only in the Himalayas, and are not migratory. They are always found near water, generally running water. The nest is a shallow compact structure of mosses and roots and fibres placed on banks or rocks, and the eggs are speckled in all the species of which the breeding is known.

Wagtails, (*Budytes, Motacilla, Nemoricola*).—Are very migratory birds. Only two appear to be permanent residents in the plains of India: one the Indian pied wagtail (*M. maderaspatana*), the other a very anomalous form, the black-breasted wagtail (*Nemoricola indica*), which is rare every where, and of which the nest has never been taken. Of the remainder, three species (*M. luzionensis, M. melanope*, and *B. calcaratus*) are known to breed in the Himalayas. The rest probably migrate still further north; breeding in Turkistan. In habits they are all alike keeping to plains near water or moist fields, building a shallow nest of roots and hair on the ground and laying speckled eggs.

Pipits, (*Pipastes, Anthus, Corydalla, Agrodroma, Heterura*).—Are as a rule migratory, though many of them are permanent residents in some parts of India. One of the tree pipits (*P. montanus*) appears to be confined to the Nilgiris. The others are cold weather visitants to the plains, retiring to the alpine Himalayas to breed. So also with the true pipits (*Anthus* as restricted), which are known to breed on this side of the snows. Of the titlarks (*Corydalla*), one (*C. rufula*) is a very common permanent resident throughout the plains. The others are only cold weather migrants. Of the stone pipits (*Agrodroma*), one (*A. griseorufescens*) is a cold weather visitant to the plains, but breeds in the north-western Himalayas; another (*A. campestris*) is abundant in the cold weather, and is said to breed in the plains, but this requires confirmation; the third (*A. cinnamomea*) is confined to the Nilgiris, where it is a permanent resident. The genus *Heterura*, of which there is only one species in India, is confined to the Himalayas, where it is a permanent resident. All the pipits make their nest on the ground, sheltered by grass, on open plains or hill sides, and lay richly blotched or spotted eggs.

Thrush tits, (*Cochoa*).—Are a very remarkable group of birds. They are confined to the eastern Himalayas, frequent forests at moderate elevations, and in their nidification and eggs much resemble blackbirds. There are only two species in India, both rare.

Shrike tits, (*Pteruthius*).—Are confined to the Himalayas. Of one kind (*P. rufiventer*), the nest has never been found. Of the other (*P. erythropterus*), the egg is one of the rarest in collections. The shrike tits are arboreal in their habits, frequent well-wooded slopes at moderate elevations. They lay speckled eggs in a basket-shaped nest of moss and roots hung from a fork near the top of a tree.

Hill tits, (*Allotrius, Cutia, Leioptila, Leiothrix, Siva, Minla, Proparus, Ixulus, Yuhina, Myzornis, Erpornis*).—Are also confined to the Himalayas, and with few exceptions to the eastern Himalayas and such outlying ranges as the Khasia hills. They are very arboreal in their habits, frequent well-wooded tracts, and generally associate in small flocks. They usually make rather massive cup-shaped nests, about five to ten feet from the ground, and lay spotted eggs, in which the markings frequently form a zone at the large end. One species (*Yuhina nigrimentum*) is known to lay pure white eggs, and another (*Myzornis pyrrhoura*) is believed to lay unspotted eggs also. As a rule these birds are not migratory, but breed wherever they are found.

Tits, (*Zosterops, Sylviparus, Cephalopyrus, Egithaliscus, Lophophanes, Parus, Machlolophus, Melaniparus, Melanochlora*).—Are as a rule confined to the Himalayas. One (*Zosterops palpebrosus*) is found throughout India as a permanent resident. One (*Parus cinereus*) is found in all wooded hills. Another (*Parus nuchalis*) is only found in central and south India. Another (*Machlolophus jerdoni*) is only found in the hills of south India. All the rest are confined to the Himalayas, and a great number of them are found in the eastern Himalayas only. They are not as a rule migratory, and are by no means shy, often associating in small flocks. The nest and eggs of *Zosterops palpebrosus* are quite aberrant (the eggs are pale unspotted blue). The nest of *Sylviparus* is unknown. So also are those of *Melaniparus* and *Melanochlora*. The nest of *Egithaliscus* is like that of the bottle tits in England, while all the others are typically "parine" in their nidification, building in holes, in walls, or decayed trees, and laying spotted eggs.

Hedge sparrows, (*Accentor*).—There are several kinds of hedge sparrows found in the upper regions of the Himalayas; but nowhere else in India. They are not migratory, and their nests and eggs as far as is known are similar to those of the hedge sparrow in England.

Ravens and crows, (*Corvus*).—Ravens are found only in the Himalayas and western continental India. They frequent open country, and do not appear to be entirely migratory, though they wander far in the cold weather. Crows are found all over India. Their nests and eggs are all of one general type, which is well known.

Jackdaws, (*Colæus*).—One species, the common jackdaw (*C. monedula*) is found in the north-west Himalayas, where it is a permanent resident. Its habits are well known. It migrates to the Punjab in the winter, but does not breed there.

Nutcrackers, (*Nucifraga*).—Are confined to the Himalayas, chiefly the western Himalayas. They keep to rather high elevations, frequent pine forests, and in habits closely resemble jays and magpies. They are not migratory.

Magpies, (*Pica*).—Two species occur in the alpine Himalayas, where they are permanent residents. Their habits are identical with those of the English magpie.

Jays, (*Garrulus, Urocissa, Cissa*).—Are found only in the Himalayas within the Indian limit. They keep to open forests, are not migratory, and feed partly on the ground. The eggs of all are profusely spotted, and the nest is generally a loose structure of twigs, with a slight inner casing of fine roots.

Tree pies, (*Dendrocitta*).—Are found throughout India in wooded country. Their habits and nests are very similar to those of the jays, and they do not migrate, but the eggs are less thickly spotted.

Choughs, (*Fregilus, Pyrrhocorax*).—Are permanent residents in the alpine Himalayas; but their breeding in this country has only very recently been ascertained. They nestle in holes, in rocks, and in buildings, and their eggs are similar to those of the European chough. A few migrate as far south as the Punjab in the cold weather.

Starlings, (*Sturnus*).—Are cold weather visitants to the plains of India, migrating north and west to breed. One only (*S. nitens*) breeds within our limits in Kashmir and the extreme north-west Punjab. They build in holes and lay unspotted blue eggs.

Mynahs, (*Sturnopastor, Acridotheres, Temenuchus, Pastor, Saraglossa, Eulabes*).—As a rule these birds are not migratory. The genus *Pastor* perhaps more properly belongs to the starlings. The only species of *Pastor* that occurs here (*P. roseus*) is very migratory, and does not breed in this country. The true mynahs (*Acridotheres, Temenuchus, Sturnopastor*) are very domestic, and are found almost everywhere. The stare (*Saraglossa*) is confined to the Himalayas, and the grackles (*Eulabes*) to warm forest country. All build in holes, except the pied mynah (*S. contra*) which makes a conspicuous nest like a truss of hay in the outer fork of a bare tree. The eggs of the rose-coloured pastor (*P. roseus*) are not known. The true mynahs lay unspotted blue eggs. But the eggs of the stare and of the grackles are all spotted.

Weaver birds, (*Ploceus*).—Are highly gregarious, but not migratory. They are somewhat locally distributed, and prefer wooded country near long grass and water. They lay pure white eggs.

Munias, (*Munia, Estrelda*).—Are all permanent residents in some part of India. They wander a good deal in the cold weather, and frequent grass jungle near water or open glades in forests. They make large rough globular nests and lay pure white eggs.

Sparrows, (*Passer*).—Are widely distributed and do not as a rule migrate, though in the winter they associate in flocks. Their eggs are all profusely spotted.

Buntings, (*Emberiza, Euspiza, Melophus*).—Are usually migratory birds, found in this country chiefly in the cold weather. Two species (*Emberiza striolata* and *Melophus melanicterus*) are permanent residents and breed in the plains. Two or three kinds of buntings breed in the Himalayas, but all the rest go further north or west to breed. They frequent open ground or rocks with scanty jungle. The corn buntings (*Euspiza)* are generally found in cultivated ground. They all nestle on or close to the ground, under shelter, and the eggs are spotted and often scrawled with fine hair-like lines.

Finches, (*Hesperiphona, Mycerobas, Pyrrhula, Pyrrhoplectes, Loxia, Hæmatospiza, Propyrrhula, Carpodacus, Propasser, Procarduelis, Pyrrhospiza, Callacanthis, Carduelis, Chrysomitris, Metoponia, Fringilla, Montifringilla, Fringillauda*).—A few finches wander to the foot of the hills in the winter, but the common rose finch (*Carpodacus erythrinus*) is the only one found in the plains of India. All the others occur in the Himalayas only, chiefly at high elevations. They are all more or less migratory. Of arboreal habits, frequenting forests and wooded tracts, and of their breeding, very little is known. All the eggs of this group that are known are prettily, some very handsomely, marked.

Bush larks, (*Mirafra*).—Are spread throughout the plains of India. They frequent open forests, grass jungle, and edges of cultivation, are not migratory, build on the ground in short grass, and lay profusely spotted eggs.

Finch larks, (*Ammomanes, Pyrrhalauda*).—Are also permanent residents of the plains of India frequenting drier and more open ground and avoiding cultivation. They are widely distributed. Their eggs are profusely speckled.

Larks, (*Calandrella, Melanocorypha, Alaudala, Otocoris, Spizalauda, Alauda, Galerita, Certhilauda*).—Are more or less migratory, associating in flocks in the cold weather, but many species breed in India. The short-toed larks (*Calandrella*), the calandra larks (*Melanocorypha)*, the horned larks (*Otocoris*), and probably also the desert larks (*Certhilauda*) are merely cold weather visitants, and do not breed at all within our limits. The Himalayan sky lark (*A. dulcivox*) breeds only in the Himalayas, while the others breed in suitable localities throughout the country. The sky larks (*Alauda*) affect damp grassy spots. The sand larks (*Alaudala*) frequent the sandy beds of large rivers. All the others are found in dry, open, or cultivated plains. They all build on the ground and lay spotted eggs.

Pigeons, (*Treron, Crocopus, Osmotreron, Sphenocercus, Carpophaga, Alsocomus, Palumbus, Palumbæna, Columba*).—There are several well-marked groups of pigeons. The green pigeons (*Treron, Crocopus, Osmotreron, Sphenocercus*) are forest-loving, fruit-eating birds, partly gregarious, and wandering a good deal during the winter, though all are permanent residents of the Indo-Malayan region, and the species that occur in India breed there too. The imperial pigeons (*Carpophaga*) are similar in their habits, but even more confined to dense forests. The wood pigeons (*Alsocomus, Palumbus*) are more migratory, more shy, and with one exception confined to mountain ranges. The stock pigeon (*Palumbæna*) is strictly migratory, visiting India in the cold weather only, in vast flocks. The true pigeons (*Columba*) are gregarious, and are probably permanent residents where they occur, but this has only been ascertained in the case of the common blue pigeon (*C. intermedia*). All pigeons lay either one or two pure white eggs on a small rough platform of sticks.

Doves, (*Macropygia, Turtur, Chalcophaps*).—Are less gregarious than pigeons. They all breed in India. Only one, Sykes' turtle dove (*T. meena*), appears to wander much from its breeding place. They feed almost entirely on the ground, and are very widespread in this country. They lay two pure white eggs on a tiny platform of sticks.

Sandgrouse, (*Pterocles, Syrrhaptes*).—Are usually only cold weather visitants to this country. They associate in large flocks, and frequent dry, open, or cultivated plains. The painted sandgrouse (*P. fasciatus*) affects rocky ground, and the Thibetan sandgrouse (*Syrrhaptes tibetanus*) is only found in the Himalayas at great elevations. Two only of the sandgrouse, the common and the painted, are known to breed with any regularity in this country. Their eggs are richly coloured and blotched. In shape they are elongated and cylindrical. The eggs of a third kind P. *lichtensteini* have lately been taken in Sind.

Pheasants, (*Pavo, Polyplectron, Lophophorus, Ceriornis, Euplocamus, Ithaginis, Pucrasia, Phasianus, Gallophasis*).—With the exception of the peacock (*Pavo cristatus*), which is found in wooded tracts throughout India, the *Phasianidæ* are confined to the Himalayas. They are found at all elevations, but only in forest country, with dense undergrowth. They are all permanent residents, breeding on the mountains, and descending into the valleys in the winter to feed. The eggs of many of them are boldly blotched, while others approach closely to the eggs of domestic fowls.

Jungle fowl, (*Gallus*).—Are more tropical birds, being found in dense thickets and forests throughout the country. They too are permanent residents, breeding where found. The eggs are like those of the Cochin-China fowls.

Spur fowl, (*Galloperdix*).—Are confined to rocky ridges and the dense jungles that fringe their bases in central and southern India where they breed. They are shy and wary, and conceal themselves in the densest cover. The eggs vary from creamy white to "cafe au lait."

Grouse, (*Tetraogallus, Lerwa*).—Are only found near the snow in the alpine Himalayas. They lay boldly blotched eggs as far as has been ascertained, and frequent grassy and rocky slopes near snow.

Partridges, (*Perdix, Francolinus, Caccabis, Ammoperdix, Ortigornis, Arboricola*).—Of the true partridges only one (*P. hodsoniæ*) is found in India. It frequents the alpine Himalayas at great altitude. The black and painted partridges (*Francolinus*) frequent thick jungle and grass near water and cultivation. The rock partridges (*Caccabis, Ammoperdix*) frequent rocky hills and open grassy slopes. Of the grey partridges one (*O. gularis*) is a swamp partridge found only in the Terais, the other is common where there is cover throughout the plains. Wood partridges (*Arboricola*) are only found in the Himalayas in dense under-wood in forests, and are difficult to flush. Partridges do not migrate and breed wherever found. The eggs of the chukor are spotted. All other partridges lay unspotted, buff, or cream coloured eggs.

Quails, (*Perdicula, Coturnix, Excalfatoria, Turnix*).—Some of the quails are migratory, but all that occur in India breed more or less in this country. The bush quails (*Perdicula*) frequent jungle and underwood, so does the blue-breasted quail (*E. chinensis*). The other quails affect cultivation or grassy plains. The eggs of the bush quails are like miniature partridges' eggs. The eggs of the true quails (*Coturnix*) are boldly blotched; and those of the bustard quails and button quails are profusely spotted and speckled.

Bustards, (*Eupodotis, Houbara, Sypheotides, Otis*).—The great bustard (*E. edwardsii*) is a permanent resident in the arid portions of continental India, frequenting low scrub and scanty grass jungle. The florikin (*S. bengalensis*) is a permanent resident in the dense grass jungles of eastern upper India. The likh (*S. auritus*) is found throughout India in the cold weather in suitable localities, but as yet it has only been known to breed in the Deccan among tufts of grass on cotton soil. The houbara and the true bustards (*Otis*) are only found in the arid plains of the extreme north-west. All the bustards lay dark-coloured handsomely marked eggs.

Plovers, (*Cursorius, Rhinoptilus, Glareola, Squatarola, Charadrius, Œgialites, Vanellus, Chettusia, Lobivanellus, Sarciophorus, Hoplopterus, Esacus, Œdicnemus, Strepsilas, Dromas, Hæmatopus*).—Plovers are more or less gregarious and widely spread in India. They frequent open country, avoiding forests entirely as a rule, and feeding on the ground in ploughed or fallow fields. The grey plover (*Squatarola helvetica*), the golden plover (*Charadrius longipes*), all the ringed plovers (*Œgialites*), except *Œ. curonicus*, the crested lapwing (*Vanellus cristatus*), the true lapwings (*Chettusia*), and the oyster catcher (*Hæmatopus ostralegus*), are migratory and only visit this country in the cold season. The remainder are either known or believed to breed in India. The courier plovers (*Cursorius*), the wattled lapwings (*Lobivanellus, Sarciophorus*), and the stone plover (*Œdicnemus*) breed in fields or plains away from water. Of the breeding of the genus *Rhinoptilus* nothing is known, but they frequent scanty jungle on rocky hills. The swallow plovers (*Glareola*), the ringed plovers (*Œgialites*), the spur-winged plovers (*Hoplopterus*), and the great stone plover (*Esacus*) lay their eggs on the bare sand in the beds of great rivers. While the turnstone (*Strepsilas interpres*) and the crab plover (*Dromas ardeola*) lay on the sand on the sea-coast. The eggs of all plovers are dark-coloured and richly marked.

Cranes, (*Grus, Anthropoides*).—The only crane that permanently resides in India is the sarus (*Grus antigone*). It feeds in open plains and fields, but breeds on islands in swamps among rushes. All the other cranes are migratory visiting India in the winter in large flocks. The eggs are spotted or blotched.

Snipe, (*Scalopax, Gallinago, Rhynchæa*).—The painted snipe (*R. bengalensis*) is the only permanent resident. It is somewhat local and affects thick weeds in marshy places. The woodcock (*S. rusticola*) visits the lower Himalayas in the winter, also the hilly portions of the south of India. A few pairs at least breed in the alpine Himalayas. The true snipe (*Gallinago*) are all migratory coming in the cold weather. A few of the common snipe *may* breed in the north-west Himalayas, but, as a rule, all the snipe go beyond Indian limits to breed. The eggs are handsomely marked.

Godwits, (*Macroramphus, Limosa, Terekia*).—Are only winter visitants. None of them breed in this country.

Curlews, (*Numenius, Ibidorhynchus*).—Are cold weather visitants and breed beyond the border.

Stints, (*Philomachus, Tringa, Eurinorhynchus, Calidris, Phalaropus*).—Are merely cold weather visitants.

Sandpipers, (*Actitis, Totanus, Himantopus, Recurvirostra*).—Are all migratory. The stilt (*H. candidus*) congregates for breeding purposes in one or more localities in the plains. The common sandpiper (*A. hypoleucus*) breeds in considerable numbers in the beds of rivers in Kashmir; but all the other birds of this class go beyond the border to lay their eggs. The eggs are spotted or blotched on a buffy ground.

Jacanas, (*Hydrophasianus, Metopidus*).—The water pheasants are permanent residents, frequenting weedy marshes. In the cold weather they retire to the moister districts, but in the rains they wander wherever there are marshes. They lay deep bronze-coloured eggs. In one species unmarked, in the other scrawled all over with fine black lines.

Coots, (*Porphyrio, Fulica, Gallicrex, Gallinula*).—Are all permanent residents, frequenting marshes and ponds or dense thickets near water. They breed both in hills and plains. Their eggs are spotted.

Rails, (*Porzana, Rallus*).—Of these birds very little is known. They frequent dense weeds and thickets near water. They breed both in the hills and plains, but are flushed with difficulty, and it is not known whether they migrate. The eggs typically are spotted.

Storks, (*Leptoptilus, Mycteria, Ciconia, Melanopelargus*).—The true storks (*Ciconia*) are cold weather visitants, and do not breed in India. The adjutants (*Leptoptilus*) have special breeding places to which they resort. While the other storks (*Mycteria* and *Melanopelargus*) breed throughout India on high trees near water. Their eggs are dingy white unspotted.

Herons, (*Ardea, Herodias, Demi-egretta, Buphus, Ardeola, Butorides*).—Are permanent residents, breeding on trees near water in all parts of India. They all lay unspotted blue eggs.

Bitterns, (*Ardetta, Botaurus*).—It is not as yet ascertained whether the common bittern (*Botaurus stellaris*) is a permanent resident, but probably it, as well as all the other bitterns, breeds in India. They frequent thick reeds in swamps, are very difficult to flush, and lay unspotted greenish eggs.

Night herons, (*Nycticorax*).—Are found near water. They are permanent residents breeding on trees, and sometimes it is said in reeds. They lay pale green eggs.

Ibises, (*Tantalus, Platalea, Anastomus, Threskiornis, Geronticus, Falcinellus*).—The glossy ibis (*Falcinellus igneus*) is a cold weather visitant, coming in in large flocks, and leaving the country when the breeding season comes. All the others are permanent residents, and are as a rule gregarious breeders, making their nests on high trees near water. The eggs of the pelican ibis (*T. leucocephalus*) are dull white; so also are those of the shell ibis (*A. oscitans*). Those of the white ibis (*T. melanocephalus*) are very pale green, and the spoonbill (*P. leucorodia*) and the king curlew (*G. papillosus*) lay spotted eggs.

Flamingoes, (*Phœnicopterus*).—Are cold weather visitants, and do not breed in this country.

Geese, (*Anser, Sarkidiornis*).—The black-backed goose (*S. melanotus*) is found throughout the country in swampy parts and is a permanent resident. All the other geese leave India to breed elsewhere. The eggs are ivory white.

Ducks and **Teal,** (*Nettapus, Dendrocygna, Casarca, Tadorna, Spatula, Anas, Chaulelasmus, Dafila, Mareca, Querquedula, Branta, Aythya, Fuligula, Clangula, Mergus*).—Almost all the ducks are migratory coming to India for the winter months only. The cotton teal (*Nettapus coromandelianus*), the two whistling teal (*Dendrocygna arcuata* and *D. major*), the spotted-billed duck (*A. pœcilorhynchus*), and the pink-headed duck (*A. caryophyllacea*) are permanent residents, and breed where they occur in the plains of India. The mallard (*Anas boschas*) and the white-eyed duck (*Aythya nyroca*) remain to breed in Kashmir. All the rest go farther north towards central Asia. The eggs are glossy white, buff or "cafe au lait."

Grebes, (*Podiceps*).—The little grebe (*P. philippinus*) is found on tanks and ponds throughout India, and is a permanent resident. The crested grebe is a winter migrant in continental India, retiring to Kashmir to breed. The eggs are dull white.

Gulls, (*Larus, Xema*); **Petrels,** (*Thallassidroma, Pelicanoides*); **Puffins** (*Puffinus*).—Are found at sea round the coast. Some of the gulls coming far inland at times. None of these birds breed within our limits, but they are believed to lay on the rocky islands of the Red sea.

Terns, (*Sylochelidon, Gelochelidon, Hydrochelidon, Seena, Sterna,*

Sternula, Thallasseus, Onochoprion, Anous).—Terns are as a rule migratory, and congregate in flocks during the breeding season. The Caspian tern (*S. caspius*) does not breed in this country; and the gull-billed tern (*G. anglicus*) only breeds in the far north-west. The marsh terns (*Hydrochelidon*) breed here and there in India gregariously on weeds floating in swamps. The true terns (*Gelochelidon, Sterna, Seena, Sternula*) lay their eggs on the bare sand in the beds of large rivers. The sea terns (*Thallasseus, Onochoprion, Anous*) lay on bare rocky islands off the sea-coast. All the terns lay handsomely marked eggs.

Skimmers, (*Rhynchops*).—Are permanent residents here, and are similar in their eggs, habits, and distribution to the true terns (*Sterna*).

Fishers, (*Phaeton, Sula, Attagen*).—Are all sea-birds which are found in Indian waters, but which are not known to breed on our coasts.

Pelicans, (*Pelecanus*).—Pelicans are widely spread throughout India in the cold weather, but of their breeding here nothing is known. They are said to build on trees.

Cormorants, (*Graculus*).—Are permanent residents in India, frequenting rivers and large tanks. They are gregarious and consequently local breeders. The breeding of the big cormorant (*G. carbo*) is not accurately known; and this bird is certainly to a great extent migratory. The eggs of cormorants are dull chalky white.

Snake Birds, (*Plotus*).—Are permanent residents in India, and are similar in their habits and eggs to the cormorants.

PART II.

INDEX.

LIST OF BIRDS THAT ARE KNOWN TO BREED IN INDIA, SHOWING DURATION OF BREEDING SEASON.

THIS list only contains those birds of which the eggs have been taken: of course, many more birds do breed here, and further research would greatly extend the list.

Column I gives the number as in Jerdon's hand-book of the Birds of India. Where no number is given in this column, it indicates a species added to the list of birds of India, since Jerdon's book was published.

Column II gives the English name of each bird. In most cases the name as given by Jerdon is adhered to. In some cases where it seemed advisable the alterations introduced by Mr. Hume in his more recent works have been adopted; and in a few cases alterations have been made which further knowledge has rendered desirable.

Column III gives the scientific name for each bird. In this column many deviations from the names as given by Jerdon, both generic and specific, will be found; but the revisions shown in Mr. Gray's hand-list have not been adopted in their entirety as they quite revolutionise the nomenclature heretofore in use, and with which we have become through Jerdon's book familiar; and though possibly Mr. Gray's list may be more scientifically correct, it is inexpedient to adopt it in this book which is written chiefly for beginners in this country, in whose hands Jerdon is the only text-book; for the disadvantage of a wholesale change, especially on merely arbitrary points, is obvious. Where it has been absolutely necessary for accuracy, I have entered the new names; and in case of a difference, the number (in Jerdon), which is quoted in Column I, will determine the bird referred to.

The remaining columns require little explanation. The portion marked off opposite each bird's name indicates the season and duration of the period in which its eggs may be found.

The breeding season thus noted includes every month in which each bird is known to breed in any locality. Where the breeding of a bird is confined for any particular season to any particular locality, a letter signifying the locality is placed over the line denoting the breeding during that month. Where no distinguishing letter is placed over the line, it indicates that the bird in that month is breeding wherever it is found.

Thus :—B. over the line signifies "Bengal."
C. „ „ "Central Provinces only."
H. „ „ "Himalayas only."
I. P. „ „ "The plains of India."
K. „ „ "Kumaon only."
M. „ „ "Moist tracts only."
N. „ „ "Nilgiris only."
P. „ „ "Punjab only."
R. „ „ "Rajputana only."
S. „ „ "South India only."
U. „ „ "Upper India."

INDEX.

LIST OF BIRDS KNOWN TO BREED IN INDIA, SHOWING PERIOD AND DURATION OF BREEDING SEASON.

Nos. in Jerdon.	English Names.	Scientific Names.	Jan.	Feb.	March.	April.	May.	June.	July.	Augt.	Sept.	Oct.	Nov.	Dec.
2	The king Vulture	Otogyps calvus	—	—	—	—								
3	The roc „	Gyps himalayensis	—	—	—								—	
4	The pale long-billed „	„ pallescens	—	—									—	
	The long-billed „	„ indicus	—	—									—	—
5	The white-backed „	„ bengalensis	—	—	—							—	—	—
	The bay „	„ fulvescens		—	—									
6	The white scavenger „	Perenopteron ginginianus	—	—	—	—	-H- —							
7	The bearded „	Gypaetus barbatus	—	—	—								—	—
9	The shaheen Falcon	Falco perigrinator	—											
	The black-capped „	„ atriceps		—	—									
11	The lagger „	„ jugger	—	—	—									
16	The red-headed Merlin	Lithofalco chicquera	—	—	—	—	-P- —							
17	The Kestril	Tinnunculus alaudarius		—	-N- —	—	—	-H- —						
18	The lesser „	Erythropus cenchris					—	—						
21	The Goshawk	Astur palumbarius				—								
23	The Shikra	Micronisus badius				—	—	—						
24	The sparrow Hawk	Accipiter nisus					—	—						
	The dove „	„ melaschistus				—	—	—						
27	The imperial Eagle	Aquila mogilnik		—	—	—								
28	The spotted „	„ nœvia				—	—	—						
29	The Indian tawny „	„ vindhyana	—	—	—	—	-M- —	—					—	—
30	The long-legged „	„ hastata				—	—	—						
31	The booted „	„ pennata		—										
32	The black „	Neopus malaiensis	—											
33	Bonellis' „	Nisaetus Bonellii	—	—	—	—								—
36	The Nepal hawk „	Spizaetus nipalensis	—	—	—	—	—							
	The changeable hawk „	„ caligatus		B— —	—	—	—	—						

Nos. in Jerdon.	English Names.	Scientific Names.	Jan.	Feb.	March.	April	May.	June.	July.	Augt.	Sept.	Oct.	Nov.	Dec.
38	The short-toed Eagle	Circaetus gallicus		—	—	—								
39	The crested serpent „	Spilornis cheela			—	—								
	The lesser Indian harrier „	„ minor					—							
41	The bar-tailed fishing „	Polioaetus ichthyaetus	—	— ?										
	The Himalayan fishing „	„ plumbeus	—			K								
42	The ring-tailed fishing „	Haliaetus leucoryphus	—	—								—	—	—
43	The white-bellied sea „	„ leucogaster	—	—										—
45	The long-legged Buzzard	Buteo canescens	—	—	—	—								
48	The white-eyed „	Poliornis teesa			—	—	—							
55	The brahminy Kite	Haliastur indus	—	—	—	—								
56	The common „	Milvus govinda	—	—	—	—							B	B
	The greater Indian „	„ major	—	—	—	—	—							
57	The crested honey Buzzard	Pernis cristata				—	—	—	—					
59	The black-winged Kite	Elanus melanopterus	—	C		—	U			R				C
60	The Indian screech Owl	Strix indica	—	C	—	U	—							C
61	The grass „	Scelostrix caudida										—	—	
65	The mottled wood „	Bulacca sinensis	L	C	—	U								C
64	The Himalayan brown wood „	„ newarensis					—							
69	The rock-horned „	Ascalaphia bengalensis	—	—	—	—								
70	The dusky-horned „	„ coromanda	—	—	—	—								—
72	The brown fish „	Ketupa ceylonensis	—	—	—									C
74	The Indian scops „	Ephialtes pennatus			—	—	—							
	The bare-foot scops „	„ spilocephalus			—	—	—							
75	The Nepal scops „	„ lettia					—							
	The plume-foot scops „	„ plumipes					—							
	Pennant's scops „	„ griseus	—	—	—	—								
76	The spotted Owlet	Athene brama		—	—	—								
77	The jungle „	„ radiata				—	—							
79	The large barred „	„ cuculoides			—	—	—							

Nos. in Jerdon.	English Names.	Scientific Names.	Jan.	Feb.	March.	April.	May.	June.	July.	Augt.	Sept.	Oct.	Nov.	Dec.
80	The collared pigmy Owlet	Glaucidium Brodiei				—	—							
82	The common Swallow	Hirundo rustica				—	—							
83	The Nilgiri house „	„ domicola		-	—	—	—	-						
84	The wire-tailed „	„ ruficeps		-	—	—	—		-	—	-			
85	The great Indian mosque „	„ daurica				-	—	—	—	-				
							-N-							
	The mosque „	„ erythropygia				-	—	—	—	-				
86	The Indian cliff „	Hirundo fluvicola		-	—	-			-	—	-			
88	The dusky sand Martin	Cotyle subsoccata	—	—	-									
89	The common sand „	„ sinensis	—		-	—	-						—	—
				-C-		-N-						-U-		
90	The dusky crag „	„ concolor	—	—	-	-	—		—		-	—		
91	The crag „	„ rupestris				—	-							
92	The house „	Chelidon urbica							-	-				
93	The Kashmir „	„ cashmirensis				—	—							
100	The common Indian Swift	Cypselus abyssinicus		-	—	—	—	—	—	—				
	The Palm roof „	„ infumatus			—	—	—							
102	The Palm „	„ batassiensis			—	-		-	—					
103	The Southern hill Swiftlet	Collocalia unicolor				-	—	-						
	Horsfield's „	„ linchi			—									
104	The Indian crested Swift	Dendrochelidon coronatus				-	—	-						
106	The Sikkim Frogmouth	Otothrix Hodgsoni					—							
107	The jungle Nightjar	Caprimulgus indicus				—	—							
					-N-				-O-					
108	The Nilgiri „	„ Kelaarti		-	—	—	—	—	—	-				
109	The large Bengal „	„ albonotatus			-	—	—	-						
111	The Ghat „	„ atripennis					—							
112	The common Indian „	„ asiaticus				—	—	—	-					
114	Franklin's „	„ monticolus				-	—	—	—	—				
	Unwin's „	„ Unwini					—	-						
116	Hodgson's Trogon	Harpactes Hodgsoni				—	—							
117	The common Bee eater	Merops viridis			-	—	—	-						

Nos. in Jerdon.	English Names.	Scientific Names.	Jan.	Feb	March.	April.	May.	June.	July.	Augt.	Sept.	Oct.	Nov.	Dec
118	The blue-tailed Bee eater	Merops philippensis			—	—	—	—						
119	The chestnut-headed „	„ quinticolor			—	—								
120	The Egyptian „	„ ægyptius					—	—						
121	The European „	„ apiaster					—	—						
122	The blue-ruffed „	Nyctiornis Athertoni				—	—							
123	The common Roller	Coracias indica			—	—	—	—						
125	The European „	„ garrula					—	—	—					
126	The broad-billed „	Eurystomus orientalis				—	—	—	—					
127	The Indian stork-billed Kingfisher	Pelargopsis gurial				—	—							
129	The white-breasted „	Halcyon smyrnensis			—	—	—	—	—					
134	The little Indian „	Alcedo bengalensis			—	—	—	—						
136	The pied „	Ceryle rudis		—	—	—								
138	The yellow-throated Broadbill	Psarisomus Dalhousiæ				—	—	—						
140	The great Indian Hornbill	Homraius bicornis				—	—	—						
144	The Northern grey „	Meniceros bicornis				—	—	—						
147	The Northern rose-band Paroquet	Palæornis sivalensis				—								
148	The rose-ringed „	„ torquatus		—	—	—								
149	The rose-headed „	„ purpureus			—	—	—							
150	The slaty-headed „	„ schisticeps			—	—								
152	The red-breasted „	„ javanicus			—	—								
153	The Indian Loriquet	Loriculus vernalis			—	—	—							
154	The Himalayan pied Woodpecker	Picus himalayanus				—	—	—						
156	The lesser black „	„ caphtharius				—	—	—						
157	The Indian spotted „	„ macei				—	—	—						
159	The brown-fronted „	„ brunneifrons				—	—							
160	The yellow-fronted „	„ mahrattensis		—	—	—								
161	The rufous-bellied pied „	Hypopicus hyperythrus				—	—							
163	The Himalayan pigmy „	Yungipicus pygmæus				—	—							
164	The Southern pigmy „	„ Hardwickii			—	—								
167	The Southern golden-backed „	Chrysocolaptes delesserti	—	—										—

Nos. in Jerdon.	English Names.	Scientific Names.	Jan.	Feb.	March.	April.	May.	June.	July.	Augt.	Sept.	Oct	Nov.	Dec.
170	The scaly-bellied green Woodpecker	Gecinus squamatus				—	—							
171	The lesser Indian green „	„ striolatus				—	—							
172	The black-naped green „	„ occipitalis					—	—						
180	The common gold-back „	Brachypternus aurantius				—			—					
186	The speckled Piculet	Vivia innominata				—	—							
191	The Marshall's Barbet	Megalæma Marshallorum						—	—					
192	Hodgson's green „	„ Hodgsoni					—	—						
193	Franklin's green „	„ caniceps				—	—							
194	The small green „	„ viridis				—	—							
195	The blue-throated „	„ asiatica					—							
196	The golden-throated „	„ Franklinii					—							
197	The crimson-breasted „	Xantholæma hæmacephala			—	—	—							
199	The common Cuckoo	Cuculus canorus						—	—					
201	The hoary-headed „	„ poliocephalus						—						
204	The hill „	Cuculus striatus						—						
207	The large hawk „	Hierococcyx sparverioides							—					
212	The pied crested „	Coccystes melanoleucus						—	—	—				
214	The Koel	Eudynamis orientalis					—	—	—	—				
217	The common Coucal	Centropus rufipennis		—	—	B —	—	—	—	—	—			
218	The lesser „	„ viridis						—						
219	The southern Sirkeer	Taccocua leschenaulti			—									
220	The Bengal „	„ sirkee					—	—	—	—				
225	The Himalayan red Honey Sucker	Œthopyga miles					—	—						
229	The maroon-backed „	„ nipalensis					—	—						
231	The black-breasted „	„ saturata					—	—						
232	The amethyst-rumped „	Leptocoma zeylanica	—	—	—		B —	—	—		—	—	—	—
233	The tiny „	„ minima	N		U		C	&	U		—	—		
234	The purple „	Arachnechthra asiatica	—	—	—	—	—	—	B —	—	—			
238	Tickell's Flower Pecker	Dicæum minimum			—	—	—	—						
239	The Nilgiri „	„ concolor	—	—	—	—								

Nos in Jerdon.	English Names.	Scientific Names.	Jan.	Feb.	March.	April.	May.	June.	July.	Augt.	Sept.	Oct.	Nov.	Dec.
240	The thick-billed Flower Pecker	Piprisoma agile		U		H								
241	The fire-breasted "	Myzanthe ignipectus												
243	The Himalayan Tree Creeper	Certhia himalayana												
	Hodgson's "	" Hodgsoni												
247	The red-winged Wall Creeper	Tichodroma muriaria												
248	The white-tailed Nuthatch	Sitta himalayensis												
249	The white-cheeked "	" leucopsis												
250	The chestnut-bellied "	" castaneiventris												
253	The velvet-fronted "	Dendrophila frontalis												
254	The Hoopoe	Upupa epops												
255	The Indian "	" nigripennis												
256	The Indian grey Shrike	Lanius lahtora												
257	The rufous-backed "	" erythronotus												
	The pale rufous-backed "	" caniceps												
258	The grey-backed "	" tephronotus												
259	The black cap "	" nigriceps												
260	The bay-backed "	" vittatus												
265	The common wood "	Tephrodornis ponticeriana												
267	The little pied "	Hemipus picatus												
	The Himalayan pied "	" capitalis												
268	The pied cuckoo "	Volvocivora Sykesii												
269	The dark grey cuckoo "	" melaschistus												
270	The large grey cuckoo "	Graucalus macei												
271	The large Minivet	Pericrocotus speciosus												
272	The orange "	" flammeus												
273	The short-billed "	" brevirostris												
275	The rosy "	" roseus												
276	The small "	" peregrinus												
278	The common Drongo Shrike	Dicrurus albirictus												

Nos. in Jerdon.	English Names.	Scientific Names.	Jan.	Feb.	March	April.	May	June.	July.	Augt.	Sept.	Oct.	Nov.	Dec.
280	The long-tailed drongo Shrike	Dicrurus longicaudatus				—	-							
	Walden's „	„ waldeni					—	-						
281	The white-bellied „	„ cœrulescens					-	-						
282	The bronzed „	Chaptia œnea			-	—	—	-						
283	The oar-tailed „	Bhringa remifer					—	-						
284	The Northern racket-tailed „	Edolius paradiseus				—	-							
286	The hair-crested „	Chibia hottentota				-	-	-						
287	The ashy swallow Shrike	Artamus fuscus			-	—	-							
288	The paradise Flycatcher	Tchitrea paradisei					-	—	-					
290	The black-naped azure „	Myiagra azurea					-	—	-					
291	The white-throated Fantail	Leucocerca fuscoventris					-	-	-					
292	The white-browed „	„ aureola		-	—	-	-	—	—	-				
293	The white-spotted „	„ pectoralis				-	—	—	-					
294	The yellow-bellied „	Chelidorhynx hypoxanthus					—	-						
295	The grey-headed Flycatcher	Cryptolopha cinereocapilla				-	—	—	-					
296	The sooty „	Hemichelidon fuliginosa					-	-						
300	The black and orange „	Ochromela nigrorufa			-	—	-							
301	The verditer „	Eumyias melanops			-	—	—	—	-					
302	The Nilgiri blue „	„ albicaudata			-	-								
304	The blue-throated Redbreast	Cyornis rubeculoides					—	-						
305	The southern blue „	„ banyumas					—	-						
306	Tickell's blue „	„ tickelliæ					—	—						
310	The white-browed blue Flycatcher	Muscicapula superciliaris					—	—						
314	The fairy „	Niltava sundara				-	-							
315	McGregor's fairy „	„ macgrigoriœ				-	—	-						
316	The great fairy „	„ grandis				-	—	-						
320	The slaty „	Siphia leucomelanura					-	-						
321	The rufous-breasted „	„ superciliaris				-	—	-						
	The grey robin „	Erythrosterna parva					-	-						
324	The white-tailed robin „	„ hyperythra				-	—	-						

Nos. in Jerdon.	English Names.	Scientific Names.	Jan	Feb	March.	April.	May	June	July.	Augt	Sept.	Oct.	Nov	Dec.
327	The chestnut-headed Wren	Tesia castaneocoronata				—	—							
331	The tailed hill „	Pneopyga caudata				—	—							
333	The Nepal „	Troglodytes nipalensis					—	—						
	The Kashmir „	„ neglectus					—	—						
338	The white-browed Shortwing	Brachypteryx cruralis				—	—							
339	The rufous-bellied „	Callene rufiventris				—	—							
	The white-bellied „	„ albiventris				—	—							
343	The yellow-billed whistling Thrush	Myiophonus temminckii				—	—	—						
342	The Malabar „ „	„ horsfieldii			—	—								
344	The Nepal ground „	Hydrornis nipalensis					—	—						
345	The Indian ground „	Pitta bengalensis							—	—				
346	The green-breasted ground „	„ cucullata				—	—							
347	The brown water Ouzel	Hydrobata asiatica	—	—	—	—	—							
351	The blue rock Thrush	Petrocossyphus cyaneus					—	—						
352	The chestnut-bellied chat „	Orocetes erythrogastra				—	—							
353	The blue-headed „ „	„ cinclorhynchus				—	—	—						
355	The rusty-throated bush „	Geocichla citrina				—	—	—						
356	The dusky „ „	„ unicolor					—	—						
358	The variable pied Blackbird	„ dissimilis					—							
357	Ward's pied „	Turdulus wardii					—	—						
360	The Nilgiri „	Merula simillima			—	—	—							
361	The grey-winged „	„ boulboul				—	—	—	—	—				
362	The white-collared Ouzel	„ albocincta				—	—							
363	The grey-headed „	„ castanea				—	—	—						
368	The Indian missel Thrush	Turdus hodgsoni				—	—	—						
371	The small-billed Mountain „	Oreocincla dauma					—	—						
382	The striated Jay „	Grammatoptila striata						—						
385	The yellow-eyed Babbler	Pyctorhis sinensis						—	—	—				
388	The Nepal quaker Thrush	Alcippe nipalensis			—	—	—	—	—					
389	The Nilgiri „ „	„ poiocephala	—	—	—	—	—	—	—					

Nos. in Jerdon.	English Names.	Scientific Names.	Jan.	Feb.	March.	April.	May.	June	July.	Augt.	Sept.	Oct.	Nov.	Dec.
390	The black-headed quaker Thrush	Alcippe atriceps						—	—					
391	The black-headed wren Babbler	Stachyris nigriceps					—	—						
392	The red-billed " "	" pyrrhops						—	—					
393	The red-headed " "	" ruficeps				—	—	—						
395	The yellow-breasted " "	Mixornis rubricapillus					—							
396	The red-capped " "	Timalia pileata					—			—				
397	The rufous-bellied " "	Dumetia hyperythra						—	—	—				
398	The white-throated " "	" albogularis						—						
399	The spotted " "	Pellorneum ruficeps			—	—								
	The Nepal spotted " "	" nipalensis						—	—					
400	The rufous-necked scimitar "	Pomatorhinus ruficollis				—	—							
404	The southern " "	" horsfieldii		—	—	—	—							
405	The rusty-cheeked " "	" erythrogenys				—	—	—						
406	The slender-billed " "	Xiphoramphus superciliaris					—	—						
407	The white-crested laughing Thrush	Garrulax leucolophus				—	—	—	—					
408	The grey-sided " "	" cœrulatus					—	—						
410	The rufous-necked " "	" ruficollis					—							
411	The white-throated " "	" albogularis				—	—	—						
412	The black-gorgetted " "	" pectoralis				—		—	—					
413	The necklaced " "	" moniliger					—	—						
414	The white-spotted " "	" occellatus					—							
415	The red-headed " "	Trochalopteron erythrocephalum					—	—	—	—				
417	The plain-coloured " "	" subunicolor					—	—						
418	The variegated " "	" variegatum				—	—	—	—					
420	The blue-winged " "	" squamatum					—	—						
421	The red-throated " "	" jugulare					—	—	—					
422	The crimson-winged " "	" phœniceum					—							
423	The Nilgiri " "	" cacchinans		—	—	—	—							
425	The streaked " "	" lineatum				—	—	—	—	—	—			
426	The bristly " "	" setafer					—	—						

Nos in Jerdon.	English Names.	Scientific Names.	Jan.	Feb.	March.	April.	May.	June.	July.	Augt.	Sept.	Oct.	Nov.	Dec.
428	The hoary Barwing	Actinodura nipalensis				—	—	—						
429	The black-headed Sibia	Sibia capistrata					—	—	—					
	The Assam "	" gracilis							—					
430	The magpie "	" picaoides						—						
432	The Bengal Babbler	Malacocercus canorus			—	—	—	—	—					
433	The white-headed "	" griseus				—	—	—				—		
434	The jungle "	" malabaricus					—	—				—		—
435	The rufous-tailed "	" somervillii					—	—						
436	The large grey "	" malcolmi			—	—	—	—	—	—	—	—	—	
438	The striated bush "	Chattarrhœa caudata	—	—	—	—	—	—	—	—	—	—		—
439	The striated reed "	" earlii			—	—				—	—			
440	The striated marsh "	Megalurus palustris					—							
441	The grass "	Chætornis striatus									—			
444	The Himalayan black Bulbul	Hypsipetes psaroides				—	—	—						
445	The Nilgiri black "	" nilgiriensis			—	—	—	—						
447	The rufous-bellied "	" mcClellandi				—	—	—						
450	The yellow-browed bush "	Criniger ictericus			—	—	—							
451	The white-throated "	" flaveolus							—					
452	The white-browed bush "	Ixos luteolus						—			—			
456	The black-crested yellow "	Rubigula flaviventris					—							
458	The white-cheeked crested "	Otocompsa leucogenys				—	—	—	—					
459	The white-eared " "	" leucotis					—	—	—	—				
460	The red-whiskered "	" emeria			—	—	—							
	The southern " "	" fuscicaudata	—	—	—	—	—	—						
461	The common Bengal "	Pycnonotus pygœus				—	—	—						
462	The common Madras "	" pusillus		· —	N —	—	· —	· —	U —	· —	—			
463	Jerdon's green "	Phyllornis jerdoni			·	B —		·	C —	—				
467	The black-backed "	Iora zeylanica							—	—				
468	The white-winged green "	" typhia			· —	B —	—	·	B —					
469	The fairy Blue Bird	Irena puella	—	—										

Nos. in Jerdon.	English Names.	Scientific Names.	Jan	Feb.	March.	April.	May.	June	July.	Augt.	Sept.	Oct.	Nov.	Dec.
470	The Indian golden Oriole	Oriolus kundoo					—	—	—	—				
472	The black-headed „	„ melanocephalus				—	—	—						
475	The magpie Robin	Copsychus saularis			—	—	—	—	—					
476	The Shama	Kittacincla macroura				—	—							
477	The white-tailed Bluchat	Myiomela leucura					—							
479	The southern brown-backed Robin	Thamnobia fulicata			—	—	—							
480	The brown-backed „	„ cambaiensis			—	—	—	—	—					
481	The black Bushchat	Pratincola caprata			—	—	—	—						
482	The southern black „	„ atrata			—	—	—							
483	The common Indian „	„ indica			—	—	—	—	—					
486	The iron grey „	„ ferrea				—	—	—	—					
494	The brown Rockchat	Cercomela fusca			—	—	—	—	—					
504	The blue-headed Redstart	Rutacilla cœruleocephala				—								
505	The plumbous water Robin	„ fuliginosa					—	—						
506	The white-capped Redstart	Chæmorrornis leucocephala					—							
507	The blue Woodchat	Larvivora cyana			—	—								
508	The white-breasted blue „	Ianthia rufilata					—	—						
511	The golden „	Tarsiger chrysœus								—				
513	The white-tailed Ruby throat	Calliope pectoralis						—						
515	The large reed Warbler	Acrocephalus brunnescens					—	—						
516	The lesser „ „	„ dumetorum					—	—						
517	The paddy field „	„ agricolus						—						
	The brown-breasted hill „	Dumeticola brunneipectus							—	—				
	The streaked-scrub „	Drymœca inquieta		—	—	—								
523	The fulvous-breasted hill „	Horornis fulviventer							—					
526	The strong-footed „ „	„ fortipes						—	—					
529	The large „ „	Horeites major							—					
	The pale „ „	„ pallidus					—	—						
						B	—							
530	The Indian Tailor Bird	Orthotomus longicauda				—	—	—	—	—				
532	The yellow-bellied Wren Warbler	Prinia flaviventris							—	—				

Nos in Jerdon.	English Names.	Scientific Names.	Jan.	Feb.	March.	April.	May.	June.	July.	Augt.	Sept.	Oct.	Nov.	Dec.
533	Adams's Wren Warbler	Prinia adamsi										—		
534	The ashy „ „	„ socialis			—	—	—	—	—	—	—			
535	Stewart's „ „	„ stewarti						—	—	—				
537	The grey-capped „ „	„ cinereocapilla							—					
538	Hodgson's „ „	„ hodgsoni						—	—					
539	The rufous Grass „	Cisticola schœnicola			—			—	—	—	—	—		
542	The Bengal „ „	Graminicola bengalensis							—	—				
543	The common Wren „	Drymoipus inornatus							—	—	—	—		
	The earth brown „ „	„ terricolor						—	—	—	—			
544	The long-tailed „ „	„ longicaudatus							—	—	—			
	Jerdon's „ „	„ jerdoni								—				
	The great „ „	„ insignis							—	—				
546	The allied „ „	„ neglectus							—	—	—			
	The fuscous „ „	„ fuscus				—	—	—	—					
	The great rufous „ „	„ rufescens								—				
547	The brown Hill „	Suya criniger					—	—						
548	The dusky „ „	„ fuliginosa					—	—						
549	The black-throated „ „	„ atrogularis				—	—	—						
550	The streaked Wren „	Burnesia lepida		—	—						—	—		
551	The rufous-fronted „ „	Franklinia buchanani					—	—	—	—	—	—		
552	The aberrant Tree „	Neornis flavolivacea					—	—	—					
	Blyth's aberrant „ „	„ assimilis					—							
553	Sykes' Warbler	Hyppolais rama				—				—				
	Tytler's Tree „	Phylloscopus tytleri					—	—						
563	The large-crowned „	Reguloides occipitalis					—	—	—					
565	The crowned „	„ superciliosus					—	—						
566	The Dalmatian „	„ proregulus					—	—						
570	The lesser black-browed „	Culicopeta cantator					—							
571	The black-eared „	Abrornis schisticeps				—	—							
572	The grey-headed „	„ xanthoschistus				—								

Nos. in Jerdon	English Names.	Scientific Names.	Jan'	Feb.	March.	April.	May.	June.	July.	Augt	Sept.	Oct.	Nov.	Dec.
	The grey-faced Warbler	Abrornis chloronotus					—	—						
573	The white-browed „	„ albosuperciliaris			—	—	—							
	The chestnut-headed „	„ castaneiceps					—	—						
580	The Indian golden-crested Wren	Regulus himalayensis					—	—						
582	The Indian Whitethroat	Sylvia affinis					—	—						
584	The western-spotted Forktail	Henicurus maculatus				—	—	—						
586	The slaty-backed „	„ schistaceus					—	—	—					
587	The little „	„ scouleri					—							
	The eastern-spotted „	„ guttatus					—	—						
589	The Indian pied Wagtail	Motacilla maderaspatana	S- —		—	—	—							S- -
590	The white-faced „	„ luzionensis					—	—						
592	The grey and yellow „	„ melanope						—						
	The black-backed yellow-headed „	Budytes calcaratus					—							
596	The Indian Pipit	Anthus arboreus					—	—						
597	The Tree „	„ maculatus					—	—						
598	The Nilgiri „	„ montanus				—	—							
600	The Indian Tit Lark	„ rufulus			—	-B —	—		-C -					
605	The ruddy Pipit	„ rosaceus					—	—						
603	The Nilgiri Tit Lark	Agrodroma cinnamomea			—	—	—							
604	The brown Rock Pipit	„ griseorufescens				—	—	—	—					
606	The upland „	Heterura sylvana				—	—	—	—					
607	The purple Thrush Tit	Cochoa purpurea						—						
608	The green „ „	„ viridis						—						
609	The red-winged Shrike „	Pteruthius erythropterus						—						
614	The red-billed Hill „	Leiothrix luteus				—	—	—	—	—				
615	The silver-eared „ „	„ argentarius					—	—						
616	The stripe-throated „ „	Siva strigula					—	—						
617	The blue-winged „ „	„ cyanouroptera					—	—						
618	The red-tailed „ „	Minla ignotincta					—	—						
619	The chestnut-headed „ „	„ castaneiceps					—	—						

Nos. in Jerdon.	English Names.	Scientific Names.	Jan.	Feb.	March.	April.	May.	June.	July.	Augt.	Sept.	Oct.	Nov.	Dec.
621	The golden breasted Hill Tit	Proparus chrysœus					—							
623	The yellow naped „ „	Ixulus flavicollis					—	-						
624	The rusty headed „ „	„ occipitalis					—	-						
626	The stripe throat crested „ „	Yuhina gularis					—	-						
628	The black-chinned „ „	„ nigrimentum					—	-						
629	The fire-tailed „ „	Myzornis pyrrhoura					—							
631	The Indian white-eyed „	Zosterops palpebrosus	-	-H —	& —	N —	—	—	-I —	P —	- -			
633	The firecap „	Cephalopyrus flammiceps				-	-							
634	The red-capped „	Egithaliscus erythrocephalus			—	—	-							
638	The crested-black „	Lophophanes melanolophus			—	-	—							
644	The mountain „	Parus monticolus			-	—	—	-						
645	The Indian grey „	„ cinereus	-N -	N —	- —	—								
647	The yellow-cheeked „	Machlolophus xanthogenys				—	-							
654	The rufous-breasted Accentor	Accentor strophiatus					—	—	-					
	Jerdon's „	„ jerdoni					-	-						
657	The Raven	Corvus corax	—	—	-								—	
659	The Indian carrion Crow	„ corone					-	-						
660	The bow-billed Corby	„ culminatus		-	—	—								
661	The Himalayan „	„ intermedius					—							
663	The common „	„ impudicus				—	—	—						
665	The Jackdaw	„ monedula				-	—	-						
666	The Himalayan Nutcracker	Nucifraga hemispila			-	-								
668	The Himalayan Magpie	Pica bottanensis			—									
669	The Himalayan Jay	Garrulus bispecularis			-	—	—	-						
670	The black-throated „	„ lanceolatus				-	—	-						
671	The red-billed blue „	Urocissa occipitalis				—	—	-						
672	The yellow-billed blue „	„ flavirostris					—	—	—	-				
673	The green „	Cissa venatoria				—	-							
674	The Indian Treepie	Dendrocitta rufa				-	—	—	-					
676	The Himalayan „	„ himalayanus					-	—	—					

Nos. in Jerdon.	English Names.	Scientific Names.	Jan.	Feb.	March.	April.	May.	June.	July.	Augt.	Sept.	Oct.	Nov.	Dec.
678	The long-tailed Treepie	Dendrocitta leucogastra			—	—								
682	The bright Starling	Sturnus nitens				—	—	—						
683	The pied Mynah	Sturnopastor contra					—	—	—	—				
	The Burmese pied „	„ superciliaris				—	—							
684	The common „	Acridotheres tristis					—	—	—	—				
685	The bank „	„ ginginianus				—	—	—	—					
					I	P		H						
686	The jungle „	„ fuscus		—	—	—	—	—	—					
687	The brahminy „	Temenuchus pagodarum					—	—	—	—				
688	The grey-headed „	„ malabaricus					—	—						
691	The spotted-winged Stare	Saraglossa spiloptera				—	—							
692	The southern hill Mynah	Eulabes religiosa			—	—								
693	The large hill „	„ intermedia			—	—								
694	The common Weaver Bird	Ploceus baya				—	—	—	—	—	—			
695	The striated „ „	„ manyar								—	—			
696	The black-throated „ „	„ bengalensis									—			
697	The black-headed Munia	Munia malacca							—			—		
											B			
698	The chestnut-bellied „	„ rubroniger						—	—	—	—			
699	The spotted „	„ undulata				—	—		—	—				
700	The rufous-bellied „	„ pectoralis							—					
				C			B		N					
701	The white-backed Munia	„ striata	—			—			—					
702	Hodgson's „	„ acuticauda						—						
703	The pin-tailed „	„ malabarica	—	—					—	—	—	—	—	—
704	The Indian Amadavat	Estrelda amandava	—	—					—	—			—	—
705	The green „	„ formosa					—		—					—
706	The Indian house Sparrow	Passer indicus		—	—	—	—	—						
708	The cinnamon-headed „	„ cinnamomeus					—	—						
710	The tree „	„ montanus					—		—					
										H				
711	The yellow-throated „	„ flavicollis				—	—		—					
713	The meadow Bunting	Emberiza cia					—	—	—					
	The striolated „	„ striolata											—	

Nos. in Jerdon.	English Names.	Scientific Names.	Jan.	Feb.	March.	April.	May.	June.	July.	Augt.	Sept.	Oct.	Nov.	Dec.
718	The white-capped Bunting	Emberiza stewarti						—	—					
719	The grey-headed „	„ fucata					—	—	—					
724	The crested black and chestnut „	Melophus melanicterus				—	—	—	—	—				
725	The black and yellow Grosbeak	Hesperiphona icterioides					—	—						
732	The orange Bullfinch	Pyrrhula aurantiaca							—					
737	The Circassian rose Finch	Carpodacus rubicilla							—					
748	The red-browed „	Callocanthis burtoni							—					
750	The Indian Siskin	Chrysomitris spinoides							—	—				
754	The Bengal Bush Lark	Mirafra assamica						—						
756	The red-winged „ „	„ erythroptera			—	—	—	—	—	—	—			
757	The singing „ „	„ cantillans			—	—		—	—					
758	The rufous-tailed Finch „	Ammomanes phœnicura		—	—	—								
759	The desert „ „	„ luscitanica					—	—						
760	The black-bellied „ „	Pyrrhalauda grisea	—	—	—	—	—	—	—	—				
762	The Eastern Sand „	Alaudala raytal		—	—	—	—							
	The Punjab „ „	„ adamsi			—	—	—							
765	The Northern crown crest „	Spizalauda simillima						—	—	—				
766	The Himalayan Sky „	Alauda dulcivox					—	—						
767	The Indian „ „	„ gulgula			—	—	—							
	The Nilgiri „ „	„ australis			—	—	—	—			—	—		
768	The Malabar crested „	„ malabarica		—	—	—				—	—	—		
769	The common „ „	Galerita cristata			—	—	—							
	The lesser „ „	„ boysii			—	—	—							
772	The Bengal green Pigeon	Crocopus phœnicopterus					—	—						
773	The Southern „ „	„ chlorigastra			—	—	—	—						
774	The orange-breasted „ „	Osmotreron bicincta				—								
775	The grey-fronted „ „	„ malabarica		—		—								
778	The Kokla „ „	Sphenocercus sphenurus				—	—	—	—					
781	The bronze-backed Imperial Pigeon	Carpophaga insignis					—	—						
788	The speckled wood „	Alsocomus hodgsoni						—						

Nos. in Jerdon.	English Names.	Scientific Names.	Jan.	Feb.	March.	April.	May.	June.	July.	Augt.	Sept.	Oct.	Nov.	Dec.
784	The Himalayan wood Pigeon	Palumbus casiotis					—	—						
786	The Nilgiri „ „	„ elphinstonii				—		—						
788	The Indian blue rock „	Columba intermedia	—	—	—	—	—	—						
791	The bar-tailed tree Dove	Macropygia tusalia					—	—	—					
792	Hodgson's turtle „	Turtur rupicola					—	—		—				
793	Sykes' „ „	„ meena	—	—	—	—								—
794	The brown „ „	„ cambaiensis	—	—	—	—	—	—	—	—	—	—		
795	The spotted „	„ suratensis			—	—	—	—						
796	The Indian ring „	„ risorius	—	—	—	—	—	—	—	—	—			—
797	The ruddy „ ,	„ humilis	—	—	—	—	—	—						
798	The emerald „	Chalcophaps indicus		—	—	—	—	—	—					
800	The painted sand Grouse	Pterocles fasciatus				—	—						—	
802	The common „ „	„ exustus	—		—	—	—	—	—		—	—	—	—
803	The Peacock	Pavo cristatus						—	—	—	—	—		
804	The Moonal	Lophophorus impeyanus					—							
805	The red Argus	Ceriornis satyra					—							
806	The black-headed „	„ melanocephala					—							
808	The Koklas	Pucrasia macrolopha					—							
809	The cheer Pheasant	Phasianus wallichii					—							
810	The white-crested Kalij „	Gallophasis albocristatus			—	—	—							
811	The black-backed „ „	„ melanotus					—	—	—					
812	The red jungle Fowl	Gallus ferugineus			—	—	—							
813	The grey „ „	„ sonneratii		—	—	—	—					—	—	—
814	The red spur „	Galloperdix spadiceus		—	—	—	—	—						
815	The painted „ „	„ lunulosus			—	—	—							
816	The snow Pheasant	Tetraogallus himalayensis					—	—						
817	The snow Partridge	Lerwa nivicola					—	—						
	Hodgson's „	Perdix hodgsoniæ							—					
818	The black „	Francolinus vulgaris					—	—	—	—				
819	The painted „	„ pictus							—	—	—			

Nos. in Jerdon.	English Names.	Scientific Names.	Jan.	Feb.	March.	April.	May.	June.	July.	Augt.	Sept.	Oct.	Nov.	Dec.
820	The chukor Partridge	Caccabis chukor				—	—	—	—					
821	The susee „	Ammoperdix bonhami				—	—							
822	The grey „	Ortygornis ponticeriana			—	—	—	—			—	— P.	—	
823	The Kyah „	„ gularis			—	—	—							
824	The Peora „	Arboricola torqueola						—	—					
826	The jungle bush Quail	Perdicula cambaiensis			—					—	—	—	—	—
827	The rock „ „	„ asiatica			—	—								
828	The red-billed „ „	„ erythrorhyncha	—	—	—						—	—		
829	The common „	Coturnix communis			—	—								
830	The rain „	„ coromandelicus								—	—	—		
831	The blue-breasted „	Excalfatoria sinensis							—					
832	The Bustard „	Turnix taigoor							—	—	—			
833	The Himalayan „ „	„ plumbipes					—	—	—					
834	The large Button „	„ tanki								—				
835	The lesser „ „	„ dussumieri				—				—				
836	The Indian Bustard	Eupodotis edwardsii			—	—	—	—	—	—				
838	The Florikin	Sypheotides bengalensis						—	—					
839	The Likh „	„ auritus									—	—		
840	The Indian courier Plover	Cursorius coromandelicus			—	—	—	—	—					
	The cream-coloured „ „	„ gallicus			—	—	—	—	—					
843	The lesser swallow „	Glareola lactea			—	—								
846	The greater shore „	Œgialites leschenaulti					—	—						
847	Pallas's „ „	„ mongolicus					—	—						
849	The ringed „	„ curonicus		—	—	—	—							
855	The red-wattled „	Lobivanellus goensis			—	—	—	—	—	—				
856	The yellow-wattled . „	Sarciophorus bilobus			—	—	—							
857	The spur-winged „	Hoplopterus malabaricus			—	—								
858	The great Indian stone „	Esacus recurvirostris			—	—	—							
859	The „ „	Œdicnemus crepitans		—	—	—	—	—	—	—				
863	The Sarus Crane	Grus antigone						—	—	—				

Nos. in Jerdon.	English Names.	Scientific Names.	Jan.	Feb.	March.	April.	May.	June.	July.	Augt.	Sept.	Oct.	Nov.	Dec.
867	The Woodcock	Scolopax rusticola					—							
873	The painted Snipe	Rhynchœa bengalensis			—	B —					—			
893	The common Sandpiper	Actitis hypoleucus					—	—						
898	The Stilt	Himantopus candidus				—	—	—						
900	The bronze-winged Jacana	Metopidus indicus							—	—	—			
901	The pheasant-tailed „	Hydrophasianus sinensis							—	—				
902	The purple Coot	Porphyrio poliocephalus							—	—				
903	The common „	Fulica atra					—	—	—	—				
904	The water Cock	Gallicrex cristatus							—	—				
905	The „ Hen	Gallinula chloropus					H —		—	—				
906	Blythe's „ „	„ burnesii								—				
907	The white-breasted „ „	Porzana phœnicura							—	—				
908	The brown Rail	„ akool					—	—	—	—				
910	Baillon's Crake	„ pygmœa						H —	—	—				
911	The ruddy Rail	„ fusca							—	—				
915	The Adjutant	Leptoptilus argala											—	
917	The black-necked Stork	Mycteria australis									—	—	—	—
920	The white-necked „	Melanopelargus episcopus						—	—	—	—		S	—
922	The great Heron	Ardea sumatrana							—	—				
923	The common „	„ cinerea			—	—		—	—	—				
924	The purple „	„ purpurea				C —	C —	—	—	—	—			
925	The white „	Herodias alba							—	—				S —
926	The little „ „	„ egrettoides							—	—				S —
927	The little Egret	„ garzetta							—	—				S —
929	The cattle „	Buphus coromandus							—	—				S —
930	The little pond Heron	Ardeola grayi						—	—	—				S —
931	The little green Bittern	Butorides javanicus							—	—				
932	The black „	Ardetta flavicollis							—					
933	The chestnut „	„ cinnamomea					—	—	—	I —	P —			
934	The yellow „	„ sinensis						—						
935	The little „	„ minuta						—						

Nos. in Jerdon.	English Names.	Scientific Names.	Jan.	Feb.	March.	April.	May.	June.	July.	Augt.	Sept.	Oct.	Nov.	Dec.
937	The Night Heron	Nycticorax griseus				—	H —		—	—				
938	The pelican Ibis	Tantalus leucocephalus									—	—		
939	The Spoonbill	Platalea leucorodia							—	—	—			
940	The shell Ibis	Anastomus oscitans						—	—	—				
941	The white "	Threskiornis melanocephalus						—	—	—				
942	The King Curlew	Geronticus papillosus			—	C —	—	—	—	—	—		S —	—
949	The bar-headed Goose	Anser indicus					—							
950	The black-backed "	Sarkidiornis melanotus							—	—	—			
951	The cotton Teal	Nettapus coromandelianus							—	—				
952	The Whistling "	Dendrocygna arcuata						—	—	—				
953	The large " "	" major								—				
954	The Brahminy Duck	Casarca rutila					—							
958	The Mallard	Anas boschas					—	—						
959	The spotted-billed Duck	" pœcilorhyncha								—	—			
960	The pink-headed "	" caryophyllacea						—	—					
969	The white-eyed "	Aythya nyroca					—	—						
974	The crested Grebe	Podiceps cristatus					—							
975	The little "	" philippensis					H —	& —	N —	—	—			
983	The gull-billed Tern	Gelochelidon anglicus				—								
984	The whiskered "	Hydrochelidon indicus						—	—	—				
985	The large river "	Sterna seena			—	—								
987	The black-bellied "	" javanica			—	—								
988	The little "	Sternula minuta			—	—								
989	The large sea "	Thallaseus cristatus						—						
990	The small " "	" bengalensis						—						
991	The little black-naped "	Onochoprion melanauchen					—	—	—					
995	The Scissorbill	Rhynchops albicollis			—	—								
1005	The common Cormorant	Graculus carbo				—	—							
1006	The lesser "	" fuscicollis								—	—			
1007	The little "	" javanicus								—	—			
1008	The Indian Snake Bird	Plotus melanogaster	S —	—					U —	—				

PART III.

CALENDAR.

THE columns of the accompanying calendar give the leading details for each month. The wording is necessarily brief, as the space is limited.

The first column gives the number in Jerdon's Hand-Book for reference. Where no number is given in this column, the bird has been added to the Indian list since Jerdon's book was published.

The next column gives the generally accepted English name. Jerdon's names have been adhered to in almost every case.

The third columu is the scientific name. In this no alteration has been made, unless clearly proved to be necessary.

The next column "shape of nest."

And the one following "site of nest," need no comment.

The column headed "geographical range in breeding season" gives roughly the extent of country in which the bird is known to breed at one time or another, but it does not follow that it breeds throughout the whole of the range in that particular month.

The last column "particulars for the month" gives actual facts as ascertained by experience, leaving the reader to draw his own iuference. Representative dates have been chosen so far as possible when more than one date was available; for instance, if the season is beginning, the earliest date has been selected; and if the season is nearly over, the latest date has been taken. Similarly, in regard to localities, only one or two could be specified, and the same rule has been followed. Where the breeding is over a wide stretch of country, the two limits are given. Where any particular climate is more favorable, the typical place has been selected; of course, when only one nest has been found, the date of that is given, and there can be no selection, but the places and dates are records in every case of actual ascertained facts.

JANUARY.

January is in all parts of the country the month for the larger birds of prey. Of the fifty-six kinds of birds known to breed at this time, twenty-eight belong to this order (*Raptores*).

In the Himalayas, with the exception of a solitary instance of a nest of the brown water ouzel (*Hydrobata asiatica*), none but the nests of raptores have been found. Vultures, eagles, falcons, and kites are either building or laying, and as these birds are comparatively few in numbers, with great powers of flight, it is necessary to explore over a large extent of country to get many eggs; both birds and nests are conspicuous. Eyries can generally be marked down in the course of the morning's ride, and arrangements made afterwards for obtaining the eggs; a matter often of no small difficulty, as, whether the nest is on a ledge of the rock itself or in a tree, it is generally on the face of a precipice, which it requires both skill and nerve to surmount.

In the Punjab, besides the birds of prey, the raven, the striated bush babbler, and the dusky sand martin have eggs. Watch should be kept on all the large birds of prey, and every large solitary tree should be scanned, as it is on such trees that nests of eagles, vultures, &c., will be found. These nests are conspicuous from a distance. I have often seen and noted them while passing along on a railway journey, returning when opportunity offered to examine the nest.

In the North-West Provinces the Indian hoopoe, the sand martin, the pin-tailed munia, the blue rock pigeon, the common sand grouse, and the doves have eggs, as well as the vultures and eagles, and falcons and some of the owls.

In Bengal, the sand martin is the only bird now breeding in any quantities, besides the birds of prey.

In Central India, the dusky crag martin, the munias and amadavats, and doves have eggs, besides the birds of prey which lay everywhere at this period.

In South India, the large birds of prey are few in number, but the eggs of many other kinds may now be sought for. Some species of woodpeckers, martins, honey suckers, flower peckers, quaker thrushes, bulbuls, bluebirds, wagtails, finch larks, doves, quail, and water birds are already known to breed there at this season, and it is probable

MARSHALL DEL

NEST OF THE KING VULTURE.

(Otogyps calvus.)

that further search will lead to the discovery of many others. Our knowledge of that part of India is comparatively very incomplete.

Besides the birds noted in the list, there are many that are known to lay early in February, and which may possibly sometimes lay in the end of January; at all events they will be building in the present month, and careful watch should be kept over their movements.

Among these may be noted in the HIMALAYAS the *black-capped falcon* and the *imperial eagle.*

In the PUNJAB, the *bay vulture* and the *imperial eagle*, these are both rare birds, and few collections contain specimens of their eggs taken in India.

In the NORTH-WEST PROVINCES, the *spotted owlet* begins to lay towards the end of the month, as also the *little ringed plover*, for which watch should be kept on the sands in the beds of big rivers, more especially on the flat sandy islands left by the receding floods.

In CENTRAL INDIA, the *bay vulture* is building, and the *grey partridge* commences to pair.

In SOUTHERN INDIA, the *kestril* commences building in the Nilgiris, also the *red spur fowl*, while in Travancore the *booted eagle*, the *grey fronted green pigeon*, and the *grey jungle fowl* are pairing and preparing their nests.

JANUARY.

Nos. in Jerdon.	English Names.	Scientific Names.	Shape of Nest.	Site of Nest.	Geographical Range in Breeding Season.	Particulars for the Month.
2	The king Vulture	Otogyps calvus ...	A large platform.	On the tops of high trees.	Throughout continental India.	The Deccan; eggs.
3	The roc "	Gyps himalayensis ...	Ditto ...	On ledges of cliffs.	The Himalayas only	Kangra, 23rd; eggs.
4	The pale long-billed "	" pallescens ...	Ditto ...	Ditto ...	Western and central India.	Ajmir, 25th; eggs.
	The long billed "	" indicus ...	Ditto ...	At tops of high trees	The plains of upper India.	Lower Bengal; eggs.
5	The white-backed "	" bengalensis ...	Ditto ...	Near tops of large trees.	Throughout continental India.	Throughout the month.
6	The white scavenger "	Perenopteron ginginianus	Platform ...	On cliffs or large trees.	Throughout India ...	Nest building begins.
7	The bearded ,	Gypaetus barbatus ...	A large platform.	On ledges of cliffs...	The Himalayas and Suleiman range.	Kangra, 2nd; eggs.
9	The shahin Falcon	Falco perigrinator ...	Ditto ...	Ditto ...	Locally throughout India.	Raipur (C. P.), 25th; eggs.
11	The laggar "	" juggur ...	Ditto ...	On high trees or cliffs.	The dry plains of upper India.	Throughout the month,
16	The red-headed Merlin	Lithofalco chicquera ...	A compact massive cup.	In forks of trees ...	Throughout the plains	Fatehgurh (N. W. P.), 9th; eggs.
29	The Indian tawny Eagle	Aquila vindhyana ...	A large platform.	On high trees ...	The dry parts of upper India.	Hansi, Agra; eggs.
32	The black ,	Neopus malaiensis ...	Ditto ...	On ledges of cliffs...	The Himalayas ...	Bussahir, 4th; Kooloo, 7th; eggs
33	Bonellis "	Nisaetus bonellii ...	Ditto ...	On cliffs or high trees.	Throughout India ...	Aligurh, 20th; Kangra, 25th; eggs.
36	The Nipal hawk "	Spizaetus nipalensis ...	Ditto ...	On high trees. ...	The Himalayas ...	Bussahir, 5th; eggs (very early).
41	The bar-tailed fishing "	Polioaetus ichthyaetus	Ditto ...	Ditto ...	Eastern and peninsular India.	(Requires confirmation).
	The Himalayan , "	" plumbeus ...	Ditto ...	Ditto ...	The Himalayas ...	Nest building begins.
42	The ring-tailed " "	Haliaetus leucoryphus	Ditto ...	On high trees by water.	Throughout northern India.	Breeding season ends.

43	The white-bellied Sea „	„ leucogaster	Ditto ...	On high trees ...	All round the coasts ...	Calcutta, 28th ; eggs.
45	The long-legged Buzzard	Buteo canescens ...	Irregular platform.	On high trees or cliffs.	Punjab and north-western Himalayas . .	Kooloo, 10th ; eggs.
55	The Brahminy Kite	Haliastur indus ...	Ditto ...	On high trees near water.	Throughout the plains	Nest building begins.
56	The common „	Milvus govinda ...	Ditto ...	In forks of trees ...	Throughout India ...	Bengal and south India ; eggs.
	The greater Indian „	„ major ...	Ditto ...	Ditto ...	The western Himalayas.	Nest building begins.
59	The black-winged „	Elanus melanopterus ...	Shallow compact cup.	Ditto ...	Throughout India (locally).	Sumbhulpur (C. P.), 10th ; eggs.
60	The Indian screech Owl	Strix indica ...	None ...	In holes in trees or buildings.	Throughout the plains	A few stragglers breed.
65	The mottled wood „	Bulacca sinensis ...	Ditto ...	In holes or hollows on large trees.	Ditto ...	Ditto.
69	The rock-horned „	Ascalaphia bengalensis	Ditto ...	On ledges of banks	Throughout India ...	Ditto.
70	The dusky-horned „	„ coromanda	A large platform.	In forks of large trees	Throughout the plains	Throughout the month.
72	The brown fish „	Ketupa ceylonensis ...	None ...	In clefts of rocks or old trees	Throughout India ...	Etawah ; eggs.
	Pennant's scops „	Ephialtes griseus ...	Ditto ...	In holes in trees ...	Throughout continental India.	Breeding season begins.
88	The dusky sand Martin	Cotyle subsoccata ...	A loose cup.	In holes in river bank (gregarious.)	Northern India ...	Etawah, 11th ; eggs.
89	The Indian „ „	„ sinensis ...	Ditto ...	Ditto (do.) ...	Throughout India (late in south).	Calcutta ; eggs.
90	The dusky crag „	„ concolor ...	A deep semicircular cup	Against buildings or rocks.	Throughout India (locally).	Jhansi, Saugor ; eggs.
167	The southern golden-backed Woodpecker	Chrysocolaptes delesserti	None ...	In artificial holes in trees.	Hills of south India ...	Throughout the month.
232	The amethyst rumped Honeysucker	Leptocoma zeylanica ...	Pear-shaped, with side entrance.	Hanging from tips of branches.	Lower Bengal and peninsular India.	A few stragglers breed
234	The purple „	Arachnechthra asiatica	Ditto ...	Ditto ...	Throughout India proper.	The Nilgiris ; eggs.
239	The Nilgiri Flower-pecker	Dicœum concolor ...	Purse-shaped, with front entrance.	Hanging from twigs in thick foliage	The Nilgiris ...	Kotagiri, 24th ; eggs.
254	The Indian Hoopoe	Upupa nigripennis ...	A few feathers or leaves	In holes in trees or walls.	Throughout India ...	Allahabad, 25th ; eggs.

Nos. in Jerdon.	English Names.	Scientific Names.	Shape of Nest	Site of Nest.	Geographical Range in Breeding Season.	Particulars for the Month.
347	The brown water Ouzel	Hydrobata asiatica ...	A large ball of moss.	In clefts of rocks near water.	The Himalayas only ...	Masuri, 18th; eggs.
389	The Nilgiri quaker Thrush	Alcippe poiocephala ...	A deep massive cup.	In forks of bushes or saplings.	The hills of south India.	Kotagiri, 21st; eggs.
438	The striated bush Babbler	Chattarhœa caudata ...	Cup-shaped	In low bushes or tufts of grass.	Throughout the plains	Hansi (Punjab), 3rd; eggs
	The southern red-whiskered Bulbul	Otocompsa fuscicaudata	A small neat cup.	In isolated bushes	The hills of south India.	Travancore; eggs.
469	The fairy Bluebird	Irena puella ...	A loose straggling cup.	In forks of small trees.	Southern India ...	Assamboo hills; eggs.
589	The Indian pied Wagtail	Motacilla maderaspatana	A shallow cup.	In holes in walls or on banks.	Throughout the plains	Madras, 20th; eggs.
631	The Indian white-eyed Tit	Zosterops palpebrosus	A tiny regular cup.	Hung from twigs in trees or bushes.	Throughout India ...	Nilgiris; eggs.
657	The Raven	Corvus corax ...	A large compact cup.	In forks of solitary trees.	Western continental India.	Sambhur, 24th; eggs.
701	The white-backed Munia	Munia striata ...	A large domed oval.	In small trees or thorny bushes.	The peninsular and eastern India.	Raipur (C. P.), 2nd; eggs.
703	The pin-tail „	„ malabarica ...	Ditto ...	In small trees (or in eaves of houses).	Throughout India proper.	Etawah (N. W. P.). 22nd; eggs.
704	The Indian Amadavat	Estrelda amandava ...	Ditto .	In low thick bushes	Locally throughout India.	Raipur (C. P.); eggs.
760	The black-bellied finch Lark	Pyrrhalauda grisea ...	A tiny shallow pad.	On ground near clod or tussock.	Throughout the plains	Poona (Bo.); eggs.
788	The Indian blue rock Pigeon	Columba intermedia ...	A small platform	On ledges of buildings chiefly.	Throughout India ...	Upper India; eggs.
793	Sykes's turtle Dove	Turtur meena ...	A tiny platform.	In low trees or among thick foliage.	Peninsular and eastern India.	Sumbhulpur (C. P.); eggs.
794	The brown turtle „	„ cambaiensis ...	Ditto ...	In low trees or bushes.	Throughont the plains	Etawah (N. W. P.), 1st; eggs.
796	The Indian ring „	„ risorius ...	Ditto ...	Ditto ...	Ditto ...	Cawnpur, 1st; eggs.
797	The ruddy ring „	„ humilis ...	Ditto ...	Ditto ...	Ditto (but local) ...	Nepal Terai; eggs.
802	The common Sandgrouse	Pterocles exustus ...	None ...	On open ground in fallow fields.	The dry plains of upper India.	Eastern Punjab; eggs.
828	The red-billed bush Quail	Perdicula erythrorhyncha.	Ditto ...	On the ground under shelter.	The Nilgiris ...	Kotagiri; eggs.
1008	The Indian snake Bird	Plotus melanogaster	A rough platform.	On trees growing in water.	Throughout India ...	South of Madras; eggs.

MARSHALL DEL

NEST OF THE THICK BILLED FLOWER PECKER.

(Piprisoma agile.)

FEBRUARY.

In this month the birds of prey continue to lay, while other kinds commence. The eggs of several swallows and martins may now be found. Parrots, woodpeckers, and other climbing birds are pairing, and even commence excavating the holes for their nests. Several kinds of larks have eggs, others are pairing and building. Doves, of course, are breeding in this as in every other month. The spotted doves, which are more regular than the others, are commencing to build, and the jungle bush quail are pairing in all parts of the country.

In the Himalayas, the roc vulture, the lammergeyer, the black-capped falcon, the hawk eagles, buzzards, kites, and water ouzels have eggs, while the *large barred owlet* and the *common Indian bushchat* are pairing and building throughout the range, and the *red-capped tit* and *crested black tit* begin to build in the eastern portions. The *Himalayan magpie* in all probability has eggs in this month.

In the Punjab, the vultures, falcons, eagles, Pennant's scops owls, the hoopoe, the grey shrike, the streaked scrub warbler, and the raven have eggs throughout the month, and the *rufous grass warbler*, the *common quail*, the *big bustard*, and in some places the *common heron* are building their nests.

In the North-west Provinces, the laying season is fairly beginning. In addition to the vultures, falcons, eagles, &c., no less than seven kinds of owls have eggs. Swallows and martins begin laying; so do also the parrots, the purple honey-sucker, the flower-peckers, the streaked wren warbler, the bow-billed corby, the house sparrow, the finch larks and sand larks, the emerald dove, the ringed plover and the stone plover: and besides these, the following kinds should be watched as they commence building their nests, and possibly laying also during this month:—the *Indian scops owl*, the *palm swift*, the *rose-headed parroquet*, the *chestnut-bellied nuthatch*, the *common woodshrike*, the *brown-backed robin*, the *black bushchat*, the *common quail*, and the *spur-winged plover*. The *common heron* too begins building in parts of Oudh, and the *river terns* and *scissor bills* are now congregating on the islands, where in the next month they will breed.

In Bengal, the eggs of the long-billed vulture and white-bellied sea eagle and changeable hawk eagle, and brahminy kite may be taken. The common sand martin is still laying. The yellow-fronted woodpecker has eggs, while the *palm roof swift* in the Garo hills, the *red-breasted parroquet*, the *common woodshrike*, and the *red jungle fowl* in the sub-Himalayan tracts are pairing off and preparing their nests. Here too the *river terns* and *scissor bills* are congregating.

In Central India, the vultures and the brahminy kite, probably also the owls, and whatever species of eagles are found there, have eggs still. The cliff swallow and dusky crag martin are hatching their first brood. The pied kingfisher, the crimson-breasted barbet, the amethyst rumped honey-sucker, the Indian amadavat, and the finch-larks have eggs throughout the month, while the *painted spur fowl*, and probably also the *flower-peckers*, *nuthatches*, *woodpeckers*, *parrots*, *larks*, and some *plovers* are pairing. The *river terns* and *scissor bills* will also probably congregate here too in this month.

In Southern India, the breeding season is by this time further advanced than in the north. The kestril has eggs throughout the month in the Nilgiris. In the far south, eggs of the booted eagle may be taken, and also those of the common kite, the Nilgiri nightjar, the golden-backed woodpecker, the Nilgiri flower-pecker, the velvet-fronted nuthatch, the quaker thrushes, babblers, laughing thrushes, bulbuls, and bluebirds throughout the peninsular. In the Nilgiris the eggs of the white-eyed hill tit may be found, and the Indian grey tit, the jungle mynah, the crested larks, green pigeons, doves, jungle fowl, spur fowls, grey partridges, and bush quail are also sitting. In the extreme south the eggs of the snake bird, and possibly some other water birds, may still be found, but the season for them is virtually over. The following kinds are also commencing to pair and build their nests, and should be watched particularly towards the end of the month:—The *southern sirkeer*, the *little pied* (*flycatcher*) *shrike* (*Hemipus picatus*), the *spotted wren babbler*, the *black bulbul*, the *robins*, *bush chats*, *Nilgiri tit lark*, *long-tailed treepie*, and *Nilgiri sky lark*. Of these latter the eggs have not as yet been taken before the beginning of March.

FEBRUARY.

Nos. in Jerdon.	English Names.	Scientific Names.	Shape of Nest.	Site of Nest.	Geographical Range in Breeding Season.	Particulars for the Month.
2	The king Vulture	Otogyps calvus ...	A large platform.	On tops of high trees.	Throughout continental India.	Hansi, 20th; Agra, 10th; eggs.
3	The roc ,,	Gyps himalayensis ...	Ditto ...	On ledges of cliffs	The Himalayas only ...	Kangra, 20th, young; 28th, eggs.
4	The pale long-billed ,,	,, pallescens ...	Ditto ...	Ditto ...	Western and central India.	Ajmir, Aboo, Pachmari.
	The , ,,	,, indicus ...	Ditto ...	At tops of high trees.	The plains of upper India.	Calcutta, 5th; eggs.
5	The white-backed ,,	,, bengalensis ...	Ditto ...	Near tops of large trees.	Throughout continental India.	Agra, 10th, young; Punjab, eggs.
	The bay ,,	,, fulvescens ...	Ditto ...	Ditto ...	North-west and central India.	Lahore, eggs; Satpura hills.
6	The white scavenger ,,	Perenopteron ginginianus.	Platform ...	On cliffs or large trees.	Throughout India ...	A few stragglers breed.
7	The bearded ,,	Gypaetus barbatus ...	A large platform.	On ledges of cliffs..	The Himalayas and Suleiman range.	Kangra, 10th; eggs.
11	The black-capped Falcon	Falco atriceps ...	Ditto ...	Ditto ...	Ditto ...	Kooloo, 6th; eggs.
	The laggar ,,	,, juggur ...	Ditto ...	On high trees or cliffs.	The dry plains of upper India.	Etawah, 15th; Jhelum, 12th; eggs.
16	The red-headed Merlin	Lithofalco chicquera ...	A compact massive cap.	In forks of trees ...	Throughout the plains..	Fatehgurh (N. W. P.), 4th; eggs.
17	The Kestril	Tinnunculus alaudarius	A large platform.	On ledges of cliffs	Himalayas, Nilgiris, and Suleiman range ...	Nilgiris, 21st, 28th; eggs.
27	The imperial Eagle	Aquila mogilnik ...	Ditto ...	On tops of trees ...	The Punjab and western Himalayas.	Hansi, 22nd; eggs.
29	The Indian tawny ,,	,, vindhyana ...	Ditto ...	In high trees ...	The dry plains of upper India.	Hansi, 15th, eggs; Agra, 8th; young.
31	The booted ,,	,, pennata ...	Ditto ...	Ditto ...	Southern India ...	Salem, 21st; eggs.
33	Bonellis ,,	Nisaetus bonellii ...	Ditto ...	On cliffs or high trees.	Throughout India ...	Kangra, 5th; eggs.
36	The Nepal hawk ,,	Spizaetus nipalensis ...	Ditto ...	On high trees ...	The Himalayas ...	Masuri, 21st; eggs
	The changeable hawk ,,	,, caligatus ...	Ditto ...	Ditto ...	Bengal and sub-Himalayas.	Calcutta, 15th; eggs.

Nos. in Jerdon.	English Names.	Scientific Names.	Shape of Nest.	Site of Nest.	Geographical Range in Breeding Season.	Particulars for the Month.
38	The short-toed Eagle	Circaetus gallicus ...	A large platform...	Usually on high trees.	The dry plains of upper India.	Hansi, 6th, 26th ; eggs.
41	The bar-tailed fishing „	Polioaetus ichthyaetus	Ditto ...	On high trees near water.	Eastern and peninsular India.	(Requires confirmation.)
42	The ring-tailed fishing „	Haliaetus leucoryphus	Ditto ...	Ditto ...	Throughout northern India.	A few stagglers breed still.
43	The white-bellied sea „	„ leucogastra	Ditto ...	On high trees ...	All round the coast ...	Calcutta, 5th ; eggs.
45	The long-legged Buzzard	Buteo canescens ...	Irregular platform...	On high trees or cliffs.	The Punjab and western Himalayas.	Kooloo, 24th ; eggs.
55	The brahminy Kite	Haliastur indus ...	Ditto ...	On high trees near water.	Throughout the plains	Calcutta, 11th ; Raipur (C. P.), 10th ; eggs.
56	The common „	Milvus govinda ...	Ditto ...	In forks of trees ...	Throughout India ...	Allahabad, 20th ; eggs ; Nilgiris ; young.
	The greater Indian „	„ major ...	Ditto ...	Ditto ...	The western Himalayas.	A few stragglers breed.
60	The Indian screech Owl	Strix indica ...	None ...	In holes in trees or buildings.	Throughout the plains	Etawah (N. W. P.), 17th ; eggs.
65	The mottled wood „	Bulacca sinensis ...	Ditto ...	In holes or hollows on large trees.	Ditto ...	Etawah (N. W. P.), 27th ; eggs.
69	The rock-horned „	Ascalaphia bengalensis	Ditto ...	On ledges of banks	Throughout India proper.	Saharunpur (N. W. P.), 27th ; eggs.
70	The dusky-horned „	„ coromanda	A large platform.	In forks of large trees.	Throughout the plains	Meerut (N. W. P.), 12th ; eggs.
72	The brown fish „	Ketupa ceylonensis ...	None ...	In clefts of rocks or large trees.	Throughout India ...	Saharunpur (N. W. P.), 24th ; eggs.
	Pennant's scops „	Ephialtes griseus ...	Ditto ...	In holes in trees ...	Central and upper India	Hansi, 10th ; eggs.
76	The spotted Owlet	Athene brama ...	Ditto ...	In holes in trees or buildings.	Throughout India ...	Allahabad, 20th ; eggs.
83	The Nilgiri house Swallow	Hirundo domicola ...	Semi-circular saucer.	In buildings or eaves.	Nilgiris, Ceylon, Tennaserim.	Nest building begins.
84	The wire-tailed „	„ ruficeps ...	Ditto ...	Under bridges or on rocks by water.	Throughout India ...	Etawah (N. W. P.), 25th ; eggs.
86	The Indian cliff „	Hirundo fluvicola ...	Retort-shaped	On cliffs near water or buildings (gregarious).	Northern and central India.	First brood begins.

88	The dusky sand Martin	Cotyle subsoccata ...	A loose cup.	In holes in river banks (gregarious.)	Northern India ...	Cawnpur, 13th; eggs.
89	The common sand ,,	,, sinensis ...	Ditto ...	Ditto ...	Throughout India (rare in south).	Calcutta, 20th; young.
90	The dusky crag ,,	,, concolor ...	A deep semi-circular cup.	Against buildings or rocks.	Throughout India (locally.)	Jhansi, 10th; ditto.
100	The common Indian Swift	Cypselus abyssinicus...	Semi-globular.	Against buildings (gregarious).	Ditto ...	Nest building begins.
108	The Nilgiri Nightjar	Caprimulgus kelaarti	None ...	On the ground often near bushes.	Southern, extending to central India.	Nilgiris, 24th; eggs.
136	The pied Kingfisher	Ceryle rudis ...	Ditto ...	In holes in river banks.	Throughout the plains..	Raipur (C. P.), 8th; eggs.
147	The northern rose-band Paroquet	Palæornis sivalensis ...	Ditto ...	In holes in decayed trees.	Punjab and western Himalayas.	Dehra Doon, 20th; eggs.
148	The rose ringed ,,	,, torquatus ...	Ditto ...	Ditto ...	Throughout the plains.	Agra, 5th; Saharunpore, 20th; eggs.
160	The yellow-fronted Woodpecker	Picus mahrattensis ...	Ditto ...	In artificial holes in trees.	Ditto ...	Manbhum, 27th; eggs.
167	The southern golden-backed ,,	Chrysocolaptes delesserti.	Ditto ...	Ditto ...	The hills of south India.	Nilgiris, 3rd; eggs.
197	The crimson-breasted Barbet	Xantholæma hæmacephala.	Ditto ...	Ditto ...	Throughout the plains	Raipur (C. P.); eggs.
232	The amethyst-rumped Honeysucker	Leptocoma zeylanica	Pear-shaped, with side entrance.	Hanging from tips of branches.	Lower Bengal and peninsular India.	Raipur (C. P.), 19th; eggs
234	The purple ,,	Arachnechthra asiatica	Ditto ...	Ditto ...	Throughout India proper.	Allahabad, 18th; eggs.
239	The Nilgiri Flower-pecker	Dicæum concolor ...	Purse shaped, with front entrance.	Hanging from twigs in thick foliage.	The Nilgiris ...	Ootacamund, 20th; eggs.
240	The thick-billed ,,	Piprisoma agile ...	Ditto ...	Hanging from thin branches.	Throughout India ...	Allahabad, 25th; eggs.
253	The velvet-fronted Nuthatch	Dendrophila frontalis	None ...	In holes in trees ...	The hilly regions of India.	Kotagiri, Nilgiris, 10th; eggs.
255	The Indian Hoopoe	Upupa nigripennis ...	Ditto ...	In holes in trees or buildings.	Throughout India ...	Sambhur, 22nd; eggs.
256	The Indian grey Shrike	Lanius lahtora ...	A thick massive cup.	In thorny bushes or small trees.	Throughout the dry plains.	Delhi, 19th; eggs.
292	The white-browed Fantail	Leucocerca aureola ...	A tiny cup ..	In trees or horizontal branches.	Throughout continental India.	Nest building begins.
347	The brown water Ouzel	Hydrobata asiatica ...	A large ball of moss.	In clefts of rocks near water.	The Himalayas ...	Dehra Doon; eggs.

Nos. in Jerdon.	English Names.	Scientific Names.	Shape of Nest.	Site of Nest.	Geographical Range in Breeding Season.	Particulars for the Month.
389	The Nilgiri quaker Thrush	Alcippe poiocephala ...	A deep massive cup.	In forks of bushes or saplings.	The hills of south India.	Kotagiri, Nilgiris; eggs.
404	The southern scimitar Babbler	Pomatorhinus horsfieldii.	Large globular domed.	On the ground in a bush or tussock.	Ditto ...	Ditto ditto ditto.
423	The Nilgiri laughing Thrush	Trochalopteron cacchinans.	A deep massive cup.	In forks of bushes or saplings.	The Nilgiris ...	Ditto ditto ditto.
438	The striated bush Babbler	Chattarhœa caudata...	Cup-shaped	In low bushes or clumps of grass.	Throughout the plains	A few stragglers breed.
——	The southern red-whiskered Bulbul	Otocompsa fuscicaudata	A small neat cup.	In isolated bushes..	The hills of south India.	Kotagiri, Conoor; eggs.
462	The common Madras „	Pycnonotus pusillus ...	Ditto ...	In small trees or bushes.	Throughout the plains	Nilgiris; eggs.
469	The fairy Bluebird	Irena puella ..	A loose straggling cup.	In forks of small trees.	Southern India ...	AssambooHills, 2nd; eggs.
——	The streaked scrub Warbler	Drymœca inquieta ...	Large globular domed.	In low thorny shrubs.	The trans-Indus hills...	Nowshera; eggs.
550	The „ wren „	Burnesia lepida ...	Ditto ...	In clumps of grass on islands.	Northern India ...	Fatehgurh (N. W. P.), 24th; eggs.
631	The Indian white-eyed Tit	Zosterops palpebrosus	A tiny regular cup.	Hung from twigs in trees or shrubs.	Throughout India ...	Kotagiri, Nilgiris; eggs.
645	The Indian grey „	Parus cinereus ...	Shallow pad	In holes in walls or trees.	In all wooded hills ...	Ootacamund, 17th; eggs.
657	The Raven	Corvus corax ...	A large compact cup.	In forks of solitary trees.	Western continental India.	Jhelum, Punjab, 19th; eggs.
660	The bow-billed Corby	„ culminatus ...	Ditto ...	Ditto ...	Throughout the plains	Allahabad, 18th; eggs.
686	The jungle Mynah	Acridotheres fuscus ...	None ...	In holes in trees or buildings.	In all wooded hills ...	The Nilgiris; eggs.
703	The pin-tailed Munia	Munia malabarica ...	A large domed oval.	In small trees, shrubs, or eaves...	Throughout India proper.	Allahabad, 9th; eggs.
704	The Indian Amadavat	Estrelda amandava ...	Ditto ...	In low thick bushes	Locally throughout India.	Raipur (C. P.), 25th; eggs.
706	The Indian house Sparrow	Passer indicus ...	A globular mass.	In and about houses	Throughout India ...	Allahabad, 9th; eggs.
758	The rufous-tailed finch Lark	Ammomanes phœnicura	A slight circular pad.	On the ground near clod or tussock ...	Throughout India, south of Agra.	The Deccan; eggs.

760	The black-bellied finch Lark	Pyrrhalauda grisea ...	A tiny shallow pad.	Ditto ...	Throughout the plains.	Etawah (N. W. P.), 22nd ; eggs.
762	The eastern sand „	Alaudala raytal ...	Ditto ...	On the ground under tussocks or tamarisk.	Eastern continental India.	Cawnpur ; eggs.
768	The Malabar crested „	Alauda malabarica ...	A shallow saucer.	On the ground near tiny bushes or grass.	Southern India ...	Nest building begins.
775	The grey-fronted green Pigeon	Osmotreron malabarica	A small platform.	On outer boughs of trees.	The hills of south India.	Assamboo Hills, 24th ; eggs
788	The Indian blue rock „	Columba intermedia...	Ditto ...	On ledges of buildings chiefly.	Throughout India ...	A few stragglers breed.
793	Sykes' turtle Dove	Turtur meena ...	A tiny platform.	In low trees in thick foliage.	Peninsular and eastern India.	Breed quite irregularly.
794	The brown turtle „	„ cambaiensis ...	Ditto ...	In low trees or bushes.	Throughout the plains.	Ditto.
796	The Indian ring „	„ risorius ...	Ditto ...	Ditto ...	Ditto ...	Ditto.
797	The ruddy ring „	„ humilis ...	Ditto ...	Ditto ...	Ditto (but local)...	Ditto.
798	The emerald „	Chalcophaps indicus ...	A shallow saucer.	In thick trees or bushes.	In all densely wooded tracts.	Dehra Doon, 25th ; eggs.
813	The grey jungle Fowl	Gallus sonneratii ...	A few dry leaves.	On the ground in dense cover.	The hills of central and south India.	Malabar ; eggs.
814	The red spur „	Galloperdix spadiceus	Ditto ...	Ditto ...	Ditto ...	Kotagiri, Nilgiris ; eggs.
822	The grey Patridge	Ortygornis ponticeriana	Ditto ...	On the ground in bushes or grass ...	The open plains of India	Berar ; eggs.
828	The red-billed bush Quail	Perdicula erythorhyncha.	None ...	On the ground under shelter.	The Nilgiris ...	Kotagiri, Nilgiris ; eggs.
849	The ringed Plover	Œgialites curonicus ...	Ditto ...	On the ground by sandy rivers	Throughout India ...	Cawnpur ; eggs.
859	The stone „	Œdicnemus crepitans	Ditto ...	On the ground near bushes or trees.	Throughout India (locally).	Etawah (N. W. P.); eggs.
1008	The Indian snake Bird	Plotus melanogaster ...	A rough platform.	On trees standing in water.	Throughout the plains.	South of Madras ; eggs.

MARCH.

THE birds of prey are still in full season, and though many of the larger kinds have ceased to lay their places are filled by others, especially among the owls. Most of the bee eaters, kingfishers, parrots, woodpeckers, barbets, nuthatches, larks, plovers, and terns are either laying or building, and several species of swifts, goatsuckers, shrikes, flycatchers, thrushes, babblers, bulbuls, chats, warblers, titlarks, jays, mynahs, and game birds are beginning to lay.

In the HIMALAYAS, the king vulture is still laying, also the bearded vulture (*Lammergeyer*), the black-capped falcon, and Bonelli's eagle. The crested serpent eagle, the long-legged buzzard and the greater Indian kite, and several of the owls are laying. The slaty-headed paroquet and the scaly-bellied green woodpecker have eggs. The white-tailed and velvet-fronted nuthatches, the hoopoe, the bronzed drongo, the ashy swallow shrike, the verditer flycatcher, the Nepal quaker thrush, the white-browed warbler, the white-eyed tit, the red-capped, crested black, and mountain tits, the nutcracker, magpie and jay, the large hill mynah, the tree sparrow, and the white-crested king pheasant all begin laying; and the *goshawk, Himalayan fishing eagle, collared pigmy owlet, common swallow, crag and Kashmir martins, Hodgson's trogon, roseband paroquet, woodpeckers, piculets, flower-peckers, tree-creepers, raquet-tailed drongos, chestnut-bellied chat thrush, white-collared ouzels, missel thrush, red-headed wren babbler, rufous-necked and rusty-cheeked scimitar babblers, black gorgetted laughing thrush, iron grey bushchat, blue-headed redstart, black-eared and grey-headed warblers, western spotted forktails, yellow-cheeked tits, blue magpies, green jays,* and *spotted-winged stares* are all pairing and building.

In the PUNJAB, the vultures, hawks, falcons, and true eagles are still laying, also the short-toed eagle. The buzzards and several owls commence laying. The dusky crag martin, the pied kingfisher, the grey shrike, the babblers, the streaked scrub warbler, the streaked wren warbler, the raven, the larks, doves, the common sandgrouse, the common quail, the big bustard, most of the plovers, the common heron, the king curlew, most of the terns, and the scissor bill have eggs during the month; and the *painted sandgrouse*, the *seesee partridge*, the *lesser button quail*, and the *gull-billed terns* are pairing and making their nests.

In the NORTH-WEST PROVINCES, the white scavenger vulture

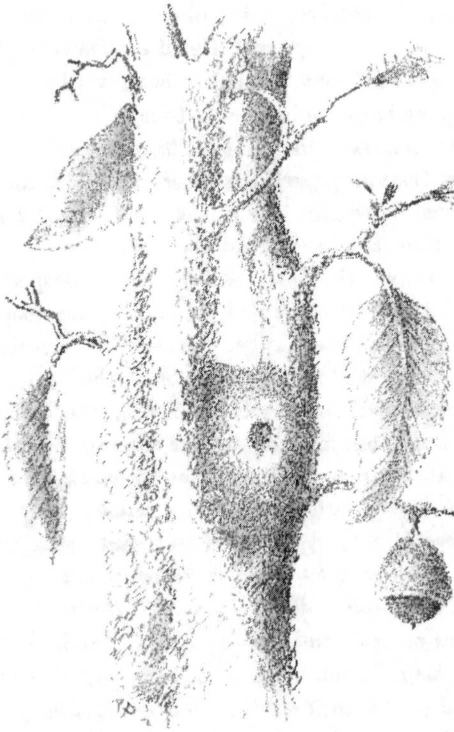

MARSHALL DEL

NEST OF THE RED-HEADED TIT.

(Egithaliscus erythrocephalus.)

and a few of the king vultures are the only vultures with eggs at this season. The laggar falcon, the red-headed merlins, the changeable hawk eagles, buzzards, kites, and most of the owls, are still laying. All the swallows and martins, the blue-tailed bee eater, the roller, the parrots, woodpeckers and barbets, the flower-peckers, honey suckers, nuthatches, robins, chats, titlarks, carrion crows, larks of all kinds, green pigeons, emerald doves, grey partridges, bush quail, common quail, most of the plovers, the river terns, and the scissor bills have all got eggs. The following birds not included in the list that follows begin building during the month, and should be watched:—The *shikra hawk*, the *jungle owlet*, the *blue-ruffed bee eater*, the *northern grey hornbill*, the *large grey cuckoo shrike*, *Sykes' warbler*, and the *common cormorant*.

In Bengal, the palm roof swift in the Garo hills lays throughout the month. The large Bengal nightjar, the white-breasted kingfisher, the red-breasted paroquet, the Indian loriquet, the yellow-fronted woodpecker, Franklin's green barbet, the koel, honey suckers, flower-peckers, the common wood shrike, the common babbler, the red-whiskered and white-winged green bulbul, the black-headed oriole, the black crow, Sykes' turtle dove, the red jungle fowl, the kyah partridge, plovers, river terns, and scissor bills all have eggs. The species that commence nest-building during the month are *Jerdon's green bulbul*, the *shama robin*, and the *white-backed munia*.

In Central India, the cliff swallows, crag martins, blue-tailed bee eater, little kingfisher, rock chat, rufous-tailed finch lark, painted spur fowl, and plovers are the characteristic species that lay during the month, but many of the species that breed at this time in northern, and particularly southern India, breed also now in central India. The species that begin building in this month are the *jungle nightjar* and the *purple heron*.

In Southern India, the kestril is still laying, and probably some of the owls. The jungle nightjar, chestnut-headed bee eater, little kingfisher, lesser green woodpecker, the green barbet, the sirkeer, flower-pecker, some shrikes, flycatchers, thrushes, blackbirds, quaker thrushes, babblers, laughing thrushes, bulbuls, robins, chats, the ashy wren warbler, titlark, tits, long-tailed treepie, mynahs, larks, grey jungle fowl, red spur fowl, and red-winged bush quail are the kinds that breed throughout the month. The *white-bellied short wing* in the Pulneys, and the *green pigeons* and *Nilgiri wood pigeons* commence building their nests.

MARCH.

Nos. in Jerdon.	English Names.	Scientific Names.	Shape of Nest.	Site of Nest.	Geographical Range in Breeding Season.	Particulars for the Month.
2	The king Vulture	Otogyps calvus ...	A large platform.	On tops of high trees	Throughout continental India.	Kangra, 2nd; Hansi, 6th 14th; eggs.
3	The roc „	Gyps himalayensis ...	Ditto ...	On ledges of cliffs..	The Himalayas only...	Kangra, young; season ends.
5	The white-backed „	„ bengalensis ...	Ditto ...	Near tops of large trees.	Throughout continental India.	Salt range, 10th; eggs.
	The bay „	„ fulvescens ...	Ditto ...	Ditto ...	North-west and central India.	Lahore, 7th; eggs.
6	The white scavenger „	Perenopteron ginginianus.	Platform ...	On cliffs or large trees.	Throughout India ...	Meerut, 24th; Salt range 21st; eggs.
7	The bearded „	Gypaetus barbatus ...	A large platform.	On ledges of cliffs..	The Himalayas and Suleiman range.	Kangra, 14th; eggs; season ends.
	The black-capped Falcon	Falco atriceps ...	Ditto ...	Ditto ...	Ditto ...	Kangra, 10th; eggs; season ends,
11	The laggar „	„ juggur ...	Ditto ...	On high trees or cliffs.	The dry plains of upper India.	Mainpuri, 2nd; Kumaon, 25th; eggs.
16	The red-headed Merlin	Lithofalco chicquera...	A compact massive cup.	In forks of trees ...	Throughout the plains	Allahabad, 27th; eggs.
17	The Kestril	Tinnunculus alaudarius	A large platform.	On ledges of cliffs..	Himalayas, Nilgiris, and Suleiman range.	Nilgiris, 1st; eggs.
27	The imperial Eagle	Aquila mogilnik ...	Ditto ...	On tops of trees ...	The Punjab and western Himalayas.	Upper Punjab; eggs.
29	The Indian tawny „	„ vindhyana ...	Ditto ...	In high trees ...	The dry plains of upper India.	Hansi; eggs.
33	Bonelli's „	Nisaetus bonellii ...	Ditto ...	On cliffs or high trees.	Throughout India ...	Kumaon; eggs.
36	The Nepal hawk „	Spizaetus nipalensis ...	Ditto ...	On high trees ...	The Himalayas ...	Masuri, 5th, 18th; eggs.
	The changeable „ „	„ caligatus ...	Ditto ...	Ditto ...	Bengal and sub-Himalayan forests.	Kumaon, Bhabur.
38	The short-toed „	Circaetus gallicus ...	Ditto ...	Usually on high trees.	The dry plains of upper India.	Hansi, 6th, 26th; Saharunpur, 13th; eggs.
39	The crested serpent „	Spilornis cheela ...	Ditto ...	In thick forks of trees.	The sub-Himalayas ...	Masuri, 20th; eggs.

No.	Name	Species	Nest	Site	Distribution	Remarks
45	The long-legged Buzzard	Buteo canescens ...	Irregular platform.	On high trees or cliffs	The Punjab and western Himalayas.	Bussahir, 1st; Jhelum; eggs.
48	The white eyed „	Policrnis teesa ...	A small platform.	In forks of trees ...	The dry plains of continental India.	Etawah, 28th; eggs.
55	The brahminy Kite	Haliastur indus ...	Irregular platform.	On high trees near water.	Throughout the plains	Allahabah, 26th; eggs.
56	The common „	Milvus govinda ...	Ditto ...	In forks of trees ...	Throughout India ...	Meerut, 23rd; eggs.
	The greater Indian „	„ major ...	Ditto ...	Ditto ...	The western Himalayas.	Kooloo, Kashmir.
60	The Indian screech „	Strix indica ...	None ...	In holes in trees or buildings.	Throughout the plains	Lucknow, Alygarh, Jaipore; eggs.
65	The mottled wood „	Bulacca sinensis ...	Ditto ...	In holes or hollows on large trees.	Ditto ...	Hansi, 16th; Etawah, 3rd; eggs.
69	The rock horned „	Ascalaphia bengalensis	Ditto ...	On ledges of banks.	Throughout India ...	Saharunpur, 26th; young; 28th; eggs.
70	The dusky „ „	„ coromanda	Ditto ...	On forks of large trees.	Throughout the plains	A few stragglers breed.
72	The brown fish „	Ketupa ceylonensis ...	Ditto ...	In clefts of rocks or large trees.	Throughout India ...	Saharunpur, 10th; eggs; season ends.
74	The Indian scops „	Ephialtes pennatus ...	Ditto ...	In holes in trees ...	In all well-wooded tracts.	The Doab; eggs.
	The barefoot „ „	„ spilocephalus	Ditto ...	Ditto ...	The Himalayas ...	Masuri, 19th; eggs.
	Pennant's „ „	„ griseus ...	Ditto ...	Ditto ...	Central and upper India	Etawah, 10th; Hansi, 25th; eggs.
76	The spotted Owlet	Athene brama ...	Ditto ...	In holes in trees or buildings.	Throughout India ...	Allahabad, 27th; eggs.
79	The large barred „	„ cuculoides ...	Ditto ...	In holes in trees ...	The Himalayas ...	Kangra, Kumaon; eggs.
83	The Nilgiri house Swallow	Hirundo domicola ...	Semi-circular saucer.	In buildings or caves.	Nilgiris, Ceylon, Tenaserim.	Throughout the month.
84	The wire-tailed „	„ ruficeps ...	Ditto ...	Under bridges or on rocks by water.	Locally throughout India.	Etawah, 8th; eggs.
85	The Indian cliff „	„ fluvicola ...	Retort shaped.	On cliffs near water or buildings (gregarious).	Northern and central India.	Ajmir, Dehra Doon; eggs.
88	The dusky sand Martin	Cotyle subsoccata ...	A loose cup	In holes in river banks (gregarious)	Northern India ...	Etawah, 12th; eggs.
89	The common „ „	„ sinensis ...	Ditto ...	Ditto do. ...	Throughout India (rare in south).	Cawnpur, 15th; eggs.
90	The dusky crag „	„ concolor ...	Semi-circular cup.	Against buildings or rocks.	Locally throughout India.	Central Provinces; eggs.
100	The common Indian Swift	Cypselus abyssinicus ...	Semi-globular	Against buildings (gregarious).	Throughout India ...	Meerut, 14th; eggs.

Nos. in Jerdon.	English Names.	Scientific Names.	hape of Nest.	Site of Nest.	Geographical Range in Breeding Season.	Particulars for the Month.
102	The palm Swift	Cypselus batassiensis	A tiny watch pocket.	On leaves of the toddy palm.	Locally throughout the plains.	Mirzapur, 18th ; eggs.
——	The palm roof "	, infumatus ...	Ditto ...	On huts thatched with palm leaves.	Garo and north Cachar Hills.	Asalu ; eggs.
——	Horsfield's Swiftlet	Collocalia linchi ...	A small cup.	In caves and on houses.	The Andamans and Nicobars.	Macpherson's Straits, 9th ; eggs.
103	The southern hill "	" unicolor ...	Small semi-circular saucer.	In caves or on rocks	The Nilgiris and Assamboo Hills.	Travancore, 20th ; eggs.
108	The Nilgiri Nightjar	Caprimulgus kelaarti	None ...	On the ground often near bushes.	Southern, extending to central India.	Kotagiri, Raipur.
109	The large Bengal "	, albonotatus	Ditto ...	Ditto ...	Wooded parts of upper India.	Manbhum, 28th ; eggs.
117	The common Bee eater	Merops viridis ...	Ditto ...	In deep holes in banks or plains.	Throughout India proper	Breeding season begins.
118	The blue tailed "	" philippensis ...	Ditto ...	In deep holes in banks.	Ditto ...	Hoshungabad, Oude ; eggs.
119	The chestnut-headed ,	, quinticolor ...	Ditto ...	Ditto ...	In wooded hilly country.	Nilgiris ; eggs.
123	The common Roller	Coracias indica ...	Ditto ...	In holes in trees or buildings.	Throughout India proper.	Allahabad, 28th ; eggs.
129	The white-breasted Kingfisher	Halcyon smyrnensis ...	Ditto ...	In holes in river banks or wells.	Ditto ...	Mergui, 25th ; eggs.
134	The little Indian "	Alcedo bengalensis ...	Ditto ...	In holes in banks by rivers.	Ditto ...	Nilgiris, 25th; Deccan, 15th; eggs.
136	The pied "	Ceryle rudis ...	Ditto ...	Ditto ...	Throughout the plains	Jhelum, 20th ; eggs.
147	The northern roseband Paroquet	Palæornis sivalensis ...	Ditto ...	In holes in decayed trees.	The Punjab and western Himalayas.	Dehra Doon ; eggs.
148	The rose-ringed "	" torquatus ...	Ditto ...	Ditto ...	Throughout the plains	Allahabad, 25th ; eggs.
149	The rose-headed "	" purpureus ...	Ditto ...	Ditto ...	Continental India, west of Oude.	Saharunpur, 10th ; eggs.
150	The slaty-headed "	" schisticeps ...	Ditto ...	Ditto ...	The Himalayas ...	Kumaon ; eggs.
152	The red-breasted "	" javanicus ...	Ditto ...	Ditto ...	Sub-Himalayas, east of the Ganges.	Very little known.
153	The Indian Loriquet	Loriculus vernalis ...	Ditto ...	Ditto ...	North-eastern India ...	Ditto.

160	The yellow-fronted Woodpecker	Picus mahrattensis ...	None ...	In artificial holes in trees.	Throughout the plains	Manbhum, 5th; Cawnpur, 27th; eggs.
164	The southern pigmy ,,	Yungipicus hardwickii	Ditto ...	Ditto ...	Ditto ...	Seetapur, Etawah; eggs.
170	The scaly-bellied green ,,	Gecinus squamatus ...	Ditto ...	Ditto ...	The Himalayas ...	Breeding season begins.
171	The lesser Indian ,, ,,	,, striolatus ...	Ditto ...	Ditto ...	Throughout eastern and southern India.	Ditto
180	The common gold back ,,	Brachypternus aurantius.	Ditto ...	Ditto ...	Throughout the plains	Etawah, 11th, 23rd; eggs.
193	Franklin's green Barbet	Megalæma caniceps ...	Ditto ...	Ditto ...	Continental India ..	Manbhum, 15th; eggs.
194	The small green ,,	,, viridis ...	Ditto ...	Ditto ...	Peninsular India ...	Nilgiris; eggs.
197	The crimson-breasted ,,	Xantholæma hæmacephala.	Ditto ...	Ditto ...	Throughout the plains	Throughout the month.
214	The Koel	Eudynamys orientalis	Habits parasitic.	Eggs laid in crows' nests.	Ditto ...	Calcutta, 15th; eggs.
219	The southern Sirkeer	Taccocua leschenaulti	A large irregular cup.	In thick bush jungle.	The hills of south India.	Nilgiris; eggs.
232	The amethyst rumped Honey-sucker	Leptocoma zeylanica	Pear-shaped, side entrance	Hanging from tips of branches.	Lower Bengal and peninsular India.	Manbhum, 27th; eggs.
234	The purple ,,	Arachnechthra asiatica	Ditto ...	Ditto ...	Throughout the plains	Saharunpur, Cawnpur, 31st; eggs.
238	Tickell's Flower-pecker	Dicœum minimum ...	Ditto ...	Ditto ...	Bombay, central and N. E. India.	Manbhum, 16th; eggs.
239	The Nilgiri ,	,, concolor ...	Purse-shaped, front entrance.	Hanging from twigs in thick foliage.	The Nilgiris ...	Ootacamund, 3rd; eggs.
240	The thick-billed ,,	Piprisoma agile ...	Ditto ...	Hanging from thin branches.	Throughout India ...	Benares, 6th, young; Manbhum, 4th; eggs.
248	The white-tailed Nuthatch	Sitta himalayensis ...	A shallow pad	In hollows in trees	The Himalayas only ...	Kumaon; season begins.
250	The chestnut-bellied ,,	,, castaneiventris ...	None ...	Ditto ...	Locally throughout the plains.	The Doab; do.
253	The velvet-fronted ,,	Dendrophila frontalis	Ditto ...	Ditto ...	The hilly regions of India.	The sub-Himalayas; do.
254	The Hoopoe	Upupa epops ...	Ditto ...	In holes in trees or buildings.	The western Himalayas.	Kashmir; do.
255	The Indian ,,	,, nigripennis ...	Ditto ...	Ditto ...	Throughout India ...	Saharunpur, 9th; eggs.
256	The Indian grey Shrike	Lanius lahtora ...	A thick massive cup.	In small trees or thorny bushes.	Throughout the dry plains. ...	Hansi, 29th; Salt range, 16th; eggs.
257	The rufous-backed ,,	,, erythronotus ...	Ditto ...	Ditto ...	Throughout India ...	Etawah, 18th; eggs.
	The pale ,, ,,	,, caniceps ...	Ditto ...	Ditto ...	The hilly regions of India.	Nilgiris; season begins.
265	The common wood ,,	Tephrodornis ponticeriana.	A neat shallow cup.	In horizontal forks of trees.	Throughout the plains	Manbhum; Saharunpur, 20th; eggs.

Nos. in Jerdon.	English Names.	Scientific Names.	Shape of Nest.	Site of Nest.	Geographical Range in Breeding Season.	Particulars for the Month.
267	The little pied Shrike	Hemipus picatus ...	A tiny shallow cup.	In horizontal forks of trees.	Southern India ...	Ootacamund, 8th ; eggs.
282	The bronzed drongo „	Chaptia œnea ...	A broad saucer.	Ditto ...	In forests throughout India.	Nepal ; season begins.
287	The ashy swallow „	Artamus fuscus ...	Ditto ...	On horizontal boughs or clumps.	Locally throughout India.	Nepal ; do.
292	The white-browed Fantail	Leucocerca aureola ...	A tiny cup...	In trees on thin branches.	Throughout continental India.	Etawah, 29th ; eggs.
300	The black and orange Flycatcher	Ochromela nigrorufa..	Large and globular.	Low down in bushes or clumps.	The Nilgiris only ...	Ootacamund ; eggs.
301	The verditer „	Eumyias melanops ...	A thick cup	In holes in banks often under bridges.	The Himalayas ...	Nest building begins.
302	The Nilgiri blue „	„ albicaudata...	Ditto ...	Ditto ...	The Nilgiris ...	Conoor, 13th ; eggs.
344	The Malabar whistling Thrush	Myiophonus horsfieldii.	A massive saucer.	On ledges of rocks near water.	The hills of south India.	Kotagiri, 22nd ; eggs.
347	The brown water Ouzel	Hydrobata asiatica ...	A large ball of moss.	In clefts of rocks near water.	The Himalayas only ...	Kangra, 12th, 20th ; eggs.
360	The Nilgiri Blackbird	Merula simillima ...	A massive cup.	In forks of trees or saplings.	The Nilgiris ...	Conoor, 25th ; eggs.
388	The Nepal quaker Thrush	Alcippe nipalensis ...	A deep massive cup.	In low thick bushes	The eastern Himalayas	Nepal ; season begins.
389	The Nilgiri „ „	„ poiocephala ...	Ditto ...	In thick bushes or saplings.	The hills of south India. ...	Nilgiris, 28th ; eggs.
399	The spotted wren Babbler	Pellorneum ruficeps ...	A loose domed cup.	On the ground against a bush.	Southern India ...	Kotagiri ; eggs.
404	The southern scimitar „	Pomatorhinus horsfieldii	Large globular domed.	On the ground in bush or tussock.	The hills of south India.	Ditto ; do.
423	The Nilgiri laughing Thrush	Trochalopteron cacchinans.	A deep massive cup.	In forks of small trees or bushes.	The Nilgiris ...	Ditto ; do.
432	The Bengal Babbler	Malacocercus canorus..	A loose straggling cup.	In thick bushes or small trees.	The plains of continental India.	Nest building begins.
436	The large grey „	„ malcolmi	Cup-shaped	In thorny trees or bushes.	Throughout the plains	Kotagiri, Cawnpur, 20th ; eggs.
438	The striated bush „	Chattarhœa caudata ...	Ditto ...	In low bushes or clumps.	Ditto	A few stragglers breed.

439	The striated reed Babbler	Chattarhœa earlii ...	A neat compact cap.	In reeds or clumps of grass.	Locally in continental India.	Saharunpur, 24th; Delhi, 28th; eggs.
445	The Nilgiri black Bulbul	Hypsepetes nilgiriensis	A rough shallow cup.	In dense bushes or parasites on trees.	The Nilgiris ...	Conoor, 14th; eggs.
450	The yellow-browed bush „	Criniger icterious ...	A small shallow cup.	Suspended from forks in thick foliage.	The hills of south India	Conoor, 20th; eggs.
460	The red-whiskered „	Otocompsa emeria ...	Ditto ...	In thick bushes or creepers.	The moist parts of upper India.	Oude and Bengal; eggs.
	The southern „ „	„ fuscicaudata	A small neat cup.	In isolated bushes	The hills of south India	Conoor, 13th; eggs.
462	The common Madras „	Pycnonotus pusillus ...	Ditto ...	In small trees or bushes.	Throughout the plains	The Nilgiris; eggs.
468	The white-winged green „	Iora typhia ...	A tiny cup...	In trees near tips of boughs.	Plains of upper India	Calcutta, 31st; eggs.
472	The black-headed Oriole	Oriolus melanocephalus	A neat deep cup.	In high trees hung from outer forks.	Eastern continental India.	Calcutta (doubtful).
475	The magpie Robin	Copsychus saularis ...	A shallow saucer.	In holes in trees or walls.	Throughout India ...	The Wynaad, 29th; eggs.
479	The southern brown-backed „	Thamnobia fulicata ...	A small cup	In holes in buildings or on the ground sheltered.	Southern India ...	Poona, 29th; December, 27th; eggs.
480	The brown-backed „	„ cambaiensis	Ditto ...	Ditto ...	Northern India ...	Cawnpur, 31st; Saharunpur, 26th; eggs.
481	The black bush Chat	Pratincola caprata ...	A shallow pad	On the ground under shelter.	The Himalayas and upper India.	Saharunpur, 27th; eggs.
482	The southern black „ „	„ atrata ...	Ditto ...	In holes in banks or walls.	The hills of south India	Conoor, 25th; Kotagiri; eges.
483	The common Indian „ „	„ indica ...	A small cup	Ditto ...	The Himalayas and N. W. Punjab.	Kumaon; eggs.
494	The brown rock „	Cercomela fusca ...	A shallow pad	Ditto ..	The dry parts of continental India.	Etawah, 23rd; Ajmir, 29th; eggs.
507	The blue wood „	Larvivora cyana ...	Ditto ...	In holes in decayed trees.	The Himalayas and Nilgiris.	Ootacamund, 15th; eggs.
	The streaked scrub Warbler	Drymœca inquieta ...	Large globular domed.	In low thorny shrubs	The trans-Indus hills	Nowshera, 16th; eggs.
534	The ashy wren „	Prinia socialis ...	A cup sewn in leaves.	Hanging in low bushes.	Southern India ...	Ootacamund; eggs.
539	The rufous grass ,	Cisticola schœnicola ...	A deep narrow purse.	Low down in tufts of grass.	Throughout the plains	Delhi; eggs.
550	The streaked wren „	Burnesia lepida ...	Large globular domed.	In clumps of grass on tamarisk islands	Northern India ...	Fatehgurh, 13th; Delhi, 28th; eggs.

Nos in Jerdon.	English Names.	Scientific Names.	Shape of Nest.	Site of Nest.	Geographical Range in Breeding Season.	Particulars for the Month.
573	The white-browed Warbler	Abrornis albosupercilia-ris.	Globular domed.	On the ground in mossy banks.	The Himalayas ...	Kangra, Kumaon; eggs.
589	The Indian pied Wagtail	Motacilla maderas patana.	A shallow pad	On the ground or buildings near water.	Throughout the plains	Etawah, 14th; eggs.
600	The Indian Tit-lark	Corydalla rufula ...	A shallow saucer.	On the ground by clod or tussock.	Throughout India ...	Saharunpur, 24th; eggs.
603	The Nilgiri "	Agrodroma cinnamomea	Ditto ...	Ditto ...	The Nilgiris ...	Segoor pass; eggs.
631	The Indian white-eyed Tit	Zosterops palpebrosus	A tiny regular cup.	Hung from twigs in trees or bushes.	Throughout India ...	Kumaon, Nilgiris, eggs.
634	The red-capped "	Egithaliscus erythro-cephalus.	Ovoidal domed.	Wedged in forks of stunted trees.	The Himalayas ...	Bhootan; eggs.
638	The crested black "	Lophophanes melanolo-phus.	A shallow pad	In holes in walls or trees.	Ditto ...	Kumaon, Sikkim; eggs.
644	The mountain "	Parus monticolus ...	A rough mass of feathers.	Ditto ...	Ditto ...	Ditto.
645	The Indian grey "	" cinereus ...	A shallow pad	Ditto ...	In all wooded hilly regions.	The Nilgiris; eggs.
657	The Raven	Corvus corax ...	A large compact cup.	In forks of solitary trees.	Western continental India.	Season nearly over.
660	The bow-billed Corby	" culminatus ...	Ditto ...	Ditto ...	Throughout the plains	Etawah, 14th; Tanaserim, 21st; eggs.
666	The Himalayan Nutcracker	Nucifraga hemispila ...	Ditto ...	High up in pine trees.	The western Himalayas	Season ends.
668	The Himalayan Magpie	Pica bottanensis ...	Ditto (domed)	In high trees ...	The eastern Himalayas	Ditto.
669	The Himalayan Jay	Garrulus bispecularis...	A neat compact cup.	In thick forks of large trees.	The Himalayas ...	Nepal; eggs.
678	The long-tailed Treepie	Dendrocitta leucogastra	A loose cup	On small trees or saplings.	The forests of south India.	Assamboo hills, 9th; eggs.
686	The jungle Mynah	Acridotheres fuscus ...	None ...	In holes in trees or buildings.	In all wooded hills ...	The Nilgiris; eggs.
692	The southern hill "	Eulabes religiosa ...	Ditto ...	In holes in trees ...	Southern India ...	Travancore, 23rd; eggs.
693	The large hill "	" intermedia ...	Ditto ...	Ditto ...	The eastern sub-Himalayas.	Nepal and Kumaon Bhabur
703	The pin-tailed Munia	Munia malabarica ..	A large dome oval.	In thick bushes, small trees, or eaves.	Throughout India proper.	Etawah; eggs.

706	The Indian house Sparrow	Passer indicus ...	A globular mass.	In or about houses	Throughout India ...	Throughout the month.
710	The tree "	" montanus ...	Ditto ...	In holes in trees or buildings.	The eastern Himalayas	Sikkim; eggs.
756	The red-winged bush Lark	Mirafra erythroptera...	A shallow pad	On the ground near tussock.	The dry plains of continental India.	The Doab; eggs.
757	The singing " "	" cantillans ...	A pad (sometimes domed)	Ditto ...	Ditto (but local)	Hansi, 28th; eggs.
758	The rufous-tailed finch "	Ammomanes phœnicura	A slight circular pad.	On the ground by clod or tussock.	Throughout India, south of Agra.	Raipur (C. P.); eggs.
760	The black-bellied " "	Pyrrhalauda grisea ...	A tiny shallow pad.	Ditto ...	Throughout the plains	Etawah, 11th, 21st; eggs.
762	The eastern sand "	Alaudala raytal ...	A tiny saucer	On the ground near grass or tiny bush.	Eastern continental India.	Cawnpur; eggs.
	The Punjab " "	" adamsi ...	Ditto ...	Ditto ...	Western continental India.	Jhelum, 20th; eggs.
767	The Indian sky "	Alauda gulgula ...	Ditto ...	Ditto ...	Plains of continental India.	Throughout the month.
	The Nilgiri " "	" australis ...	Ditto ...	Ditto ...	The hills of south India	Nilgiris; season begins.
768	The Malabar crested "	" malabarica ...	Ditto ...	Ditto ...	Southern India ...	Ditto; ditto.
769	The common " "	Galerita cristata ...	Ditto ...	Ditto ...	The dry plains of continental India.	Salt range, 25th; eggs.
	The lesser " "	" boysii ...	Ditto ...	Ditto ...	Ditto ...	Saharunpur, 20th; eggs.
773	The southern green Pigeon	Crocopus chlorigastra	A small platform.	In small trees or bushes.	Throughout the plains (except Bengal).	Etawah, 23rd; Behar, 27th; eggs.
788	The Indian blue rock "	Columba intermedia ...	Ditto ...	On ledges of buildings chiefly.	Throughout India ...	Throughout the month.
793	Sykes's turtle Dove	Turtur meena ...	A tiny platform.	In low trees in thick foliage.	Peninsular and eastern India.	Hill Tipperah, 26th; eggs.
794	The brown " "	" cambaiensis ...	Ditto ...	In low trees or bushes.	Throughout the plains	Throughout the month.
795	The spotted "	" suratensis ...	Ditto ...	Ditto ...	In all wooded parts ...	Ditto.
796	The Indian ring "	" risorius ...	Ditto ..	Ditto ...	Throughout India proper.	Ditto.
797	The ruddy " "	" humilis ...	Ditto ...	Ditto ...	Ditto (but local)	Ditto.
798	The emerald "	Chalcophaps indicus ...	A shallow saucer.	In low thick trees or bushes.	In all densely wooded tracts.	Dehra Doon; eggs.
* 802	The common Sandgrouse	Pterocles exustus ...	None ...	On the bare ground	The dry plains of continental India.	Sirsa, 1st, 21st; Fatehgurh, 2nd; eggs.
810	The white-crested kalij Pheasant	Gallophasis albocristatus	A shallow pad	On the ground in dense cover.	The Himalayas ...	Dehra Doon, 28th; eggs.

Nos. in Jerdon.	English Names.	Scientific Names.	Shape of Nest.	Site of Nest.	Geographical Range in Breeding Season.	Particulars for the Month.
812	The red jungle Fowl	Gallus ferrugineus ...	A few dry leaves.	On the ground in dense cover.	The sub-Himalayas, Madras, and C. P.	Pegu, 20th ; eggs.
813	The grey ,, ,,	,, sonneratii ...	Ditto ...	Ditto ...	The hills of central and south India.	Kotagiri ; eggs.
814	The red spur ,,	Galloperdix spadiceus	Ditto ...	Ditto ...	South India extending to Bundelkund	Nilgiris ; eggs.
815	The painted ,, ,,	,, lunulosus	Ditto ...	Ditto ...	The eastern peninsular to Central Provinces.	Raipur (C. P.) ; eggs.
822	The grey Partridge	Ortygornis ponticeriana	Ditto ...	On the ground in bushes or grass.	The open plains of India proper.	Saharunpur ; eggs.
823	The kyah ,,	,, gularis ...	Ditto ...	Ditto ...	The sub-Himalayan Terais.	Breeding season begins.
826	The jungle bush Quail	Perdicula cambaiensis	Ditto ...	On the ground in long grass.	Throughout India locally	Throughout the month.
827	The rock ,, ,,	,, asiatica ...	Ditto ...	Ditto ...	Ditto ...	Etawah ; eggs.
828	The red-billed ,, ,,	,, erythrorhyncha.	Ditto ...	On the ground under shelter.	The Nilgiris ...	Kotagiri ; eggs.
829	The common ,,	Coturnix communis ...	Ditto ...	Ditto ...	Northern India ...	Hansi, 25th ; Allahabad, 25th ; eggs.
836	The Indian Bustard	Eupodotis edwardsii ...	None ...	On the ground in scanty grass jungle	The dry parts of continental India.	Sirsa, 12th, 20th ; eggs.
840	The Indian courier Plover	Cursorius coromandelicus.	Ditto ...	On the ground in waste or fallow land.	In all dry plains, except Punjab.	Oude, Etawah ; eggs.
	The cream-colored ,, ,,	,, gallicus ...	Ditto ...	Ditto ...	The Punjab ...	Sirsa, 14th ; eggs.
843	The lesser swallow ,,	Glareola lactea ...	Ditto ...	On sandy banks and islands (gregarious).	Continental India ...	Etawah, 12th ; Cawnpur, 23rd ; eggs.
849	The ringed ,,	Ægialites curonicus ...	Ditto ...	On the sand in river beds.	Throughout India ...	Manbhum ; Sumbhulpur ; eggs.
855	The red-wattled ,,	Lobivanellus goensis ...	Ditto ...	On the ground on raised spots.	Ditto ...	Etawah, 13th ; Sambhur, 25th ; eggs.
856	The yellow-wattled ,	Sarciophorus bilobus ...	Ditto ...	On the ground in waste or fallow land.	In dry plains throughout India.	Breeding season begins.
857	The spur-winged ,,	Hoplopterus malabaricus	Ditto ...	On the sand in river beds.	Throughout India ...	Cawnpur, 12th, 30th ; Oude, 8th ; eggs.

858	The great Indian stone Plover	Esacus recurvirostris...	None ...	On the sand in river beds.	Throughout India ...	Etawah, 12th; Cawnpur, 23rd; eggs.
859	The stone ,,	Œdicnemus crepitans	Ditto ...	On the ground near bushes or trees.	Ditto (but locally)	Cawnpur, 18th; eggs.
923	The common Heron	Ardea cinerea ...	A loose platform.	On large trees (gregarious.)	Ditto (do) ...	Oude, Hansi, 26th; eggs.
942	The king Curlew	Geronticus papillosus	Ditto ...	High up in large trees.	Throughont the plains	Delhi, 28th; eggs.
985	The large river Tern	Sterna seena ...	None ...	On the sand in river beds (gregarious).	Throughout India proper.	Etawah, 13th; Cawnpur, 23rd; Calcutta, 26th; eggs.
987	The black-bellied ,,	,, javanica ...	Ditto ...	Ditto (do.)	Ditto ...	Etawah, 13th; Jhelum, 15th; the Deccan and Calcutta; eggs.
988	The little ,,	Sternula minuta ...	Ditto ...	Ditto (do.)	Ditto ...	Benares, 30th; eggs.
995	The Scissor-bill	Rhynchops albicollis ...	Ditto ...	Ditto (do.)	Ditto ...	Etawah, 15th; Cawnpur, 27th; Calcutta, 26th; eggs.

APRIL.

Breeding has by this time become more general everywhere. The kites and buzzards, the shrikes, tit larks, sparrows, doves, the common sandgrouse, jungle fowl, spur fowl, plovers, and river terns have eggs in all parts of the country. The common heron has eggs here and there in northern, western, and central India.

In the Himalayas, most of the hawks, hawk eagles, serpent eagles, the barefoot scops owl, the owlets, martins, large Bengal nightjars, trogons, most of the woodpeckers and piculets, all the barbets, (except the Marshall's barbet,) honey-suckers, treecreeper, nuthatches, hoopoe, cuckoo shrike, large minivet, some of the drongos, swallow shrikes, most of the flycatchers, shortwings, thrushes, ouzels, a few laughing thrushes, bushchats, most of the tree warblers, all the pipits, most of the true tits, crows, jackdaws, jays, the spotted winged stare, crested bunting, white-crested kalij pheasant, the chukor, and the night heron have eggs throughout the month, while the *sparrow hawk, wood owl,* the rest of the *scops owls,* the *Sikkim frogmouth, Unwin's nightjar,* the *European bee eater, black cap shrike, pied shrike, short-billed minivet, drongos, yellow-bellied fantail, red-breasts, ground thrushes, blackbirds, black-headed wren warbler,* most of the *laughing thrushes,* a few *bulbuls,* the *redstarts,* most of the remaining *warblers,* the *forktails, wagtails* and *pipits,* nearly all the *hill tits,* the *rufous-breasted accentor,* the *corby,* the *yellow-billed blue magpie,* the *grey-headed mynah,* the *sparrows, meadow bunting, skylark, imperial pigeons, turtle doves,* all the rest of the *pheasants,* the *snow partridge, bustard quail, woodcock, sandpipers, water hens, geese, ducks,* and *grebe* are pairing and commence building their nests towards the end of the month.

In the Punjab, the king vulture, the white scavenger vulture, the red-headed merlin, and Indian tawny eagle are still laying. The screech owl and scops owl, and little owlet have eggs, so also have the striated reed babblers, the rock chats, scrub warblers, treepies, the bright starlings, singing bush larks, sandlarks, crested larks, green pigeons, the seesee partridges, the common quail, button quail, big bustard, plovers, king curlew, and river terns, as well as many other

MARSHALL, DEL.

BREEDING PLACE OF THE TERNS.

birds which have been found breeding in the North-West Provinces and central India. The *Egyptian bee eaters* and *desert finch larks* commence nest building towards the end of the month.

In the NORTH-WEST PROVINCES, the shikra, the short-toed serpent eagle, buzzards, kites, and most of the owls have still got eggs. The wire-tailed and mosque swallows, the sand martins, common swifts, blue-tailed bee eaters, the kingfishers, hornbill, green barbets, cuckoo shrikes, fantails, grey babblers, bulbuls, ioras, robins, chats, Sykes's warbler, pied wagtails, treepies, bush larks, sand larks, finch larks, rock pigeons, jungle fowl, plovers, and the common cormorant are laying during this month: while the *common drongo* and the *brahminy mynah* are beginning to pair and build, also a few pairs of the *coucal* and *sirkeer* build in the eastern parts.

In BENGAL, the spotted eagle is laying. The large Bengal nightjar, the stork-billed kingfisher, the koel, the common wood shrike, the black-headed wren babbler, the red-whiskered bulbul, the common bulbul, Jerdon's green bulbul, the black-headed oriole, the shama, the tailor bird, the white-backed munia, the orange-breasted green pigeon, Sykes's turtle dove, the red jungle fowl, the kyah partridge, the common quail, and the painted snipe, all have eggs during the month, besides many others common to it and central and western India. The *long-legged and spotted eagles*, the *yellow-breasted and red-capped wren warblers*, and the *green pigeons* are beginning to pair and build.

In CENTRAL INDIA, the spotted eagle, buzzards, and kites are laying. The cliff swallow and crested swift have eggs. The jungle and Nilgiri nightjars have begun to lay, and the blue-tailed bee eaters, white-breasted kingfishers, rockchats, finch larks, painted sand-grouse, jungle fowl, spur fowl, plovers, purple herons, as well as the common herons, are sitting. The *lesser harrier eagle*, *Tickell's blue redbreast*, the *striated marsh babbler*, the *green amadavat*, and the *brown rail* begin to build towards the end of the month.

In SOUTHERN INDIA, the white scavenger vulture is still laying. The house and mosque swallows, dusky crag martins, Nilgiri nightjars, chestnut-headed bee eaters, little kingfishers, green barbets, Tickell's flower-pecker, the velvet-fronted nuthatch, white-spotted fantail, the flycatchers, shortwings, whistling thrushes, blackbirds, quaker thrushes, wren babblers, scimitar babblers, bulbuls, robins, chats, wren warblers, pipits, white-eyed tits, tit larks, treepies, jungle mynahs, hill mynahs, weaver birds, munias, larks, green pigeons, wood pigeons, jungle fowl, spur fowl, plovers, and many other kinds have eggs. The *lesser kestril* in the Nilgiris, the *ghat nightjar*, the *southern blue redbreast,* the *jungle babbler,* and the *common crow* are pairing and building by the end of the month.

APRIL.

Nos. in Jerdon.	English Names.	Scientific Names.	Shape of Nest.	Site of Nest.	Geographical Range in Breeding Season.	Particulars for the Month.
2	The king Vulture	Otogyps calvus ...	A large platform.	On tops of high trees.	Throughout continental India.	Hansi, 13th ; eggs.
6	The white scavenger „	Perenopteron gingianus.	Platform ...	On cliffs or large trees.	Throughout India ...	Hansi, 3rd, 30th ; Nilgiris, 7th, 15th ; eggs.
16	The red-headed Merlin	Lithofalco chicquera ...	A compact massive cup.	In forks of trees ...	Throughout the plains	Hansi, 5th, 28th ; eggs.
17	The Kestril	Tinnunculus alaudarius.	A large platform.	On ledges of cliffs	Himalayas, Nilgiris, and Suleiman range.	Kashmir, 28th ; eggs.
21	The Goshawk	Astur palumbarius ...	Ditto ...	Usually in pine trees high up.	The Himalayas only ...	Bussahir, 15th ; eggs.
23	The Shikra	Micronisus badius ...	A loose cup	High up in lofty trees.	Throughout India ...	The Doab ; eggs.
	The dove Hawk	Accipiter melaschistus	A small platform.	On ledges of cliffs	The Himalayas only ...	Kotegurh, 28th ; eggs.
27	The imperial Eagle	Aquila mogilnik ...	A large platform.	On tops of trees ...	The Punjab and western Himalayas.	A few stragglers breed.
28	The spotted „	„ nœvia ...	Ditto ...	In high trees ...	Central and northern India.	Raipur (C. P.) and Sikkim Terai.
29	The Indian tawny „	„ vindhyana ...	Ditto ...	Ditto ...	The dry plains of upper India.	Hansi ; eggs.
30	The long-legged ,	„ hastata ...	Ditto ...	Ditto ...	Central and northern India.	Hazara, 29th ; eggs.
33	Bonelli's „	Nisaetus bonellii ...	Ditto ...	On cliffs or high trees.	Throughout India ...	Himalayas ; eggs.
36	The Nepal hawk „	Spizaetus nipalensis ...	Ditto ...	On high trees ...	The Himalayas only ...	Masuri, 10th ; young ; Hazara, 15th ; eggs.
	The changeable hawk „	„ caligatus ...	Ditto ...	Ditto ...	Bengal and the sub-Himalayas.	Kumaon, Bhabur.
38	The short-toed „	Circaetus gallicus ...	Ditto ...	Usually on high trees.	The dry plains of upper India.	Saharunpur, 6th ; eggs.
39	The crested serpent „	Spilornis cheela ..	Ditto ...	In thick forks of trees.	The sub-Himalayan valleys.	Kangra, 5th, 11th, 25th ; eggs.
	The Himalayan fishing „	Polioaetus plumbeus ...	Ditto ...	On high trees ...	The Himalayas ...	Kumaon ; eggs.

Nos in Jerdon.	English Names.	Scientific Names.	Shape of Nest.	Site of Nest.	Geographical Range in Breeding Season.	Particulars for the Month
45	The long-legged Buzzard	Buteo canescens ..	Irregular platform.	On high trees or cliffs.	The Punjab and western Himalayas.	Kashmir ; eggs.
48	The white-eyed „	Poliornis teesa ..	A small platform.	In forks of trees ...	The dry plains of continental India.	Throughout the month.
55	The brahminy Kite	Haliastur indus ..	Triangular platform.	On high trees near water.	Throughout the plains	Saharunpur, 6th ; Raipur ; eggs.
56	The common „	Milvus govinda ...	Ditto ...	In forks of trees ...	Throughout India ...	Saharunpur, 10th ; Sambhur ; eggs.
	The greater Indian	„ major ..	Ditto ...	Ditto ...	The western Himalayas	Kashmir ; eggs.
57	The crested honey Buzzard	Pernis cristata ..	Ditto ...	Ditto ...	Locally throughout India proper.	Oude ; eggs.
59	The black-winged Kite	Elanus melanopterus ..	A shallow compact cup.	Ditto ...	Ditto ...	Dehra Doon, Rohilkhund ; eggs.
60	The Indian screech Owl	Strix indica ...	None.	In holes in trees or buildings.	Throughout the plains	Upper India ; eggs.
65	The mottled wood „	Bulacca sinensis ..	Ditto ...	In holes or hollows of large trees.	Ditto ...	Dehra Doon ; eggs.
69	The rock-horned „	Ascalaphia bengalensis	Ditto ...	On ledges of banks	Throughout India proper.	Saharunpur, 3rd, 16th ; eggs.
70	The dusky-horned ,	„ coromanda	Ditto ...	In forks of large trees.	Throughout the plains	Saharunpur 18th ; eggs ; season ends.
74	The Indian scops ,	Ephialtes pennatus ...	Ditto ...	In holes in trees ...	Locally throughout India.	Dehra Doon ; eggs.
	The barefoot , „	„ spilocephalus	Ditto ...	Ditto ...	In continental India ...	Koteguph, 30th ; Masuri ; eggs.
	Pennant's „ „	„ griseus ...	Ditto	Ditto ...	Central and northern India.	Hansi, 2nd ; eggs.
76	The spotted Owlet	Athene brama ...	Ditto ...	In holes in trees or buildings.	Throughout India ...	Hansi, 20th ; Saharunpur, 10th ; eggs.
77	The jungle „	„ radiata ..	Ditto ...	In holes in trees ...	In all wooded tracts ...	Bijnor, Allahabad, 26th ; eggs.
79	The large-barred „	, cuculoides ..	Ditto ...	Ditto ...	The Himalayas ...	Kangra, 27th ; Masuri ; eggs.
80	The collared pigmy „	Glaucidium brodiei ..	Ditto ...	Ditto ...	The Himalayas and Khasia Hills.	Masuri, Kumaon ; eggs.

82	The common Swallow	Hirundo rustica ...	Deep semi-circular cup.	In and about houses.	The Himalayas ...	Kangra, Kumaon, Naga Hills.
83	The Nilgiri house "	" domicola ...	Semi-circular saucer.	In buildings or caves.	The Nilgiris, Ceylon, Tenasserim.	Conoor, Kotagiri, Tenasserim.
84	The wire-tailed "	" ruficeps ...	Ditto ...	Under bridges or rocks by water.	Locally throughout India.	The Doab; eggs.
85	The great Indian mosque "	" daurica ...	Tubular, retort-shaped.	In caves or buildings.	The Himalayas ...	Dehra Doon, 30th; eggs.
	The " "	" erythropygia	Ditto ...	Ditto ...	Throughout India proper.	Kotagiri, 9th; eggs.
86	The Indian cliff "	" fluvicola ...	Retort-shaped	On cliffs near water or buildings (gregarious).	Continental India ...	Jodhpur, 4th; Jhansi; eggs.
89	The common sand Martin	Cotyle sinensis ...	A loose cup	In holes in river banks (gregarious).	Throughout India (rare in south.)	Oudh, 10th, 23rd; Sambhur, 15th; eggs.
90	The dusky crag "	" concolor ...	Semi-circular cup.	Against buildings or rocks.	Locally throughout India.	Nilgiris; eggs.
91	The " "	" rupestris ...	Ditto ...	Against rocks or caves.	The Himalayas ...	Chakrata; eggs.
93	The Kashmir "	Chelidon cashmirensis	Ditto ...	Ditto ...	Ditto ...	Simla; eggs.
100	The common Indian Swift	Cypselus abyssinicus	Semi-globular.	Against buildings (gregarious).	Throughout India ...	The Doab; eggs.
102	The palm "	" batassiensis	A tiny watch pocket.	On leaves of the toddy palm.	Locally throughout the plains.	First brood ends.
	The palm-roof "	" infumatus...	Ditto ...	In huts thatched with palm leaves	Garo and north Cachar hills.	Asaloo; eggs.
103	The southern hill Swiftlet	Collocalia unicolor ...	Small semi-circular saucer.	In caves or on rocks.	The Nilgiris and Assamboo hills.	Nest building begins.
104	The Indian crested Swift	Dendrochelidon coronatus.	A tiny half saucer.	On dead boughs of high trees.	The forests of India proper.	Mandla (C. P.), 6th; eggs.
107	The Indian Nightjar	Caprimulgus indicus...	None ...	On the ground often near a bush.	The forests of continental India.	Raipur (C. P.); eggs.
108	The Nilgiri "	" kelaarti ...	Ditto ...	Ditto ...	Southern extending to central India.	Raipur, Nilgiris; eggs.
109	The large Bengal "	" albonotatus	Ditto ...	Ditto ...	The wooded parts of upper India.	Masuri, 19th; Manbhum, 5th; eggs.
112	The common Indian "	" asiaticus ...	Ditto ...	Ditto ...	The plains of continental India.	Season begins.
114	Franklin's "	" monticolus	Ditto ...	Ditto ...	In wooded hills throughout India.	Ditto.

Nos. in Jerdon.	English Names.	Scientific Names.	Shape of Nest.	Site of Nest.	Geographical Range in Breeding Season.	Particulars for the Month.
116	Hodgson's Trogon	Harpactes hodgsoni ...	None ...	In holes in decayed trees.	The eastern sub-Himalayas.	Sikkim, Nepal; eggs.
117	The common Bee eater	Merops viridis ...	Ditto ...	In deep holes in banks or plains.	Throughout India proper.	Throughout the month.
118	The blue-tailed „	„ philippensis ...	Ditto ...	In deep holes in banks.	Ditto ...	Hoshungabad, 1st; Oude; eggs.
119	The chestnut-headed „	„ quinticolor ...	Ditto ...	Ditto ...	In all wooded hills ...	Nilgiris, Dehra Doon.
122	The blue-ruffed „	Nyctiornis athertoni ...	Ditto ...	Ditto* ...	Sub-Himalayas, east of Jumna.	(Requires confirmation.)
123	The common Roller	Coracias indica ...	Ditto ...	In holes in trees or buildings.	Throughout India proper.	Oude, 19th; Sambhur, 26th; eggs.
126	The broad-billed „	Eurystomus orientalis	Ditto ...	In holes in lofty trees.	Sub-Himalayas, east of Ganges.	(Requires confirmation.)
127	The Indian stork-billed Kingfisher	Pelargopsis gurial ...	Ditto ...	In holes in banks by running water.	Eastern sub-Himalayas and Bengal.	Calcutta, 25th; eggs.
129	The white-breasted „	Halcyon smyrnensis ...	Ditto ...	In holes in river banks or wells.	Throughout India proper.	Saharunpur, 25th; Sambhur, 15th; eggs.
134	The little Indian „	Alcedo bengalensis ...	Ditto ...	In holes in banks often by rivers.	Ditto ...	Allahabad, 10th; Nilgiris, 2nd; eggs
136	The pied „	Ceryle rudis ...	Ditto ...	In holes in river banks.	Throughout the plains	Saharunpur, 10th; eggs; season ends.
138	The yellow-throated Broadbill	Psarisomus dalhousiæ	Large, rough, pear-shaped.	Pendent from lofty trees.	The eastern Himalayas	Very little known.
140	The great Indian Hornbill	Homraius bicornis ...	None ...	In holes in lofty decayed trees.	The eastern sub-Himalayas.	Ditto.
144	The northern grey „	Meniceros bicornis ...	Ditto ...	In holes in decayed trees.	Throughout the plains	Mynpuri (N. W. P.), 15th; eggs.
147	The northern roseband Paroquet	Palæornis sivalensis ...	Ditto ...	Ditto ...	Punjab and western Himalayas.	Kangra; eggs.
148	The rose-ringed „	„ torquatus ...	Ditto ...	Ditto ...	Throughout the plains	Season nearly over.
149	The rose-headed „	„ purpureus...	Ditto ...	Ditto ...	Western continental India.	Ditto.
150	The slaty-headed „	„ schisticeps...	Ditto ...	Ditto ...	The Himalayas ...	Murree, 20th; eggs.
152	The red-breasted „	„ javanicus ...	Ditto ...	Ditto ...	Bengal and eastern sub-Himalayas.	Very little known.
153	The Indian Loriquet	Loriculus vernalis ...	Ditto ...	Ditto ...	North-eastern India ...	Ditto.

* It is said to lay in hollow trees.

154	The Himalayan pied Woodpecker	Picus himalayanus ...	None ...	In artificial holes in trees.	The Himalayas from Sikkim west.	Kumaon, 10th ; eggs.
156	The lesser black „	„ cathpharius ...	Ditto ...	Ditto ...	The eastern Himalayas	Nepal, Sikkim ; eggs.
157	The Indian spotted „	„ macei ...	Ditto ...	Ditto ...	The Himalayas and eastern Bengal.	Masuri, 20th ; eggs.
159	The brown-fronted „	„ brunneifrons ...	Ditto ...	Ditto ...	The western Himalayas from Nepal.	Hazara, 25th ; Kumaon ; eggs.
160	The yellow-fronted „	„ mahrattensis ...	Ditto ...	Ditto ...	Throughout the plains	Season nearly over.
161	The rufous-bellied pied „	Hypopicus hyperythrus	Ditto ...	Ditto ...	The Himalayas ...	Murree, 25th ; eggs.
163	The Himalayan pigmy „	Yungipicus pygmœus	Ditto ...	Ditto ...	The western Himalayas	Very little known.
164	The southern pigmy „	„ hardwickii	Ditto ...	Ditto ...	Throughout the plains	Season nearly over.
170	The scaly-bellied green „	Gecinus squamatus ...	Ditto ...	Ditto ...	The eastern Himalayas	Kangra, 5th ; Kumaon ; eggs.
171	The lesser Indian green „	„ striolatus ...	Ditto ...	Ditto ...	The forests of India proper.	Very little known.
172	The black naped green „	„ occipitalis ...	Ditto ...	Ditto ...	The Himalayas ...	Season commences.
180	The common gold back „	Brachypternus aurantius	Ditto ...	Ditto ...	Throughout the plains	First brood ends.
186	The speckled Piculet	Vivia innominata ...	Ditto ...	Ditto ...	The Himalayas ...	Kumaon, 10th ; eggs.
192	Hodgson's green Barbet	Megalæma hodgsoni ...	Ditto ...	Ditto ...	The lower Himalayas .	Nepal, Kumaon ; eggs.
193	Franklin's „ „	„ caniceps ...	Ditto ...	Ditto ...	The wooded parts of continental India.	Oudh, Rohilcund ; eggs.
194	The small „ „	„ viridis ...	Ditto ...	Ditto ...	The wooded parts of peninsular India.	The Nilgiris ; eggs.
195	The blue-throated „	„ asiatica ...	Ditto ...	Ditto ...	Lower Bengal and eastern Himalayas.	Very little known.
196	The golden-throated „	„ franklinii	Ditto ...	Ditto ...	The eastern Himalayas	Nepal, Sikkim ; eggs.
197	The crimson-breasted „	Xantholæma hæmacephala ...	Ditto ...	Ditto ...	Throughout the plains	Manbhum, Sambhur ; eggs.
225	The Himalayan red Honeysucker	Œthopyga miles ...	Pear-shaped, side entrance.	Hanging from tips of branches ...	The eastern Himalayas	Nepal ; eggs.
229	The maroon-backed „	„ nipalensis...	Ditto ...	Ditto ...	The eastern Himalayas and Khasia hills.	Nepal, Sikkim ; eggs.
231	The black-breasted „	„ saturata ...	Ditto ...	Ditto ...	Ditto ...	Nepal, Kumaon.
234	The purple „	Arachnechthra asiatica	Ditto ...	Ditto ...	Throughout the plains	Cawnpur. 2nd ; Allahabad, 10th, 14th ; eggs.
238	Tickell's Flower-pecker	Dicœum minimum ...	Ditto ...	Ditto ...	Bombay, central and N. E India.	Poona, 5th ; eggs.

Nos. in Jerdon.	English Names.	Scientific Names.	Shape of Nest.	Site of Nest.	Geographical Range in Breeding Season.	Particulars for the Month.
239	The Nilgiri Flower-pecker	Dicœum concolor ...	Purse-shaped, front entrance	Hung from twigs in thick foliage.	The Nilgiris ...	Season nearly over.
240	The thick-billed ,,	Piprisoma agile ...	Ditto ...	Hung from thin branches.	Throughout India ...	Season over in plains.
241	The fire-breasted ,,	Myzanthe ignipectus ...	Ditto ...	Ditto ...	The eastern Himalayas	Nepal.
243	The Himalayan Treecreeper	Certhia himalayana ...	A rough cup	In crevices of bark on high trees	The western ,,	Murree, Kashmir; eggs.
248	The white-tailed Nuthatch	Sitta himalayensis ...	A shallow pad	In natural hollows in trees.	The Himalayas ...	Kumaon, 10th; eggs; 25th; young.
250	The chestnut-bellied ,,	,, castaneiventris ...	None ...	Ditto ...	Locally throughout the plains.	Rohilkhund; season ends.
253	The velvet-fronted ,,	Dendrophila frontalis	Ditto ...	Ditto ...	The hilly parts of India.	Nilgiris.
254	The Hoopoe	Upupa epops ...	Ditto ...	In holes in trees or buildings. ...	The western Himalayas	Season begins.
255	The Indian ,,	,, nigripennis ...	Ditto ...	Ditto ...	Throughout India ...	Season ends in the north.
256	The Indian grey Shrike	Lanius lahtora ...	A thick massive cup.	In small trees or thorny bushes.	Throughout the dry plains.	Salt range, Delhi; eggs.
257	The rufous-backed ,	,, erythronotus ...	Ditto ...	Ditto ...	Throughout India ...	The dry plains; eggs.
	The pale rufous-backed ,,	,, caniceps ...	Ditto ...	Ditto ...	The hilly parts of India	Nilgiris; eggs
260	The bay backed ,,	,, vittatus ...	A neat cup	Ditto ...	Throughout India ...	Nest building begins.
265	The common wood ,	Tephrodornis ponticeriana.	A neat shallow cup.	In horizontal forks of trees.	Throughout the plains	Manbhum, 5th; eggs.
269	The dark grey cuckoo ,,	Volvocivora melaschistus.	A small saucer.	Ditto ...	The Himalayas ...	Nepal, Masuri; eggs.
270	The large grey ,, ,,	Graucalus macei ...	A broad saucer.	At tops of lofty trees.	Locally throughout India.	Oude; eggs.
271	The large Minivet	Pericrocotus speciosus	A small deep cup.	In high trees near end of branches.	The Himalayas ...	Nepal; eggs.
280	The long-tailed drongo Shrike	Dicrurus longicaudatus	A neat saucer	In horizontal forks of trees.	In the plains in moist forests.	Nest building begins.
282	The bronzed ,, ,,	Chaptia œnea ...	A broad saucer.	Ditto ...	In forests throughout India.	Nepal; eggs.
284	The northern racket-tailed ,, ,,	Edolius paradiseus ...	Ditto ...	Ditto ...	The Himalayas and eastern India.	Nepal, Kumaon; eggs.

286	The hair-crested drongo Shrike	Chibia hottentota ...	A broad saucer.	In horizontal forks of trees.	The eastern Himalayas	Nepal, Kumaon ; eggs.
287	The ashy swallow „	Artamus fuscus ...	Ditto ...	On big boughs of trees or stumps.	Locally throughout India.	Nepal ; eggs.
292	The white-browed Fantail	Leucocerca aureola ...	A tiny cup	In trees on thin horizontal branches.	Throughout continental India.	Bareilly 15th ; Etawah, 15th ; eggs.
293	The white-spotted „	„ pectoralis...	A tiny inverted cone.	Ditto ...	The hills of south India.	Kotagiri ; season begins.
295	The grey-headed Flycatcher	Cryptolopha cinereocapilla.	A watch pocket.	Against moss covered trunks of trees.	The Himalayas, Wynaad, and Nilgiris.	Dehra Doon, 10th ; Kotagiri ; eggs.
300	The black and orange „	Ochromela nigrorufa...	Large, globular, domed.	Low down in bushes or clumps.	The Nilgiris only.	Throughout the month.
301	The verditer „	Emmyias melanops ...	A thick cup	In holes in banks or under bridges.	The Himalayas ...	Kumaon, 16th; Sikkim, 30th ; eggs.
302	The Nilgiri blue „	„ albicaudata	Ditto ...	In holes in banks or under bridges.	The Nilgiris only ...	Throughout the month.
310	The white-browed blue „	Muscicapula superciliaris.	A small thick cup.	In holes or cracks in trees.	The Himalayas ...	Simla, Kumaon ; eggs.
314	The fairy „	Niltava sundara ...	A large thick pad.	In clefts of rocks or under stumps.	Ditto ...	Nepal ; season ends
315	Macgregor's fairy „	„ macgregoriæ	A large thick cup.	Ditto ...	The eastern Himalayas	Ditto ; do.
316	The great fairy „	„ grandis ...	A large thick pad.	Ditto ...	Ditto ...	Ditto ; do.
321	The rufous-breasted „	Siphia superciliaris ...	A deep cup	On the ground at foot of trees	The Himalayas ...	Ditto ; do.
324	The whitetailed robin „	Erythrosterna hyperythra.	A large deep cup.	Unknown.	The north-west Himalayas.	Kashmir ; do.
327	The chestnut-headed Wren	Tesia castaneocoronata	Large, globular, domed.	Near the ground in thick bushes.	The eastern Himalayas	Nepal ; do.
331	The tailed hill „	Pnœpyga caudata ...	A deep thick cup.	On the ground near roots or stumps.	Ditto ...	Ditto ; do.
338	The white-browed Shortwing	Brachypteryx cruralis	Globular, domed.	In creepers near roots of trees.	Ditto ...	Ditto ; do.
339	The rufous-bellied „	Callene rufiventris ...	A large thick cup.	In holes in banks or trees.	The Nilgirie ...	Ootacamund ; do.
	The white-bellied „	„ albiventris ...	A loose cup	In holes in trees ...	The Pulney hills ...	Pulneys ; do.
340	The blue-fronted „	„ frontalis ...	Globular, domed.	Ditto ...	The eastern Himalayas	(Requires confirmation)
342	The Malabar whistling Thrush	Myiophonus horsfieldii	A massive saucer.	On ledges of rocks or banks by water	The Himalayas ...	Kumaon ; season begins.
343	The yellow-billed „ „	„ temminckii	Ditto ...	Ditto ...	The hills of south India	Nilgiris ; do.

Nos. in Jerdon.	English Names.	Scientific Names.	Shape of Nest.	Site of Nest.	Geographical Range in Breeding Season.	Particulars for the Month.
346	The green-breasted ground Thrush	Pitta cucullata ...	Large, globular, domed.	On the ground in bamboos or thickets	The eastern Himalayas	Nepal ; season begins.
347	The brown water Ouzel	Hydrobata asiatica ...	A large ball of moss.	In clefts of rocks near water.	The Himalayas only....	Sutlej valley, 21st ; eggs.
352	The chestnut-bellied chat Thrush	Orocetes erythrogastra	A neat cup	In holes in banks or rocks.	Ditto ...	Kumaon, 15th ; Nepal ; eggs.
353	The blue-headed „ „	„ cinclorhynchus.	Ditto ...	Ditto (often at roots of trees)	Ditto ...	Nepal ; season begins.
355	The rusty-throated bush „	Geocichla citrina ...	A broad cup	In forks of small trees.	Ditto ...	Ditto ; do.
360	The Nilgiri Blackbird	Merula simillima ...	Ditto ...	In forks of trees or saplings.	The Nilgiris ...	Throughout the month.
361	The grey-winged „	„ boulboul ...	Ditto ...	In thick forks of trees.	The Himalayas ...	Sikkim ; season begins.
362	The white-collared Ouzel	„ albocincta ...	Ditto ...	In banks or on stumps.	Ditto ...	Kumaon ; do.
363	The grey-headed „	„ castanea ...	Ditto ...	Ditto ...	Ditto ...	Murree, 5th ; Kotegurh, 20th ; eggs.
368	The Indian missel Thrush	Turdus hodgsoni ...	Ditto ...	In thick forks of trees.	Ditto ...	Sutlej valley, 6th ; eggs.
388	The Nepal quaker „	Alcippe nipalensis ...	A deep massive cup.	In low thick bushes	The eastern Himalayas	Nepal, 1st ; eggs.
389	The Nilgiri „ „	„ poiocephala ...	Ditto ...	In forks of thick bushes or trees.	The hills of south India	Nilgiris, 5th ; eggs.
391	The black-headed wren Babbler	Stachyris nigriceps ...	Ditto ...	In grassy banks near bushes.	The eastern Himalayas	Pegu, 15th ; eggs.
393	The red-headed „ „	„ ruficeps ...	Ditto ...	In bamboo clumps chiefly.	Ditto ...	Nepal ; season begins.
399	The spotted „ „	Pellorneum ruficeps ...	A loose domed cup.	On the ground against a bush.	Southern India ...	Nilgiris ; eggs.
400	The rufous-necked scimitar „	Pomatorhinus ruficollis	Large, globular, domed.	On the ground in grass or weeds.	The eastern Himalayas	Sikkim, 25th ; eggs.
404	The southern „ „	„ horsfieldii	Ditto ...	On the ground in a bush or clump.	The hills of south India	Conoor, 7th ; eggs.
405	The rusty-cheeked „ „	„ erythrogenys.	Ditto ...	On the ground in a bush or clump.	The Himalayas ...	Masuri, Sikkim ; eggs.

407	The white-crested laughing Thrush	Garrulax leucolophus	A broad shallow cup.	In thick bushes or low trees.	The Himalayas east of Sutlej.	Nepal; season begins.
411	The white-throated " "	" albogularis...	Ditto ...	Ditto ...	The Himalayas ...	Masuri; eggs.
412	The black-gorgetted " "	" pectoralis ...	Ditto ...	In clumps of bamboos.	The eastern Himalayas	Pegu, 27th; eggs.
418	The variegated " "	Trochalopteron variegatum.	A large deep cup.	In thick bushes or trees.	The western Himalayas	Simla; season begins.
423	The Nilgiri " "	Trochalopteron cacchinans ...	Ditto ...	In forks of trees or bushes.	The Nilgiris ...	Conoor, 22nd; eggs.
425	The streaked " "	Trochalopteron lineatum.	Cup-shaped	In low bushes or banks.	The Himalayas ...	Masuri, 29th; eggs
428	The hoary Barwing	Actinodura nipalensis	A shallow cup	In holes in rocks or banks.	The eastern Himalayas	Sikkim; season begins.
432	The Bengal Babbler	Malacocercus canorus	A loose straggling cup.	In thick bushes or small trees.	The plains of continental India.	Nest building begins.
433	The white-headed "	" griseus...	Ditto ...	In thorny hedges and low trees.	The plains of south India.	Ditto.
436	The large grey "	" malcolmi	Cup-shaped	In thorny trees and bushes.	Throughout the plains	Cawnpur, 1st; eggs.
438	The striated bush "	Chattarhœa caudata ...	Ditto ...	In low bushes or clumps of grass.	Ditto ...	Saharunpur, 8th; eggs.
439	The " reed "	" earlii ...	Ditto ...	In reeds or clumps of grass.	Locally in continental India.	Saharunpur, Delhi; eggs.
444	The Himalayan black Bulbul	Hypsepetes psaroides	A neat cup	In forks of bushes or trees.	The Himalayas ...	Nest building begins.
445	The Nilgiri " "	" nilgiriensis	A rough shallow cup.	In dense bushes or clumps.	The Nilgiris ...	Throughout the month.
447	The rufous-bellied "	" macclellandi	A neat shallow saucer	Hung from a fork in thick foliage.	The eastern Himalayas	Nepal; season begins.
450	The yellow-browed bush "	Criniger ictericus ...	A small shallow cup	Ditto ...	The hills of south India	Nilgiris; eggs.
458	The white-cheeked crested "	Otocompsa leucogenys	A neat cup	In bushes or low trees.	The Himalayas ...	Hazara, 24th; Masuri; eggs.
460	The red-whiskered "	" emeria ...	Ditto ...	In thick bushes or creepers.	The moist parts of upper India.	Throughout the month.
	The southern red-whiskered "	" fuscicaudata	Ditto ...	In isolated bushes	The hills of south India	Conoor, 22nd; eggs.
461	The common Bengal "	Pycnonotus pygœus ...	A small slender cup.	In small trees or bushes.	The Himalayas and eastern Bengal.	Dera Doon and Calcutta; eggs.
462	The common Madras "	" pusillus ...	Ditto ...	Ditto ...	Throughout the plains	Kotagiri, Fatehgurh, 30th; eggs.
463	Jerdon's green "	Phyllornis jerdoni ...	A small shallow cup.	In high trees near tips of branches.	Central and southern India.	Manbhum, 4th; eggs.

Nos. in Jerdon.	English Names.	Scientific Names.	Shape of Nest.	Site of Nest.	Geographical Range in Breeding Season.	Particulars for the Month.
468	The white-winged green Bulbul	Iora typhia ...	A tiny cup	In trees near tips of boughs.	Locally throughout India.	Moradabad, 18th ; eggs.
472	The black-headed Oriole	Oriolus melanocephalus	A neat deep cup.	In high trees hung from outer forks.	Locally in eastern continental India.	Manbhum, 5th ; eggs.
475	The magpie Robin	Copsychus saularis ...	A shallow saucer.	In holes in trees or walls.	Throughout India ...	Saharunpur, 23rd ; eggs
476	The Shama	Kittacincla macroura...	Ditto ...	Ditto ...	Peninsular and eastern India.	Tenasserim, 17th ; eggs.
479	The southern brown-backed Robin	Thamnobia fulicata ..	A small cup	On the ground sheltered or in holes in walls.	Southern India ...	Poona, 3rd, 15th ; eggs.
480	The brown-backed "	" cambaiensis	Ditto ...	Ditto ...	The plains of upper India.	Saharunpur, 16th, 27th ; eggs.
481	The black Bushchat	Pratincola caprata ...	A shallow pad	On the ground under shelter.	The Himalayas and continental India.	Saharunpur, 3rd ; eggs.
482	The southern " "	" atrata ...	Ditto ...	In holes in banks or walls.	The hills of south India	Conoor, 1st, 12th ; eggs.
483	The common Indian "	" indica ...	A small cup	Ditto ...	The Himalayas and N W. Punjab.	First brood nearly over.
486	The iron grey "	" ferrea ...	Ditto ...	Ditto ...	The Himalayas ...	Kooloo, 17th ; eggs,
494	The brown Rockchat	Cercomela fusca ...	A shallow cup	Ditto ...	The dry parts of continental India.	Sambhur, 10th ; eggs.
504	The blue-headed Redstart	Rutacilla cœruleocephala.	Ditto ...	Ditto ...	The alpine Himalayas	Spitti, 16th ; eggs.
507	The blue Woodchat	Larvivora cyana ...	Ditto ...	In holes in decayed trees.	The Himalayas and Nilgiris.	Nilgiris ; eggs.
530	The Indian Tailorbird	Orthotomus longicauda	A deep cup	Among leaves sewn together ...	Throughout India proper.	Calcutta, 24th, 25th ; eggs.
	The streaked scrub Warbler	Drymœca inquieta ...	Large, globular, domed.	In low thorny shrubs	The traus-Indus Hills	Nowshera, 28th ; eggs.
534	The ashy wren "	Prinia socialis ...	A cup sewn in leaves.	Hanging low bushes	Southern India ...	Nilgiris ; eggs.
	The fuscous " "	Drymoipus fuscus ...	Deep, neat domed.	In small bushes or clumps of grass.	The Terai, Deccan, and Nilgiris.	Kotagiri ; season begins.

549	The black-throated hill Warbler	Suya atrogularis ...	Deep, neat, domed.	In small bushes or clumps of grass.	The eastern Himalayas	Nepal; season begins.
553	Sykes's „	Hyppolais rama ...	Loose, deep, domed.	In low thorny bushes	The central and N. W. Provinces.	Etawah, 1st; eggs.
571	The black-eared „	Abrornis schisticeps ...	Globular, domed.	On the ground in mossy banks.	The Himalayas ...	Throughout the month.
572	The grey-headed „	„ xanthoschistus	Ditto ...	Ditto ...	The eastern Himalayas	Nest building begins.
573	The white-browed „	„ albosuperciliaris.	Ditto ...	Ditto ...	The Himalayas ...	Murree, 16th; Kangra, 8th; eggs.
584	The western spotted Forktail	Henicurus maculatus	A massive cup	On banks or rocks near water.	The western Himalayas	Kangra, 9th; eggs.
586	The slaty-backed „	„ schistaceus	Ditto ...	Ditto ...	The eastern „	Darjeeling, 25th; eggs.
589	The Indian pied Wagtail	Motacilla maderaspatana	A shallow pad	On the ground or buildings by water	Throughout the plains	Saharunpur, 26th; Deccan; eggs.
598	The Nilgiri Pipit	Anthus montanus ...	A shallow cup	On the ground under a tuft of grass.	The Nilgiris ...	Nest building begins.
600	The Indian Titlark	Corydalla rufula ...	A shallow saucer.	On the ground under clod or tussock.	Throughout India ...	Throughout the month.
603	The Nilgiri „	Agrodroma cinnamomea	Ditto ...	Ditto ...	The Nilgiris ...	Ditto.
604	The brown rock Pipit	„ griseorufescens.	Ditto ...	Ditto ...	The western Himalayas	Nest building begins.
606	The upland „	Heterura sylvana ...	Ditto ...	Ditto ...	The Himalayas from Nepal west.	Nepal; season begins.
614	The red-billed hill Tit	Leiothrix luteus ...	A substantial cup.	In thick bushes ...	The eastern Himalayas	Darjeeling, 24th; eggs.
631	The Indian white-eyed „	Zosterops palpebrosus	A tiny cup regular.	Hung from twigs in trees or bushes	Throughout India ...	Nilgiris and Sikkim; eggs
633	The firecap „	Cephalopyrus flammiceps.	A deep thick cup.	In holes in decayed trees.	The western Himalayas	Murree, Kashmir.
634	The red-capped „	Egithaliscus erythrocephalus.	Deep, compact, domed.	Wedged in forks of stunted trees.	The Himalayas ...	Kumaon; season begins.
638	The crested black „	Lophophanes melanolophus.	A shallow pad	In holes in walls or trees.	Ditto ...	Kumaon, 12th; Simla, 10th; eggs.
644	The mountain „	Parus monticolus ...	A rough mass of feathers.	Ditto ...	Ditto ...	Throughout the month.
645	The Indian grey „	„ cinereus ...	A shallow pad	Ditto ...	In all wooded hills ...	First brood ends.
647	The yellow-cheeked „	Machlolophus xanthogenys.	Ditto ...	Ditto ...	The western Himalayas	Kumaon, Kangra; eggs.

Nos. in Jerdon.	English Names.	Scientific Names.	Shape of Nest.	Site of Nest.	Geographical Ranges in Breeding Season.	Particulars for the Month.
660	The bow-billed Corby	Corvus culminatus ...	A large compact cup.	In forks of solitary trees.	Throughout the plains	Season nearly over.
665	The Jackdaw	„ monedula ...	A small platform.	In holes in buildings or trees	The western Himalayas	Kashmir ; season begins.
666	The Himalayan Nutcracker	Nucifraga hemispila ...	A large compact cup.	High up in pine trees.	Ditto ...	Season nearly over.
669	The Himalayan Jay	Garrulus bispecularis	A neat compact cup.	On thick boughs or forks of trees.	The Himalayas ...	Nepal, 20th ; Murree, 29th ; eggs.
670	The black-throated „	„ lanceolatus	A loose shallow cup.	In small trees or saplings.	The Himalayas from Nepal west.	Murree, 20th ; Kangra, 28th ; eggs.
671	The red-billed blue „	Urocissa occipitalis ...	Ditto ...	In trees usually small ones.	The Himalayas from Nepal to Sutlej.	Kumaon, 20th ; eggs.
673	The green „	Cissa venatoria ...	Ditto ...	In trees or bamboo clumps.	The eastern Himalayas	Pegu, 10th ; eggs.
674	The Indian Treepie	Dendrocitta rufa ...	Ditto ...	In trees near the top.	Throughout continental India.	Hansi, Fatehgurh ; eggs.
678	The long-tailed „	„ leucogastra	Ditto ...	In small trees or saplings.	The forests of south India,	Travancore, 8th ; young.
682	The bright Starling	Sturnus nitens ...	None ...	In holes in trees or buildings.	The north-west Punjab.	Peshawur ; eggs.
685	The bank Mynah	Acridotheres ginginianus.	Ditto ...	In deep holes in banks or wells.	The plains of continental India.	Season commences.
686	The jungle „	Acridotheres fuscus ...	Ditto ...	In holes in trees or buildings.	In all wooded hilly regions.	The Nilgiris ; eggs.
691	The spotted-winged Stare	Saraglossa spiloptera	Ditto ...	In holes in trees ...	The Himalayas. ...	Naini Tal ; eggs.
692	The southern hill Mynah	Eulabes religiosa ...	Ditto ...	Ditto ...	Southern India ...	Travancore, 21st ; eggs.
693	The large „ „	„ intermedia ...	Ditto ...	Ditto ...	The eastern sub-Himalayas.	Season nearly over.
694	The common Weaver bird	Ploceus baya ...	A pendent retort.	In trees hung from tips of boughs.	Throughout India proper.	The extreme south.
699	The spotted Munia	Munia undulata ...	Large, oval, domed.	In thick thorny bushes usually.	In all moist wooded tracts.	Nilgiris ; eggs.
701	The white-backed „	„ striata ...	Ditto ...	Ditto ...	Peninsular and eastern India.	Manbhum, 3rd ; eggs.
708	The pin-tailed „	„ malabarica ...	Ditto ...	In small trees, thick bushes, or eaves.	Throughout India proper.	First brood nearly over.

706	The Indian house Sparrow	Passer indicus ...	A globular mass.	In and about houses.	Throughout India ...	Througout the month.
710	The tree „	„ montanus ...	Ditto ...	In holes in trees or buildings.	The eastern Himalayas	Sikkim ; eggs.
711	The yellow-throated „	„ flavicollis ...	Ditto ...	In holes in decayed trees.	Throughout India (except extreme S. E.)	Etawah (North-West Provinces) ; eggs.
724	The crested black and chestnut Bunting	Melophus melanicterus	A nest shallow cup.	In holes in banks or walls.	Locally in continental India.	Nepal, 15th ; eggs.
756	The red-winged bush Lark	Mirafra erythroptera	A shallow pad	On the ground near tufts of grass.	The dry plains of continental India.	Etawah (North-West Provinces) ; eggs.
757	The singing „ „	„ cantillans ...	A pad (sometimes domed.)	Ditto ...	Ditto (but local) ...	Hansi ; eggs.
758	The rufous-tailed finch „	Ammomanes phœnicura	A slight circular pad.	On the ground near clod or tussock.	Throughout India (south of Agra)	Hoshungabad, 28th ; eggs.
760	The black-bellied „ „	Pyrrhalauda grisea ...	A tiny shallow pad.	Ditto ...	Throughout the plains..	Etawah ; Sambhur ; eggs.
762	The eastern sand „	Alaudala raytal ...	A tiny saucer	On the ground by grass or tiny bush.	Eastern continental India.	Cawnpur ; eggs.
	The Punjab „ „	„ adamsi ...	Ditto ...	Ditto ...	Western continental India.	Jhelum ; eggs.
767	The Indian sky „	Alauda gulgula ...	Ditto ...	Ditto ...	The plains of continental India.	Throughout the month.
	Tho Nilgiri , „	„ australis ...	Ditto ...	Ditto ...	The hills of south India	The Nilgiris ; eggs.
768	The Malabar crested „	„ malabarica ...	Ditto ...	Ditto ...	Southern India ...	Mysore ; eggs.
769	The common „ „	Galerita cristata ...	Ditto ...	Ditto ...	The dry plains of continental India.	Sambhur, 19th ; eggs.
	The lesser „ „	„ boysii ...	Ditto ...	Ditto ...	Ditto ...	Season nearly over.
773	The southern green Pigeon	Crocopus chlorigastra	A small platform.	In small trees or bushes.	Throughout the plains (except Bengal.)	Hansi ; eggs.
774	The orange-breasted green „	Osmotreron bicincta ...	Ditto ...	Ditto ...	The moist forests of eastern India.	Nepal, Hill Tipperah ; eggs
775	The grey-fronted „ „	„ malabarica	Ditto ...	On outer boughs of trees.	The wooded hills of south India.	Terai Hills, 10th ; eggs.
778	The kokla „ „	Sphenocercus sphenurus.	Ditto ...	Ditto ...	The Himalayas ...	Nest building begins.
786	The Nilgiri wood „	Palumbus elphinstoni	Ditto ...	On thick boughs in dense forests.	The Nilgiris ...	Kotagiri ; eggs.
788	The Indian blue rock „	Columba intermedia ...	Ditto ...	On ledges of buildings chiefly.	Throughout India proper.	Saharunpur ; eggs.

Nos in Jerdon.	English Names.	Scientific Names.	Shape of Nest.	Site of Nest.	Geographical Range in Breeding Season.	Particulars for the Month.
793	Sykes' turtle Dove	Turtur meena ...	A tiny platform.	In low trees in thick foliage.	Peninsular and eastern India.	Hill Tipperah ; eggs.
794	The brown „ „	„ cambaiensis ...	Ditto ...	In low trees or bushes.	Throughout the plains	Throughout the month.
795	The spotted „	„ suratensis ...	Ditto ...	Ditto ...	In all wooded parts ...	Nepal, Kumaon ; eggs.
796	The Indian ring „	„ risorius ...	Ditto ...	Ditto ...	Throughout India proper.	Throughout the month.
797	The ruddy „ „	„ humilis ...	Ditto ...	Ditto ...	Ditto (but local)	Ditto.
798	The emerald „	Chalcophaps indicus...	A shallow saucer.	In low thick trees or bushes.	In all densely wooded tracts.	Masuri ; eggs.
800	The painted Sandgrouse	Pterocles fasciatus ...	None ...	On the ground by grass or tiny bush.	The rocky parts of upper India.	Sambhur, Jodhpur ; eggs.
802	The common „	„ exustus ...	Ditto ...	On the bare ground	The sandy plains of continental India.	Sirsa, Fatehgurh ; eggs.
810	The white-crested kalij Pheasant	Gallophasis albocristatus.	A shallow pad	On the ground in dense cover ...	The Himalayas ...	Dehra Doon ; eggs.
812	The red jungle Fowl	Gallus ferugineus ...	A few dry leaves.	Ditto ...	Sub-Himalayas, C. P., and Madras.	Ditto ; ditto.
813	The grey „ „	„ sonneratii ...	Ditto ...	Ditto ...	The hills of central and south India.	Kotagiri, Mount Aboo ; eggs.
814	The red spur „	Galloperdix spadiceus	Ditto ...	Ditto ...	South India extending to Bundelkhund.	Ditto ; ditto.
815	The painted „ „	„ lunulosus	Ditto ...	Ditto ..	The eastern peninsular and C. P.	Raipur (C. P.) ; eggs.
820	The Chukor	Caccabis chukor ...	Ditto ...	On the ground on grassy slopes.	Himalayas, trans-Indus, and Punjab hills.	The lower hills ; eggs.
821	The Seesee	Ammoperdix bonhami	Ditto ...	On the ground under stone or bush.	The trans-Indus hills and Salt range.	Nowshera, 10th ; eggs.
822	The grey Partridge	Ortygornis ponticeriana	Ditto ...	On the ground in bushes or grass.	The open plains of India proper.	Throughout the month.
823	The kyah „	„ gularis ...	Ditto ...	Ditto ...	The eastern sub-Himalayan Terais.	Nepal Terai.
827	The rock bush Quail	Perdicula asiatica ...	Ditto ...	On the ground in long grass.	Throughout India, locally.	First brood nearly over.

829	The common Quail	Coturnix communis ...	A few dry leaves.	On the ground under shelter.	Northern India ...	Purneah, 29th; Lahore, 14th; eggs.
835	The lesser button „	Turnix dussumieri ...	Ditto ...	Ditto ...	Locally throughout India proper.	Hansi, 16th; eggs.
836	The Indian Bustard	Eupodotis edwardsii ...	None ...	On the ground in scanty grass jungle.	The dry parts of continental India.	Sirsa, 19th; eggs.
840	The Indian courier Plover	Cusorius coromandelicus.	Ditto ...	On the ground in waste or fallow land.	In all dry plains (except Punjab).	Seetapur, Oudh; eggs.
	The cream-coloured courier Plover	Cursorius gallicus ...	Ditto ...	Ditto ...	The Punjab ...	Sirsa, 28th; eggs.
843	The lesser swallow „	Glareola lactea ...	Ditto ...	On sandy banks or islands (gregarious).	Continental India ...	Cawnpur, 3rd; Aligurh, 13th; eggs.
849	The ringed „	Œgialites curonicus ...	Ditto ...	On the sand in beds of rivers.	Throughout India ...	Central Provinces; eggs.
855	The red-wattled „	Lobivanellus goensis...	Ditto ...	On the ground on raised spots.	Ditto ...	Saharunpur, 10th; eggs.
856	The yellow-wattled „	Sarciophorus bilobus...	Ditto ...	On the ground in waste or fallow land	In dry places throughout India.	Cawnpur, 26th; eggs.
857	The spurwing „	Hoplopterus malabaricus.	Ditto ...	On the sand on islands or river banks.	Throughout India ...	Cawnpur, 3rd; Aligurh, 5th; eggs.
858	The great Indian stone „	Esacus recurvirostris	Ditto ...	Ditto ...	Ditto ...	Cawnpur, 3rd; Aligurh, 13th; eggs.
859	The „ „	Œdicnemus crepitans	Ditto ...	On the ground near bushes or trees.	Ditto (but locally)	Hansi. Etawah, Manbhum.
873	The painted Snipe	Rhynchœa bengalensis	A large pad	On the ground in wild rice or rushes.	In all moist tracts ...	Calcutta, 7th; eggs.
898	The Stilt	Himantopus candidus	None ...	On the ground in salt works (gregarious).	Near Delhi and Goorgaon.	Breeding season begins.
923	The common Heron	Ardea cinerea ...	A loose platform.	On large trees (gregarious).	Throughout India locally.	Hansi, Oude, Saugor; eggs.
924	The purple „	„ purpurea ...	Ditto ...	In thick beds of reeds (gregarious).	Throughout India proper.	Saugor; eggs.
937	The night „	Nycticorax griseus ...	Ditto ...	In high trees (sometimes in reeds).	Throughout India ...	Kashmir; eggs.
942	The king Curlew	Geronticus papillosus	Ditto ...	High up in large trees.	Throughout the plains	Hansi, 3rd; eggs.

0

Nos. in Jerdon.	English Names.	Scientific Names.	Shape of Nest.	Site of Nest.	Geographical Range in Breeding Season.	Particulars for the Month.
983	The gull-billed Tern	Gelochelidon anglicus	None ...	On the sand on islands in rivers.	The Punjab ...	Wazeerabad, 28th; eggs.
985	The large river "	Sterna seena ...	Ditto ...	Ditto (gregarious)	Throughout India ...	Cawnpur, 3rd; eggs.
987	The black-bellied ,	" javanica ...	Ditto ...	Ditto (ditto)	Ditto ...	Cawnpur, 3rd; Saharunpur, 15th, eggs.
988	The little "	Sternula minuta ...	Ditto ...	Ditto (ditto)	Ditto ...	Cawnpur, 3rd and 10th; eggs.
995	The scissor Bill	Rhyncbops albicollis ...	Ditto ...	Ditto (ditto)	Ditto ...	Cawnpur, 3rd; Jhelum, 24th; eggs.
1005	The common Cormorant	Graculus carbo ...	A loose platform.	On rocks by water (sometimes in trees.)	Upper India ...	Etawah (requires confirmation.

MARSHALL, DEL

NEST OF THE WHITE-THROATED FANTAIL.

(Leucocerca fuscoventris.)

MAY.

THIS is in all parts of India the most prolific season of the year. Nearly thirty kinds of birds of prey are still breeding, and almost all the non-climbing birds have commenced to lay. The shrikes, the common drongo, the large grey babbler, the doves, and the red wattled plover are now breeding in all parts of the country.

In the HIMALAYAS, the white scavenger vulture is still laying. The kestril, shikra, sparrow hawks, long-legged eagles, hawk eagles, serpent eagles, kites, wood owls, scops owls, owlets, mosque swallows, frogmouths, goatsuckers, European bee eater, rollers, and broadbills are laying. Most of the woodpeckers still have eggs, though for them it is late. The Marshall's barbet begins laying, while the other barbets still have eggs. The cuckoos, honey suckers, flower-peckers, tree creepers, nuthatches, hoopoes, shrikes and drongos of all kinds, flycatchers, wrens, shortwings, thrushes of all kinds, black-birds, ouzels, wren babblers, laughing thrushes, barwings, bulbuls, robins, bushchats, woodchats, water robins, reed warblers, tailor birds, warblers of all kinds, golden-crested wrens, forktails, wagtails, pipits, all the hill tits (*Leiotrichinæ*), true tits, hedge sparrows, crows, jays, magpies, starlings, mynahs, sparrows, buntings, gros-beaks, skylarks, pigeons, doves, pheasants, grouse, partridges, quail, plovers, woodcock, sandpipers, coots, bittern, herons, geese, ducks, and grebe have all begun to lay: while the *rosy minivet*, the *red-billed wren warbler*, the *magpie sibia*, the *white-tailed ruby throat*, the *paddy field warbler*, *strong-footed hill warbler*, the *golden-breasted hill tit*, *Hodgson's munia*, the *white-capped bunting*, the *speckled wood pigeon*, *Baillon's crake*, the *little bittern* and the *whiskered tern* have all begun to pair and build.

In the PUNJAB, the red-headed merlins, the sand martin, the Egyptian bee eater, the rose-headed paroquet, the speckled piculet, the common bulbul, the magpie robins, the common bushchat, the bright starling, the pied mynah, the pin-tailed munia, the desert finch lark, the sand larks, the crested lark, the common sand-grouse, the black partridge, the chukor, the seesee, the grey partridge, the big bustard, the courier plover, the great stone plover, the stone plover, the stilt, the king curlew, and the gull-billed tern are all laying: while the *white-necked storks* are pairing and building.

In the NORTH-WEST PROVINCES the true eagles, buzzards, kites, screech owl, scops owl, jungle owlet, wire-tailed swallow, goat-suckers, rollers, white-breasted and little kingfishers, hornbills, koel, concal, sirkeer, purple honey sucker, fantails, babblers, bulbuls, orioles, robins, pied wagtails, treepies, mynahs, sparrows, bush larks, finch larks, skylarks, green pigeons, rock pigeons, sandgrouse, jungle fowl, partridges, plovers, and common cormorants have eggs; and *Stewart's wren warblers*, the *Bengal bush larks*, *white-necked storks*, *shell ibis*, and *white ibis* are pairing and building.

In BENGAL, the spotted eagle, the crested swift, the white-breasted and stork-billed and little kingfishers, the amethyst-rumped honey suckers, king crows, the yellow-breasted and red-capped wren babblers, the striated marsh babblers, red-whiskered bulbuls, the black-headed oriole, the shama, titlark, sparrows, and many other kinds are laying. The *lesser concal*, the *Bengal bushlark*, the *florikin*, the *yellow bittern*, and the *pink-headed duck* are commencing to pair and build.

In CENTRAL INDIA, the shikra, the lesser harrier eagle, the white-eyed buzzard, the Nilgiri nightjar, the blue-tailed bee eater, the blue redbreasts, the striated marsh babblers, the white-eared crested bulbuls, the brown-backed robins, the brown rock chats, pied wagtails, green amadavats, the sand larks, the painted sandgrouse and the common sandgrouse, the grey jungle fowl, the spur fowl, courier plovers, wattled plovers, the brown rails, purple herons, and some others have got eggs. The *white ibis* are pairing and building towards the end of the month.

In SOUTHERN INDIA, the house and mosque swallows are laying. Also the crag martins, swiftlets, ghat nightjars, small green barbets, crimson-breasted barbets, long-tailed drongos, white-spotted fantails, grey-headed and black and orange flycatchers, blue redbreasts, short wings, blackbirds, Nilgiri quaker thrushes, scimitar babblers, laughing thrushes, babblers, black bulbuls, yellow-browed bush bulbuls, bushchats, the fuscous and ashy wren warblers, the Nilgiri pipit and Nilgiri tit lark, the white-eyed tit, the grey tit, the black crows, the common crows, the hill mynah, the weaver bird, the spotted munia and Indian amadavat, the skylark, the grey jungle fowl, the red spur fowl, and the little grebe have all got eggs during the month. Towards the end of it, the *orange minivets*, *black-headed*

***quaker thrush, white-browed bush bulbuls,* and *peafowl* commence pairing and building.**

In the ANDAMANS and NICOBARS, the *black-naped ternlet* is laying, and the *sea terns* and *gulls* begin to congregate for breeding purposes on the rocky islands in the Indian ocean and Persian gulf. The island of Astolah is well known as a breeding place.

MAY.

Nos. in Jerdon.	English Names.	Scientific Names.	Shape of Nest.	Site of Nest.	Geographical Range in Breeding Season.	Particulars for the Month.
6	The white scavenger Vulture	Perenopteron ginginianus	Platform ...	On cliffs or large trees.	Throughout India ...	The Himalayas; eggs.
16	The red-headed Merlin	Lithofalco chicquera . .	A compact massive cup.	In forks of trees ...	Throughout the plains..	The Punjab; eggs.
17	The Kestril	Tinnunculus alaudarius	A large platform.	On ledges of cliffs	Himalayas, Nilgiris, and Suleiman range.	Kangra, 27th; Kumaon; eggs.
18	The lesser "	Erythropus cenchris ...	Ditto ...	Ditto ...	The Nilgiris ...	Very little known.
23	The Shikra	Micronisus badius ...	A loose cup	High up in lofty trees.	Throughout India ...	Kashmir, 24th; C. P.; eggs.
24	The sparrow Hawk	Accipiter nisus ...	A small platform	Ditto ...	The western Himalayas	Kashmir, Gangootri; eggs.
	The dove "	" melaschistus	Ditto ..	On ledges of cliffs.	The Himalayas ...	Simla, 1st, 29th; eggs.
28	The spotted Eagle	Aquila nœvia ...	A large platform.	In high trees ...	Central and northern India.	Saharunpur, 12th, 28th; eggs.
29	The Indian tawny "	" vindhyana ...	Ditto ...	Ditto ...	The dry plains of upper India.	Saharunpur, 12th; eggs.
30	The long-legged "	" hastata ...	Ditto	Ditto ...	Central and northern India.	Oudh, 12th; Hazara, 6th; eggs.
36	The Nepal hawk "	Spizaetus nipalensis ...	Ditto ...	Ditto ...	The Himalayas only ...	Hazara, 6th; eggs.
	The changeable "	" caligatus ...	Ditto ...	Ditto ...	Bengal and the sub-Himalayas.	Kumaon, Bhabur.
38	The short-toed "	Circaetus gallicus ...	Ditto ...	Usually on high trees.	The dry plains of upper India	Breeding season ends.
39	The crested serpent "	Spilornis cheela ...	Ditto ...	In thick forks of trees.	The sub-Himalayan valleys.	Kangra; season ends.
	The lesser Indian-harrier "	" minor ...	Ditto ...	Ditto ...	The Central Provinces	Raipur (C. P.); eggs.
48	The white-eyed Buzzard	Poliornis teesa ...	A small platform.	In forks of trees ...	The dry plains of continental India.	Sambhur 29th; Meerut, 1st, 10th, 27th; eggs.
	The greater Indian Kite	Milvus major ...	Irregular platform.	Ditto ...	The western Himalayas	Kashmir; eggs.
	The crested-honey Buzzard	Pernis cristata ...	Ditto ...	Ditto ...	Locally throughout India proper.	Saharunpur, 15th, 30th; eggs.

59	The black-winged Kite	Elanus melanopterus...	A shallow compact cup	In forks of trees ...	Locally throughout India proper.	Dehra Doon (?)
60	The Indian screech Owl	Strix indica ...	None ...	In holes in trees or buildings.	Throughout the plains	Agra ; eggs.
64	The Himalayan brown wood ,,	Bulacca newarensis ...	Ditto ...	On a ledge on a low precipice.	The Himalayas ...	Simla, 25th ; eggs.
74	The Indian scops ,,	Ephialtes pennatus ...	Ditto ...	In holes in trees ...	Locally throughout India	Saharunpur (?)
	The barefoot ,, ,,	,, spilocephalus	Ditto ...	Ditto ...	The Himalayas ...	Simla, 1st ; Murree, 30th ; eggs.
75	The Nepal ,, ,,	,, lettia ...	Ditto ...	Ditto (or clefts in rocks) ...	The eastern Himalayas	Kumaon, 22nd ; eggs.
	The plume-foot ,, ,,	,, plumipes ...	Ditto ...	Ditto ...	The Himalayas ...	Simla, 13th ; eggs.
77	The jungle Owlet	Athene radiata ...	Ditto ...	Ditto ...	Locally throughout India.	The sub-Himalayas.
79	The large-barred ,,	,, cuculoides ...	Ditto ...	Ditto ...	The Himalayas ...	Kangra ; season ends.
80	The collared pigmy ,,	Glaucidium brodiei ...	Ditto ...	Ditto ...	The Himalayas and Khasia Hills.	Masuri, 1st ; Murree 30th ; eggs.
82	The common Swallow	Hirundo rustica ...	A deep semi-circular cup.	In and about houses	The Himalayas ...	Season nearly over.
83	The Nilgiri house ,,	,, domicola ...	A semi-circular saucer.	In buildings or caves	Nilgiris, Ceylon, Tenasserim.	Conoor ; eggs.
84	The wire-tailed ,,	,, ruficeps ...	Ditto ...	Under bridges or on rocks by water.	Locally throughout India.	Saharunpur, 24th ; eggs
85	The great India mosque ,,	,, daurica ...	A tubular retort.	In caves or buildings	The Himalayas ...	Kumaon, 6th ; Murree, 30th ; eggs.
	The mosque ,,	,, erythropyga .	Ditto ...	Ditto ...	Throughout India proper.	Nilgiris , season ends.
89	The common sand Martin	Cotyle sinensis ...	A loose cup	In holes in river banks (gregarious)	Throughout India (rare in south).	Jhelum ; eggs.
90	The dusky crag ,,	,, concolor ...	A semi-circular cup.	Against buildings or rocks.	Locally throughout India.	The Nilgiris ; eggs.
91	The ,, ,,	,, rupestris ...	Ditto ...	Against rocks or caves (gregarious)	The Himalayas.	Season ends.
93	The Kashmir ,,	Chelidon cashmirensis	Ditto ...	Ditto ...	Ditto ...	Ditto.
100	The common Indian Swift	Cypselus abyssinicus...	Semi-globular.	Against buildings (gregarious).	Throughout India ...	Throughout the month.
	The palmroof ,,	,, infumatus ...	A tiny watch pocket.	In palm leaf thatches.	The Garo and north Cachar hills.	Season ends.
103	The southern hill Swiftlet	Collocolia unicolor ...	A small semi-circular saucer.	In caves or on rocks (gregarious).	The Nilgiris and Assamboo hills.	Throughout the month.

Nos. in Jerdon.	English Names.	Scientific Names.	Shape of Nest.	Site of Nest.	Geographical Range in Breeding Season.	Particulars for the Month.
104	The Indian crested Swift	Dendrochelidon coronatus.	A tiny half saucer.	On dead boughs of high trees.	The forests of India proper.	Darjeeling Terai; eggs.
106	The Sikkim Frogmouth	Otothrix hodgsoni ..	A broad pad	In trees on thick branches.	The eastern Himalayas	Darjeeling, 10th; eggs.
107	The jungle Nightjar	Caprimulgus indicus ...	None ...	On the ground often near a bush.	The forests of continental India	Masuri; eggs.
108	The Nilgiri „	„ kelaarti ...	Ditto ...	Ditto ...	South extending to central India.	Central Provinces; eggs.
109	The large Bengal „	, albonotatus.	Ditto ...	Ditto ...	The forests of upper India.	Kumaon; eggs.
111	The ghat „	„ atripennis	Ditto ...	Ditto ...	The Nilgiris ...	Kotagiri, 10th; eggs.
112	The common Indian ,	„ asiaticus .	Ditto ...	Ditto ...	Locally in upper India	Saharunpur, 18th; eggs.
114	Franklin's „	„ monticolus	Ditto ...	Ditto ...	In wooded hills throughout India.	The sub-Himalayas.
	Unwin's ,	„ unwini ...	Ditto ...	Ditto ...	The north-western Himalayas.	Murree; eggs.
116	Hodgson's Trogon	Harpactes hodgsoni ...	Ditto ...	In holes in decayed trees	The eastern sub-Himalayas.	Darjeeling; eggs.
117	The common Bee eater	Merops viridis ...	Ditto ...	In deep holes in banks or plains.	Throughout India proper	Saharunpur, 10th; eggs.
118	The blue-tailed „	„ philippensis ...	Ditto ...	In deep holes in banks.	Ditto ...	Raipur (C. P); eggs.
120	The Egyptian „	„ ægyptius ...	Ditto ...	Ditto (or plains)...	The dry plains of N. W India.	Delhi; eggs.
121	The European „	„ apiaster ...	Ditto ...	Ditto ...	The western Himalayas	Kashmir; eggs.
122	The blue-ruffed „	Nyctiornis athertoni ...	Ditto ...	Ditto ...	The eastern sub-Himalayas.	(Requires confirmation).
123	The common Roller	Coracias indica ...	Ditto ...	In holes in trees or buildings.	Throughout India proper.	Saharunpur, 13th; eggs.
125	The European „	„ garrula ...	Ditto ...	Ditto ...	The western Himalayas	Kashmir; eggs.
126	The broad-billed „	Eurystomus orientalis	Ditto ...	In holes in lofty trees.	The eastern sub-Himalayas.	(Requires confirmation).
127	The Indian stork-billed King-fisher	Pelargopsis gurial ...	Ditto ...	In holes in banks by running water.	Bengal and eastern sub Himalayas.	Calcutta; eggs.

129	The white breasted Kingfisher	Halcyon smyrnensis ...	None ...	In holes in river banks or wells.	Throughout India proper.	Calcutta, 2nd ; Saharunpur, 4th, 9th ; eggs.
134	The little Indian "	Alcedo bengalensis ...	Ditto ...	In holes in banks often by rivers.	Ditto ...	Dehra Doon, Sikkim Terai.
138	The yellow-throated Broadbill	Psarisomus dalhousiæ	Large rough pear-shaped.	Pendent from lofty trees.	The eastern Himalayas	Very little known.
140	The great Indian Hornbill	Homraius bicornis ...	None ...	In holes in lofty decayed trees.	The eastern sub-Himalayas.	Kumaon, Bhabur.
144	The northern grey "	Meniceros " ...	Ditto ...	In holes in decayed trees.	Throughout the plains	Mynpuri (N. W. P.) ; 7th ; eggs.
149	The rose-headed Paroquet	Palæornis purpureus...	Ditto ...	Ditto ...	Western continental India.	Murree ; eggs.
153	The Indian Loriquet	Loriculus vernalis ...	Ditto ...	Ditto ...	Bengal and eastern sub-Himalayas.	Season nearly over.
154	The Himalayan pied Woodpecker.	Picus himalayensis ...	None ...	In artificial holes in trees.	The Himalayas ...	Kumaon ; season ends.
156	The lesser-black "	" cathpharius ...	Ditto ...	Ditto ...	The eastern Himalayas	Nepal ; eggs.
157	The Indian spotted "	" macei ...	Ditto ...	Ditto ...	The Himalayas and eastern Bengal.	Murree, Kangra ; eggs.
159	The brown-fronted "	" brunneifrons ...	Ditto ...	Ditto ...	The Himalayas from Nepal west.	Hazara, 6th ; eggs.
161	The rufous-bellied pied "	Hypopicus hyperythrus	Ditto ...	Ditto ...	The Himalayas ...	Murree ; season ends.
163	The Himalayan pigmy "	Yungipicus pygmœus	Ditto ...	Ditto ...	The western Himalayas	Kumaon ; do.
170	The scaly-bellied green "	Gecinus squamatus ...	Ditto ...	Ditto ...	The Himalayas ...	Murree ; eggs ; Simlah, 16th ; young.
171	The lesser Indian green "	" striolatus ...	Ditto ...	Ditto ...	The wooded parts of India proper.	Season nearly over.
172	The black-naped green "	" occipitalis ...	Ditto ...	Ditto ...	The Himalayas ...	Murree, 28th ; Sikkim ; eggs.
186	The speckled Piculet	Vivia innominata ...	Ditto ...	Ditto ...	Ditto ...	Hazara, 6th ; eggs.
191	The Marshall's Barbet	Megalæma marshallorum	Ditto ...	Ditto ...	Ditto ...	Nepal, 20th ; eggs.
192	Hodgson's green "	" hodgsoni ...	Ditto ...	Ditto ...	The lower Himalayas	Nepal ; eggs.
193	Franklin's " "	" caniceps ...	Ditto ...	Ditto ...	The woods of continental India.	Rohilkhund ; season ends.
194	The small " "	" viridis ...	Ditto ...	Ditto ...	The woods of peninsular India.	Nilgiris ; do.
195	The blue-throated "	" asiatica ...	Ditto ...	Ditto ...	Lower Bengal and eastern Himalayas.	Calcutta ; eggs.
196	The golden-throated "	" franklinii ...	Ditto ...	Ditto ...	The eastern Himalayas.	Nepal ; eggs.

Nos. in Jerdon.	English Names.	Scientific Names.	Shape of Nest.	Site of Nest.	Geographical Range in Breeding Season.	Particulars for the Month.
197	The crimson-breasted Barbet	Xantholæma hæmacephala.	None ...	In artificial holes in trees.	Throughout the plains	North India ; season ends.
199	The common Cuckoo	Cuculus canorus ...	(Parasitic habits.)	Eggs laid in bushchats' or pipits' nests.	The Himalayas ...	Kangra, Kumaon ; eggs.
201	The hoary-headed „	„ poliocephalus	Ditto ...	Eggs laid in warbler's nests	The western Himalayas.	Kashmir ; eggs.
204	The hill „	„ striatus ...	Ditto ...	Eggs laid in Laughing thrushes' nest	The Himalayas ...	Kashmir ; season begins.
214	The Koil	Eudynamis orientalis	Ditto ...	Eggs laid in crows' nests.	Throughout the plains	Fatehgurh (N. W.P.), 27th ; eggs.
217	The common Coucal	Centropus rufipennis...	Large, rough-domed	In dense thickets or thorny trees.	Throughout India proper.	Cawnpur, 27th ; eggs.
220	The Bengal Sirkeer	Taccocua sirkee ...	A rough shallow cup	Iu low thick trees or bushes.	The plains of upper India.	Chunar, 25th ; eggs.
225	The Himalayan red Honeysucker	Œthopyga miles ...	Pear-shaped, side entrance.	Hanging from tips of boughs.	The eastern Himalayas	Nepal ; eggs.
229	The maroon backed „	„ nipalensis	Ditto ...	Ditto ...	The eastern Himalayas and Khasia hills ...	Nepal, Sikkim ; eggs.
231	The blackbreasted „	„ saturata ...	Ditto ...	Ditto ...	Ditto ...	Kumaon ; eggs.
232	The amethyst-rumped „	Leptocoma zeylanica...	Ditto ...	Ditto ...	Lower Bengal and peninsular India.	Calcutta, 16th, 23rd ; eggs.
234	The purple „	Arachnechthra asiatica	Ditto ...	Ditto ...	Throughout India ...	Saharunpur, 11th ; Kashmir 21st ; eggs.
238	Tickell's Flowerpecker	Dicæum minimum ...	Ditto ...	Ditto ...	Bombay, central and N. E India ...	Calcutta ; eggs.
240	The thick-billed „	Piprisoma agile ...	Purse-shaped, front entrance	Hanging from thin branches.	Throughout India ...	Kotegurh, Kumaon ; eggs.
241	The fire-breasted „	Myzanthe ignipectus	Ditto ...	Ditto ...	The eastern Himalayas	Nepal ; eggs.
243	The Himalayan Treecreeper	Certhia himalayana ...	A rough cup	In crevices in bark on high trees.	The western Himalayas	Kashmir ; eggs.
	Hodgson's „	„ hodgsoni ...	Ditto ...	Ditto ...	Ditto ...	Ditto.

248	The white-tailed Nuthatch	Sitta himalayensis ...	A shallow pad.	In natural hollows in trees.	The Himalayas ...	Kumaon; season ends.
249	The white-cheeked „	„ leucopsis ...	Ditto ...	Ditto ...	The western Himalayas	Kashmir; eggs.
253	The velvet-fronted „	Dendrophila frontalis	None	Ditto ...	The hilly regions of India.	Season nearly over.
254	The Hoopoe	Upupa epops ...	Ditto ...	In holes in trees or buildings.	The western Himalayas	Kashmir, 16th; eggs.
255	The Indian „ „	„ nigripennis ...	Ditto ...	Ditto ...	Throughout India ...	Season nearly over.
256	The Indian grey Shrike	Lanius lahtora ...	A thick massive cup.	In small trees or thorny bushes.	Throughout the dry plains.	Saharunpur, 1st, 30th; eggs.
257	The rufous-backed „	„ erythronotus	Ditto ...	Ditto ...	Throughout India ...	Throughout the month.
	The pale „ „ „	„ caniceps ...	Ditto ...	Ditto ...	The hilly regions of India.	The Nilgiris; eggs.
258	The grey-backed „	„ tephronotus ...	Ditto ...	Ditto ...	The Himalayas ...	Kumaon, 23rd; eggs.
259	The black cap „	„ nigriceps ...	Ditto ...	Ditto ...	The Himalayas and east central India.	Nepal, 17th; Sikkim, 17th; eggs.
260	The bay-backed „	„ vittatus ...	A neat cup	Ditto ...	Throughout India ...	Aligurh, 28th; eggs.
	The Himalayan pied „	Hemipus capitalis ...	A small cup	On the ground under shelter.	The Himalayas. ...	Dehra Doon, 12th; eggs.
269	The dark grey cuckoo „	Volvocivora melaschistus ...	A small saucer.	In horizontal forks of trees.	Ditto ...	Throughout the month.
271	The large Minivet	Pericrocotus speciosus	A small deep cup.	In high trees near end of boughs.	Ditto ...	Dehra Doon, Nepal; eggs.
273	The short-billed „	„ brevirostris	Ditto ...	Ditto ...	Ditto ...	Nepal, 16th; eggs.
278	The common drongo Shrike	Dicrurus albirictus ...	A loose saucer.	In horizontal forks of trees.	Throughout India ...	Kumaon, 23rd; Meerut; 28th; eggs.
280	The long-tailed „ ,	„ longicaudatus	A neat saucer.	Ditto ...	The plains in moist forests.	Malabar; eggs.
	Walden's „ „	„ waldeni ...	Ditto ...	Ditto ...	The Himalayas ...	Throughout the month.
281	The white-bellied „ „	„ cœrulescens...	A loose saucer.	Ditto ...	The hilly regions of India.	Kumaon (?).
282	The bronzed „ „	Chaptia ænea ...	A broad saucer.	Ditto ...	In forests throughout India.	Nepal; eggs.
283	The oar tailed „ „	Bhringa remifer ...	Ditto ...	Ditto ...	The eastern Himalayas	Very little known.
284	The northern racket-tailed „ „	Edolius paradiseus ...	Ditto ...	Ditto ...	The Himalayas and eastern India. ...	Sikkim; eggs.
286	The hair-crested „ „	Chibia hottentota ...	Ditto ...	Ditto ...	The eastern Himalayas	Nepal, Sikkim; eggs.
287	The ashy swallow „	Artamus fuscus ...	Ditto ...	On big horizontal boughs or stumps.	Locally throughout India.	Darjeeling, 8th; eggs.
288	The paradise Flycatcher	Tchitrea paradisei ...	A small delicate cup.	On thin branches in trees.	In all moist forests throughout India.	Dehra Doon, 26th; Murree; eggs.

Nos. in Jerdon.	English Names.	Scientific Names.	Shape of Nest.	Site of Nest.	Geographical Range in Breeding Season.	Particulars for the Month.
290	The black-naped azure Flycatcher	Myiagra azurea ...	A deep compact cup.	On thin branches in trees.	In all moist forests throughout India.	Season begins.
291	The white-throated Fantail	Leucocerca fuscoventris	A tiny inverted cone.	Ditto ...	Locally in continental India.	Dehra Doon, 25th ; eggs.
292	The white-browed „	„ aureola ...	A tiny cup.	Ditto ...	Throughout continental India.	Oudh, Dehra Doon ; eggs.
293	The white-spotted „	„ pectoralis...	A tiny inverted cone.	Ditto ...	The hills of south India	The Nilgiris ; eggs.
294	The yellow-bellied „	Chelidorhynx hypoxantha...	A deep neat cup.	Ditto ...	The sub-Himalayas ...	Nepal ; eggs.
295	The grey-headed Flycatcher	Cryptolopha cinereocapilla	A watch pocket.	Against moss covered trunks of trees.	The Himalayas, Nilgiris, and Wynaad.	Kumaon, 2nd ; Nilgiris ; eggs.
296	The sooty „	Hemichelidon fuliginosa	A compact pad.	Against mossy trees or on stumps.	The western Himalayas	Kashmir, 29th ; Nepal ; eggs.
300	The black and orange „	Ochromela nigrorufa...	Large globular-domed.	Low down in bushes or clumps.	The Nilgiris only ...	Kotagiri, 11th ; eggs.
301	The verditer „	Eumyias melanops ...	A thick cup	In banks often under bridges.	The Himalayas ...	Darjeeling, 25th ; Kangra ; eggs.
304	The blue-throated Red-breast	Cyornis rubeculoides...	Ditto ...	In holes in banks or decayed trees.	Ditto ...	Nepal ; eggs.
305	The southern blue	Cyornis banyumas ...	A small thick cup.	In holes in banks or decayed trees.	Southern India ...	Mysore ; eggs.
306	Tickell's blue „	„ tickelliæ ...	Ditto ...	Ditto ...	Central and southern India.	Kotagiri, 27th ; eggs.
310	The white-browed blue Flycatcher	Muscicapula superciliaris.	Ditto ...	In holes or cracks in trees.	The Himalayas.	Throughout the month.
314	The fairy „	Niltava sundara ...	A large thick pad.	In clefts of rocks or under stumps.	Ditto ...	Sikkim, 19th ; Nepal ; eggs.
315	Macgregor's „ „	„ macgregoriæ ...	A large thick cup.	Ditto ...	The eastern Himalayas	Sikkim, 7th ; Nepal ; eggs.
316	The great „ „	„ grandis ...	A large thick pad.	Ditto ...	Ditto ...	Sikkim, Nepal ; eggs.
320	The slaty „	Siphia leucomelanura	A massive little cup.	At roots of trees in pine forests.	The western Himalayas	Kashmir, 29th ; eggs.

321	The rufous-breasted Flycatcher	Siphia superciliaris ...	A deep cup	At roots of trees in pine forest.	The Himalayas ...	Nepal; eggs.
	The grey robin „	Erythrosterna parva ...	(Unknown)	(Unknown)...	Ditto ..	Ditto.
324	The white-tailed robin „	„ hyperythra	A large deep cup.	In forks in low bushes.	The north-west Himalayas.	Kashmir; eggs.
327	The chestnut-headed Wren	Tesia castaneocoronata	Large globular, domed.	Low down in thick bushes or clumps.	The eastern Himalayas	Nepal; eggs.
331	The tailed hill „	Pnœopyga caudata ...	A deep thick cup,	On the ground near roots or stumps...	Ditto ...	Ditto.
333	The Nepal „	Troglodytes nipalensis	Globular, domed.	Low down among creepers on trees.	The Himalayas ...	Kashmir; eggs.
338	The white-browed Shortwing	Brachypteryx cruralis	Ditto ...	Ditto ...	The eastern Himalayas	Nepal; eggs.
339	The rufous-bellied „	Callene rufiventris ...	A large thick cup.	In holes in banks or trees.	The Nilgiris ...	Kotagiri, eggs; season ends.
	The white-bellied „	„ albiventris ...	A loose cup.	In holes in trees.	The Pulney hills.	Throughout the month.
343	The yellow-billed whistling Thrush	Myiophonus temminckii.	A massive saucer.	On ledges of rocks by water.	The Himalayas ...	Kangra, 20th; Hazara, 2nd; eggs.
344	The Nepal ground „	Hydrornis nipalensis..	Large globular, domed.	In banks at foot of a bush.	The eastern Himalayas	Sikkim, 10th; eggs.
346	The green-breasted „ „	Pitta cucullata ...	Ditto ...	On the ground in bamboos or thickets.	Ditto ...	Nepal; eggs.
347	The brown-water Ouzel	Hydrobata asiatica ...	A large ball of moss.	In clefts of rocks near water.	The Himalayas only ...	Simla; eggs.
351	The blue-rock Thrush	Petrocossyphus cyaneus	Cup-shaped	In holes in banks or walls.	The western Himalayas	Murree; eggs.
352	The chestnut-bellied chat Thrush	Orocetes erythrogastra	A neat cup	Ditto ...	The Himalayas ...	Kangra, 20th; eggs.
353	The blue-headed „ „	„ cinclorhynchus	Ditto ...	Ditto (often at roots of trees.)	Ditto ...	Kashmir, 29th; Kumaon, 21st: eggs.
355	The rusty-throated bush „	Geocichla citrina ...	A broad cup	In forks of small trees.	Ditto ...	Nepal, Masuri; eggs.
356	The dusky „ „	„ unicolor ...	Ditto ...	In thick forks or on stumps.	Ditto ...	Kumaon, 16th, 31st; eggs.
358	The variable pied Blackbird	„ dissimilis ...	Ditto ...	Ditto ...	Ditto ...	Kumaon, 16th; eggs (very rare.)
357	Ward's pied „	Turdulus wardii ...	Ditto ...	Ditto ...	Ditto ...	Kumaon, 22nd; eggs.
360	The Nilgiri „	Merula simillima ...	Ditto ...	In forks of trees or saplings.	The Nilgiris ...	Conoor 18th; Kotagiri; eggs.
351	The grey-winged „	„ boulboul ...	Ditto ...	In thick forks of trees.	The Himalayas ...	Kumaon, 30th; Sikkim, 20th; eggs.

Nos. in Jerdon.	English Names.	Scientific Names.	Shape of Nest.	Site of Nest.	Geographical Range in Breeding Season.	Particulars for the Month.
362	The white-collared Ouzel	Merula albocincta ...	A broad cup	In banks or on stumps.	The Himalayas ...	Kumaon, 20th; eggs; season ends.
363	The grey-headed ,,	,, castanea ...	Ditto ...	Ditto	Ditto ...	Murree, Kumaon; eggs.
368	The Indian missel Thrush	Turdus hodgsoni ...	Ditto ...	In thick forks of trees.	Ditto ...	Kumaon, 16th; Kangra; eggs.
371	The small-billed mountain ,,	Oreocincla dauma ...	Ditto ...	Ditto ...	Ditto ...	Kumaon, 29th; Kashmir, 30th; eggs.
388	The Nepal quaker Thrush	Alcippe nipalensis ...	A deep massive cup.	In low thick bushes	The eastern Himalayas	Nepal, Sikkim; eggs.
389	The Nilgiri ,, ,,	,, poiocephala...	Ditto ...	In forks of thick bushes or saplings.	The hills of south India	Nilgiris; eggs.
391	The black-headed wren Babbler	Stachyris nigriceps ...	Ditto ...	In grassy banks near roots of shrubs.	The eastern Himalayas	Darjeeling, 14th; Nepal; eggs.
393	The red-headed ,, ,,	,, ruficeps ...	Ditto ...	In bamboo clumps chiefly.	Ditto ...	Nepal; eggs.
395	The yellow-breasted ,, ,,	Mixornis rubricapillus	Deep egg-shaped domed	Low down in dense thorny bushes.	Ditto ...	Tenasserim, 6th; eggs.
396	The red-capped ,, ,,	Timalia pileata ...	Ditto ...	Ditto ...	Ditto (and Bengal) ...	Thayetmyo, 15th; eggs.
400	The rufous neck scimitar ,,	Pomatorhinus ruficollis	Large-globular; domed.	On the ground in grass or weeds.	Ditto ...	Darjeeling, 5th; Nepal; eggs.
404	The southern ,, ,,	,, horsfieldii	Ditto ...	On the ground in a bush or tussock.	The hills south of India	Nilgiris; season ends.
405	The rusty-cheeked ,, ,,	,, erythrogenys	Ditto ...	Ditto ...	The Himalayas ...	Sikkim, Nepal, 20th; eggs.
406	The slender-billed ,, ,,	Xiphoramphus superciliaris.	Ditto ...	Near the ground in grass or bushes.	The eastern Himalayas	Nepal; eggs.
407	The white-crested laughing Thrush	Garrulax leucolophus...	A broad shallow cup.	In thick bushes or low trees.	The Himalayas east of Sutlej.	Nepal; season begins.
408	The grey sided ,, ,,	,, cærulatus ...	A large deep cup.	In small trees or saplings.	The eastern Himalayas	Darjeeling; eggs.
410	The rufous-necked ,, ,,	,, ruficollis ...	Ditto ...	In bushes or low trees.	Ditto ...	Ditto.
411	The white throated ,, ,,	,, albogularis ...	A broad shallow cup.	Ditto ...	The Himalayas ...	Kumaon, 31st; Murree, 3rd; eggs.
413	The necklaced ,, ,,	,, moniliger ...	A large deep cup.	Ditto ...	The eastern Himalayas	Darjeeling, 28th; eggs.

414	The white-spotted laughing Thrush	Garrulax ocellatus ...	A massive cup	In low thickets or clumps of fern.	The Eastern Himalayas	Darjeeling; eggs.
415	The red-headed " "	Trochalopteron erythrocephalum	Ditto ...	In forks of trees or bushes.	The western Himalayas	Kumaon, 15th, 31st; eggs.
417	The plain-coloured " "	" subunicolor	Ditto ...	Ditto ...	The eastern Himalayas	Nepaul; eggs.
418	The variegated " "	" variegatum	Ditto ...	Ditto ...	The western Himalayas	Ditto.
420	The blue-winged " "	" squamatum	Ditto ...	Ditto ...	The eastern Himalayas	Darjeeling, 10th; eggs.
421	The red-throated	, rufogulare	Ditto ...	Ditto ...	Ditto ...	Dehra Doon; eggs.
422	The crimson-winged " "	" phœnicium	Ditto ...	Ditto ...	Ditto ...	Darjeeling, 4th, 23rd; eggs.
423	The Nilgiri " "	" cacchinans	Ditto ...	Ditto ...	The Nilgiris ...	Conoor; eggs.
425	The streaked " "	" lineatum	Cup-shaped	In low bushes or holes in banks.	The Himalayas ...	Throughout the month.
426	The bristly " "	" imbricatum	Ditto ...	Ditto ...	The eastern Himalayas	Nepal; eggs.
428	The hoary Barwing	Actinodura nipalensis	A shallow cup	In holes in banks or rocks.	Ditto ...	Ditto.
429	The black-headed Sibia	Sibia capistrata ...	A neat deep cup.	In outer twigs of trees or bushes.	The Himalayas ...	Nest building begins.
432	The Bengal Babbler	Malacocercus canorus	A loose straggling cup.	In thick bushes or small trees.	The plains of continental India.	Throughout the month.
433	The white-headed "	" griseus	Ditto ...	In thorny hedges or low trees	The plains of south India.	Madras; eggs.
434	The jungle "	" malabaricus.	Ditto ...	In trees or thick thorny bushes.	The hills of south India.	Nilgiris; eggs.
435	The rufous-tailed "	" somervillii.	Ditto ...	Ditto ...	The western Ghats ...	Bombay; eggs.
436	The large grey "	" malcolmi	Cup-shaped	In thorny trees or bushes.	Throughout the plains	Nilgiris; season ends.
438	The striated bush "	Chattarhœa caudata ...	Ditto ...	In low bushes or clumps of grass.	Ditto ...	Aligurh, 10th; eggs.
440	The striated marsh "	Megalurus palustris ...	Deep egg-shaped domed	In clumps of grass or reeds.	Eastern Bengal and Central Provinces.	Hoshungabad, 4th; Calcutta, 7th; eggs.
444	The Himalayan black Bulbul	Hypsepetes psaroides	A neat cup	In forks of bushes or trees.	The Himalayas ...	Throughout the month.
445	The Nilgiri " "	" nilgiriensis	A rough shallow cup.	In dense bushes or clumps.	The Nilgiris ...	Conoor; eggs.
447	The rufous-bellied "	" macclellandi	A neat shallow saucer.	Suspended from a leafy fork.	The eastern Himalayas	Nepal; eggs.

Nos. in Jerdon.	English Names.	Scientific Names.	Shape of Nest.	Site of Nest.	Geographical Range in Breeding Season.	Particulars for the Month.
450	The yellow-browed bush Bulbul	Criniger ictericus ...	A small shallow cup.	Suspended from a leafy fork	The hills of south India.	The Nilgiris; eggs.
456	The black-crested yellow „	Rubigula flaviventris...	A neat cup.	In bushes or thickets	The eastern Himalayas	Darjeeling, 16th; eggs.
458	The white-checked crested „	Otocompsa leucogenys	Ditto ...	In bushes or low trees.	The Himalayas ...	Hazara, 7th; Kumaon, 13th; eggs.
459	The white-eared „ „	„ leucotis	Ditto ...	In dense thorny bushes.	Western continental India.	Rajputana; eggs.
460	The red-whiskered „	„ emeria	Ditto ...	In thick bushes or creepers.	The moist parts of upper India.	Season nearly over.
	The southern red-whiskered „	fuscicaudata	Ditto ...	In isolated bushes...	The hills of south India.	Ditto.
461	The common Bengal „	Pycnonotus pygæus ...	A small slender cup.	In small trees or bushes.	The Himalayas and eastern Bengal.	Kumaon, 23rd; Sikkim; eggs.
462	The common Madras „	„ pusillus ...	Ditto ...	Ditto ...	Throughout the plains	The Punjab; eggs.
468	The white-winged green „	Iora typhia ...	A tiny cup...	In trees near leafy tips of boughs.	Locally throughout India.	Seetapur, Oudh, 13th; eggs.
470	The Indian golden Oriole	Oriolus kundoo ...	A neat deep cup.	In high trees hung from outer forks.	Throughout India ...	Nest building begins.
472	The black-headed „	„ melanocephalus	Ditto ...	Ditto ...	Locally in continental India.	Allahabad, Bengal; eggs.
475	The magpie Robin	Copsychus saularis ...	A shallow saucer.	In holes in trees or walls.	Throughout India ...	Throughout the month.
476	The Shama	Kittacincla macroura	Ditto ...	In holes in decayed trees.	Peninsular and eastern India.	Tenasserim, 5th; eggs.
477	The white-tailed Bluechat	Myiomela leucura ...	A deep massive cup.	On rocks under bushes or grass.	The eastern Himalayas	Darjeeling, 14th; eggs.
479	The southern brown-backed Robin.	Thamnobia fulicata ...	A small cup	On the ground sheltered or in holes.	South India ...	Ahmednagar, 25th; eggs.
480	The brown-backed „	„ cambaiensis	Ditto ...	Ditto ...	The plains of upper India.	Throughout the month.
481	The black Bushchat	Pratincola caprata ..	A shallow pad.	On the ground under shelter.	The Himalayas and continental India.	Dehra Doon, Bombay; eggs.
482	The southern black „	„ atrata ..	Ditto ...	In holes in banks or wall.	The hills of south India.	Nilgiris; season ends.

483	The common Indian Bushchat	Pratincola indica ...	A small cup.	The holes in banks or walls.	The Himalayas and N. W. Punjab.	Throughout the month.
486	The iron grey "	" ferrea ...	Ditto ...	Ditto ...	The Himalayas ...	Ditto.
494	The brown Rockchat	Cercomela fusca ...	A shallow pad.	Ditto ...	The dry parts of continental India.	Saugor; eggs.
505	The plumbous water Robin	Rutacilla fuliginosa ...	A small cup.	In niches of rocks near water.	The Himalayas ...	Kangra, Masuri; eggs.
506	The white-capped Redstart	Chæmorrornis leucocephala.	Ditto ...	In holes in perpendicular banks.	The alpine Himalayas	Kumaon throughout; the month.
508	The white-breasted blue Wood chat.	Ianthia rufilata ...	Ditto ...	In banks or under fallen trees.	The western Himalayas	Kashmir, 30th; eggs.
515	The large reed Warbler	Acrocephalus brunnescens.	A very deep cup.	Among reeds growing in water.	Ditto ...	Kashmir; eggs.
516	The lesser " "	Acrocephalus dumetorum	Globular-domed.	In thick bushes or brambles.	The Himalayas ...	Masuri, 6th; Kumaon; eggs.
	The pale hill "	Horeites pallidus ...	Large globular-domed.	In tangled brushwood.	The western Himalayas	Kashmir, 25th; eggs.
530	The Indian Tailor-bird	Orthotomus longicauda	A deep cup sewn in leaves.	In low bushes or creepers.	Throughout India ...	Darjeeling, 16th; eggs.
534	The ashy wren Warbler	Prinia socialis ...	A cup sewn in leaves.	Hanging in low bushes.	Southern India ...	Nilgiris; eggs.
	The fuscous " "	Drymoipus fuscus ...	Deep neat; domed.	In small bushes or clumps.	The Terai, Deccan; and Nilgiris.	Ditto; ditto.
547	The brown hill "	Suya criniger ...	Deep flimsy domed.	In low bushes on hill-sides.	The Himalayas ...	Kangra, 15th; Kumaon; eggs.
548	The dusky " "	" fuliginosa ...	Deep neat domed.	In low bushes on hill sides.	The eastern Himalayas	Kumaon, 19th; eggs.
549	The black-throated "	" atrogularis ...	Ditto ...	In small bushes or clumps.	Ditto ...	Nepal, Sikkim; eggs.
551	The rufous-fronted wren "	Franklinia buchanani	Deep ragged often domed.	In low bushes or scrub.	Western continental India.	Season commences.
552	The aberrant tree "	Neornis flavolivacea ...	A neat shallow cup.	In bushes or low trees.	The eastern Himalayas	Nepal, 29th; eggs.
	Blythe's aberrant " "	" assimilis ...	Ditto ...	Ditto ...	Ditto ...	Darjeeling, 18th; eggs.
	Tytler's "	Phylloscopus tytleri ...	A deep, thick cup.	At tips of upper boughs of firs.	The western Himalayas	Kashmir, 30th; eggs.
563	The large crowned "	Reguloides occipitalis	A loose cup	In holes in decayed stumps or banks.	Ditto ...	Murree, 10th; eggs.
565	The crowned "	" superciliosus	Large rough globular.	On the ground on mossy banks.	Ditto ...	Kashmir, 31st; eggs.

Nos. in Jerdon.	English Names.	Scientific Names.	Shape of Nest.	Site of Nest.	Geographical Range in Breeding Season.	Particulars for the Month.
566	The Dalmatian Warbler	Reguloides proregulus	Neat compact domed.	At tips of boughs of firs or pines.	The western Himalayas	Kashmir ; eggs.
570	The lesser black-browed ,,	Culicepeta cantator ...	A watch pocket(?)	Hung from tips of boughs.	The eastern Himalayas	Sikkim; eggs (¿)
571	The black-eared ,,	Abrornis schisticeps	Globular domed	In holes in mossy banks.	The Himalayas ..	Masuri ; eggs.
	The grey faced ,	,, chloronotus ...	Pear-shaped (?)	Hanging from twigs in bushes.	The eastern Himalayas	(Requires confirmation)
573	The white-browed ,,	,, albosuperciliaris.	Globular domed.	On the ground in moss or bushes.	The Himalayas ...	Season ends.
	The chesnut-headed ,,	,, castaniceps ...	Ditto ...	Ditto ...	The eastern Himalayas	Nepal ; eggs.
580	The Indian golden crested Wren	Regulus himalayensis	A deep pouch	Hung from twigs in fir trees.	The Himalayas ...	Sutlej valley ; eggs.
582	The Indian White-throat	Sylvia affinis ...	A shallow cup	In low bushes or thickets.	The western Himalayas	Kashmir, 27th ; eggs.
584	The western spotted forktail	Henicurus maculatus	A massive cup	On banks or rocks by water.	Ditto ...	Dehra, 12th ; Kangra ; eggs.
586	The slaty-backed ,,	, schistaceus	Ditto ...	Ditto ...	The eastern Himalayas	Darjeeling, 4th ; eggs.
587	The little ,,	, scouleri ...	Ditto ...	Ditto ...	Ditto ...	Kumaon ; eggs.
	The eastern spotted ,,	,, guttatus ...	Ditto ...	Ditto ...	Ditto ...	Darjeeling ; eggs.
589	The Indian pied Wagtail	Motacilla maderaspatana	A shallow pad	On the ground or buildings by water	Throughout the plains	Fatehgurh, Sambhur ; eggs.
590	The white-faced ,,	,, luzionensis ...	Ditto ...	Under stones or snags by rivers.	The western Himalayas	Kashmir ; eggs.
592	The grey and yellow ,,	,, melanope ...	Ditto ...	Ditto ...	Ditto ...	Kashmir, 25th ; eggs.
	The black-backed yellow-headed ,,	Budytes calcaratus ...	Ditto ...	On the ground under stones or rocks.	Ditto ...	Kashmir, 18th ; eggs.
596	The Indian Pipit	Anthus arboreus ...	A shallow cup	On the ground on grassy slopes.	The alpine Himalayas	Kooloo ; eggs.
597	The tree ,,	,, maculatus ...	Ditto ...	Ditto ...	Ditto ...	Kotegurh, Kumaon ; eggs.
598	The Nilgiri ,,	,, montanus ...	Ditto ...	On the ground under a tussock.	The Nilgiris ...	Nidivatum ; eggs.
605	The ruddy ,,	,, rosaceus ...	Ditto ...	Ditto ...	The Alpine Himalayas	Gurhwal, 27th ; eggs.
600	The Indian Titlark	Corydalla rufula ...	Ditto ...	Ditto ...	Throughout India proper.	Calcutta, 2nd, 17th ; eggs.

607	The Nilgiri Titlark	Agrodroma cinanmomea	A shallow saucer.	On the ground under clod or tuft.	The Nilgiris ...	Kotagiri, 16th ; eggs.
606	The brown rock Pipit	„ griseorufescens.	Ditto ...	Ditto ...	The western Himalayas	Murree ; eggs.
603	The upland „	Heterura sylvana ...	Ditto ...	Ditto ...	The Himalayas from Nepal west.	Nepal, 4th ; eggs.
608	The purple thrush Tit	Cochoa purpurea ...	A large deep cup.	In small trses or bushes.	The eastern Himalayas	Kumaon ; eggs.
604	The green „ „	„ viridis ...	Ditto	Ditto ...	Ditto ...	Sikkim ; eggs.
609	The red-winged shrike Tit	Pteruthius erythropterus.	A rather deep cup.	Attops of high trees	The western Hamalayas	Murree, 30th ; eggs.
614	The red-billed hill „	Leothrix luteus ...	A substantial cup.	In thick bushes ...	The eastern Himalayas	Darjeeling ; eggs.
615	The silver-eared „ „	„ argentarius...	Ditto ...	Ditto ...	Ditto ...	Nepal ; eggs.
616	The stripe-throated „ „	Siva strigula ...	Ditto ...	In slender forks of small trees.	Ditto ...	Nepal, 27th ; eggs.
617	The blue-winged „ „	„ cyanouroptera ...	Ditto ...	Ditto ...	Ditto ...	Nepal, 25th ; eggs.
618	The red-tailed „ „	Minla ignotincta ...	Ditto ...	Ditto ...	Ditto ...	Nepal, 25th ; eggs.
619	The chesnut-headed „ „	„ castaneiceps ...	A broad shallow cup.	In forks in thick bushes.	Ditto ...	Sikkim, 18th ; eggs.
622	The yellow-naped „	Ixulus flavicollis ...	Egg-shaped domed	On the ground in tufts of grass.	Ditto ...	Kumaon, 1st ; Sikkim, 14th ; eggs.
623	The rusty-headed „ „	„ occipitalis ...	A shallow cup	In forks in small trees,	Ditto ...	Sikkim, 30th ; eggs.
626	The stripe-throated crested „ „	Yuhina gularis ...	Large globular domed.	Wedged in forks of trees or rocks.	Ditto ...	Nepal ; eggs.
628	The black chinned „ „	„ nigrimentum	A neat shallow cup.	On thick forks of large trees.	Ditto ...	Sikkim ; eggs.
629	The fire-tailed „ „	Myzornis pyrrhoura ...	Ditto ...	Ditto ...	Ditto ...	Ditto, do.
631	The Indian white-eyed „	Zosterops palpebrosus	A tiny regular cup.	Hung from twigs in trees or bushes.	Throughout India ...	Kumaon, 1st ; Conoor ; eggs
633	The fire-cap „	Cephalopyrus flammiceps.	A deep thick cup.	In holes in decayed trees.	The western Himalayas	Murree, 10th ; eggs.
634	The red-capped „	Egithaliscus erythrocephalus.	Deep compact domed.	Wedged in forks of stunted trees.	The Himalayas ...	Kumaon, 10th, 30th ; Murree ; eggs.
638	The crested black „	Lophophanes melanolophus.	A shallow pad	In holes in walls or trees.	Ditto ...	Murree, 29th ; Kashmir ; eggs.
644	The mountain „	Parus monticolus ..	A rough mass of feathers.	Ditto ...	Ditto ...	Sikkim, 14th ; Kangra ; eggs.
645	The Indian grey „	„ cinereus ...	A shallow pad	Ditto ...	In all wooded hilly tracts.	Kashmir, 27th ; Conoor, 15th ; eggs.

Nos. in Jerdon.	English Names.	Scientific Names.	Shape of Nest.	Site of Nest.	Geographical Range in Breeding Season.	Particulars of the Month.
647	The yellow-cheeked Tit	Maclolophus xanthogenys.	A shallow pad	In holes in walls or trees.	The western Himalayas	Kaugra; eggs.
654	The rufous-breasted Accentor	Accentor strophiatus ...	A deep cup	On the ground in tufts of grass.	The eastern Himalayas	Nepal season begins.
	Jerdon's „	„ jerdoni ...	Ditto ...	On lower boughs of pine trees	The western Himalayas	Kashmir; eggs.
659	The Indian carrion Crow	Corvus corone ...	A large compact cup.	High up in forks of trees.	Ditto ...	Kashmir, 30th; eggs.
660	The bow-billed Corby	„ culminatus ...	Ditto ...	Ditto ...	Throughout India proper.	Nilgiris, Bareilly, 10th; eggs.
661	The Himalayan „	„ intermedius ...	Ditto ...	Ditto ...	The Himalayas ...	Hazara; eggs.
663	The common Crow	„ impudicus ...	Ditto ...	Ditto ...	Throughout India proper.	South India; eggs.
665	The Jackdaw	„ monedula ...	A small platform.	In holes in buildings or trees.	The western Himalayas	Kashmir, 30th; eggs.
669	The Himalayan Jay	Garrulus bispecularis...	A neat compact cup.	On thick boughs of large trees.	The Himalayas ...	Murree, 6th; Kumaon, 22nd; eggs.
670	The black-throated „	„ lanceolatus ...	A loose shallow cup.	In small trees or saplings.	Himalayas from Nepal west.	Kashmir, 30th; Kumaon, 31st; eggs.
671	The red-billed blue „	Urocissa occipitalis ...	Ditto ...	In trees usually small ones.	Himalayas, Nepal to Suttej.	Masuri; eggs.
672	The yellow-billed blue „	„ flavirostris ...	Ditto ...	Ditto ...	Extreme west and east Himalaya.	Murree, 10th; Sikkim; eggs.
673	The green „	Cissa venatoria ...	Ditto ...	In trees or bamboo clumps	The eastern Himalayas	Nepal, Sikkim; eggs.
674	The Indian Treepie	Dendrocitta rufa ...	Ditto ...	In trees near the top.	Throughout continental India.	Cawnpur, 24th; Meerut, 26th; eggs.
676	The Himalayan „	„ himalayensis	Ditto ...	In small trees or bushes.	The Himalayas ...	Sikkim, 14th; Masuri; eggs.
682	The bright Starling	Sturnus nitens ...	None ...	In holes in trees or buildings.	The north-west Punjab	Kashmir, 30th; Peshawar, 1st; eggs.
683	The pied Mynah	Sturnopastor contra ...	Large globular domed	In trees at ends of boughs.	Continental India ...	Saharampur, 29th; eggs.
684	The common „	Acridotheres tristis ...	None ...	In holes in trees or buildings.	Throughout India ...	Aligurh, 20th; eggs.

No.	English name	Scientific name	Nest	Situation	Locality	Remarks
685	The bank Mynah	Acridotheres ginginianus	None ...	In deep holes in banks or walls.	The plains of upper India.	Etawah ; eggs.
686	The jungle "	" fuscus ...	Ditto ...	In holes in trees or buildings.	In all wooded hilly tracts.	Himalayas ; season begins.
687	The brahminy "	Temenuchus pagodarum	Ditto ...	In holes in decayed trees.	Throughout India proper.	Aligurh, 28th ; Oudh, 25th ; eggs.
688	The grey-headed "	" malabaricus	Ditto ...	Ditto ...	The eastern Himalayas	Sikkim ; eggs.
691	The spotted-winged Stare	Saraglossa spiloptera...	Ditto ...	Ditto ...	The western "	Kumaon, Masuri eggs.
692	The southern hill Mynah	Eulabes religiosa ...	Ditto ...	Ditto ...	Southern India ...	Travancore, 22nd ; eggs.
694	The common Weaver Bird	Ploceus baya ...	A pendent retort.	Hung from tips of boughs of trees.	Throughout India proper.	South India ; eggs.
699	The spotted Munia	Munia undulata ...	Large oval domed.	Usually in thick thorny bushes.	In all moist wooded tracts.	The Nilgiris ; eggs.
703	The pin-tailed "	" malabarica ...	Ditto ...	In small trees or shrubs.	Throughout India proper	The Punjab ; eggs.
704	The Indian Amadavat	Estrelda amandava ...	Ditto ...	In thick bushes near water.	Ditto (but locally)	The Nilgiris ; eggs.
705	The green "	" formosa ...	Ditto ...	On stalks of sugarcane.	Central India ...	Saugor ; eggs.
706	The Indian house Sparrow	Passer indicus ...	A globular mass.	In and about houses	Throughout India ...	North India ; eggs.
708	The cinnamon-headed "	" cinnamomeus ...	Ditto ...	In holes in trees or buildings.	The Himalayas ...	Kumaon, 19th ; Kangra ; eggs.
710	The tree "	" montanus ...	Ditto ...	Ditto ..	The eastern Himalayas	Sikkim, 18th ; eggs.
711	The yellow-throated "	" flavicollis ...	Ditto ...	In holes in decayed trees.	Generally throughout India.	Oudh, 4th ; Bareilly; eggs.
713	The meadow Bunting	Emberiza cia ...	A shallow cup	On the ground under shelter.	The western Himalayas	Simla ; eggs.
719	The grey-headed "	" fucata ...	Ditto ...	Ditto ...	Ditto ...	Ditto ditto.
724	The crested black and chesnut "	Melophus melanicterus	A neat shallow cup.	In holes in banks or walls.	Locally in continental India.	Sikkim, Kumaon ; eggs.
725	The black and yellow Grosbeak	Hesperiphona icterioides.	Cup-shaped.	High up in trees (often pines).	The western Himalayas	Murree, 28th ; eggs.
756	The red-winged bush Lark	Mirafra erythroptera ...	A shallow pad	On the ground by tufts of grass.	The dry plains of upper India.	Aligurh, 22nd ; eggs.
759	The desert finch "	Ammomanes luscitanica	Ditto ...	On the ground by rocks or stones.	The western Punjab ...	Nowshera ; eggs.
760	The black-bellied " "	Pyrralauda grisea ...	A tiny shallow pad.	On the ground by clod or tussock.	Thoughout the plains	Aligurh, 6th ; Oudh, 4th ; eggs.
762	The eastern sand "	Alaudala raytal ...	A tiny saucer	Ditto ...	Beds of rivers east of Jumna.	Hoshungabad, 6th ; eggs.
	The Punjab " "	" adamsi ...	Ditto ...	Ditto ...	Ditto west of Jumna	Jhelum ; eggs.

Nos. in Jerdon.	English Names.	Scientific Names.	Shape of Nest.	Site of Nest.	Geographical Range in Breeding Season.	Particulars of the Month.
766	The Himalayan sky Lark	Alauda dulcivox ...	A shallow saucer.	On the ground on grassy slopes.	The western Himalayas	Kashmir, 22nd ; eggs.
767	The Indian " ,	" gulgula ...	Ditto ...	On the ground by tuft or bush.	The plains of upper India.	Saharunpur, 20th ; eggs.
	The Nilgiri "	" australis ...	Ditto ...	Ditto ...	The hills of south India	The Nilgiris eggs.
769	The common crested ,	Galerita cristata ...	Ditto ...	Ditto ...	The dry plains of upper India.	Saharunpur, 23rd ; eggs.
	The lesser " "	" boysii ...	Ditto ...	Ditto ...	Ditto ...	Salt range ; eggs.
772	The Bengal green Pigeon	Crocopus phœnicopterus.	A small platform.	On outer forks of large trees.	Bengal and sub-Himalayas to Jumna.	Saharunpur, 16th ; eggs.
773	The southern " "	" chlorigastra	Ditto ...	In small trees or bushes,	Throughout the plains (except Bengal).	Aligurh, 4th ; eggs.
778	The kokla , "	Sphenocercus sphenurus	Ditto ...	On outer boughs of trees.	Throughout the Himalayas	Kumaon ; eggs.
781	The bronze-backed imperial ,	Carpophaga insignis...	Ditto ...	Ditto ...	The eastern Himalayas	Nepal; eggs.
784	The Himalayan wood "	Palumbus casiotis ...	Ditto ...	In small trees or thorny bushes.	The western Himalayas	Hazara. 25th ; eggs.
788	The Indian blue rock "	Columba intermedia ...	Ditto ...	On ledges of buildings chiefly.	Throughout India proper.	Meerut ; eggs.
791	The bar-tailed tree Dove	Macropygia tusalia ...	A tiny platform	In outer forks of low trees.	The eastern Himalayas	Nepal, 20th ; eggs.
792	Hodgson's turtle "	Turtur pulchrata ...	Ditto ...	On outer boughs of big trees.	Throughout the Himalayas.	Kashmir ; Kumaon, 28th ; eggs
794	The brown " "	" cambaiensis ...	Ditto ...	In low trees or bushes.	Throughout the plains	Throughout the month.
795	The spotted "	" suratensis ...	Ditto ...	Ditto ...	Throughout the wooded tracts.	Ditto.
796	The Indian ring "	" risorius ...	Ditto ...	Ditto ...	Throughout the plains	Aligurh, 6th ; Kumaon, eggs
797	The ruddy " "	" humilis ...	Ditto ...	Ditto ...	Ditto (but locally)	Throughout the month.
798	The emerald "	Chalcophaps indicus	A shallow saucer.	In thick bushes or low trees.	In all densely wooded parts	Kumaon ; Masuri ; eggs.
800	The painted Sandgrouse	Pterocles fasciatus ...	None ...	On the ground by tiny bush.	The rocky parts of upper India.	Sambhur, 4th ; eggs.

802	The common Sandgrouse	Pterocles exustus ...	None ...	On the bare open ground.	The sandy plains of upper India.	Throughout the month.
804	The Moonal	Lophophorus impeyanus.	A few dry leaves.	On the ground in thick cover.	The Himalayas only ...	Kumaon, Kangra ; eggs.
805	The red Argus	Ceriorius satyra ...	Ditto ...	Ditto in forests	The eastern Himalayas	Kumaon ; eggs.
806	The black-headed „	„ melanocephala	Ditto ...	Ditto ditto ...	The western Himalayas	Hazara, 25th ; eggs.
808	The Koklass	Pucrasia macrolopha	Ditto ...	Ditto ditto ...	The Himalayas ...	Kumaon ; eggs.
809	The Cheer	Phasianus wallichii ...	Ditto ...	Ditto in grass or bushes.	Ditto ...	Masuri, Simla ; eggs.
810	The white-crested kalij Pheasant	Gallophasis albocristatus	A shallow pad	Ditto in thick cover.	Ditto ...	Kumaon, Kangra ; eggs.
811	The black-backed „ „	„ melanotus	Ditto ...	Ditto ditto ...	The eastern Himalayas	Sikkim ; eggs.
812	The red jungle Fowl	Gallus ferruginus ...	A few dry leaves.	Ditto in dense thickets.	Sub-Himalayas, C. P and Madras	Sewaliks, Pegu ; eggs.
813	The grey „ ,	„ sonneratii ...	Ditto ...	Ditto ditto ...	Hills of south and central India.	Conoor, Mr. Aboo ; eggs.
814	The red spur „	Galloperdix spadiceus	Ditto ...	Ditto ditto ...	South India to Bundelkund.	Nilgiris, Mr. Aboo ; eggs.
815	The painted „ „	„ lunulosus	Ditto ...	Ditto ditto ...	Eastern peninsular India.	Raipur, season ends.
816	The snow Pheasant	Tetraogallus himalayensis.	Ditto ...	Ditto by rock or tuft.	The alpine Himalayas	Gangootri ; eggs.
817	The snow Partridge	Lerwa nivicola ...	Ditto ...	Unknown probably among rocks.	Ditto ...	Gangootri.
818	The black „	Francolinus vulgaris	Ditto ...	On the ground in grass or crops.	Throughout upper India.	Throughout the month.
820	The Chukor	Caccabis chukor ...	Ditto ...	Ditto on grassy slopes.	Himalayas and Salt range.	Kashmir, 20th ; Salt-range ; eggs.
821	The Seesee	Ammoperdix bonhami	Ditto ...	Ditto by stone or bush.	Salt range and trans Indus hills	Nowshera, Salt range ; eggs
822	The grey Partridge	Ortygornis ponticeriana	Ditto ...	Ditto in bush or tuft.	Open plains of India proper.	Saharunpur, 17th ; eggs.
823	The kyah „	„ gularis ...	Ditto ...	Ditto ditto ..	The eastern Sub-Himalayas.	Nepal, Tarai ; eggs.
833	The Himalayan bustard Quail	Turnix plumbipes ...	Ditto ...	Ditto ditto ...	The outer Himalayas...	Sikkim ; eggs.
836	The Indian Bustard	Eupodotis edwardsii ...	None ...	On the ground in scanty grass.	The dry parts of continental India.	Sirsa, 19th ; eggs.
840	The Indian courier Plover	Cursorius coromandelicus.	Ditto ...	Do. in fallow land	All dry plains except the Punjab.	Cawnpoor ; Deccan ; eggs.
	The cream coloured „ „	„ gallicus ...	Ditto ...	Ditto ditto	The Punjab only ...	Sirsa 8th ; eggs.
846	The greater shore „	Œgialites leschenaulti	Ditto ...	On the sand near water.	The Thibetan lakes ...	Season ends.

Nos. in Jardon.	English Names.	Scientific Names.	Shape of Nest.	Site of Nest.	Geographical Range in Breeding Season.	Particulars for the Month.
847	Pallas's shore Plover	Œgialites mongolicus	None ...	On the sand near water.	The Thibetan lakes ...	Season ends.
849	The ringed „	„ curonicus ...	Ditto ...	On bare sandy islands in rivers.	Throughout India ...	Kashmir, 14th; eggs.
855	The red-wattled „	Lobivanellus goensis ...	Ditto ...	On the ground on raised spots.	Ditto ...	Saharunpur, 3rd, 31st; eggs. Nilgiris; eggs.
856	The yellow-wattled „	Sarciophorus bilobus ...	Ditto ...	Do. in fallow land	In dry parts throughout India	Chunar, Raipur; eggs.
858	The great Indian stone „	Esacus recurvirostris ...	Ditto ...	On the bare sand on river islands	Throughout India proper.	Punjab; season ends.
859	The „ „	Œdicnemus crepitans	Ditto ...	On the ground by bushes or trees.	Ditto (but locally).	Saharunpur, 14th; eggs.
867	The Woodcock	Scolopax rusticola ...	A little grass	Ditto ...	The Himalayas ...	Kumaon; eggs.
893	The common Sandpiper	Actitis hypoleucus ...	None ...	Ditto ...	The western Himalayas	Kashmir, 23rd; eggs.
898	The Stilt	Himantopus candidus	Ditto ...	On the ground in salt-works.	Near Delhi and Goorgaon.	Throughout the month.
903	The common Coot	Fulica atra ...	A large mass of weeds.	In rice or rushes in water.	Throughout India ...	Kashmir; eggs.
905	The water Hen	Gallinula chloropus ...	Ditto ...	Ditto (or on drooping boughs).	Ditto ...	Ditto; ditto.
908	The brown Rail	Porzana akool ...	A small platform	In high grass or reeds in water.	Central and upper India.	Saugor, 27th; eggs.
924	The purple Heron	Ardea purpura ...	A loose platform.	In thick beds of reeds.	Throughout India proper.	Saugor; eggs.
933	The chesnut Bittern	Ardetta cinnamomea ...	Ditto ...	In reeds or cane brakes in water.	Continental India ...	Tipperah, Kashmir; eggs.
937	The night Heron	Nycticorax grisseus ...	Ditto ...	In high trees (or in reeds).	Throughout India ...	Kashmir, 18th; eggs.
943	The king Curlew	Geronticus papillosus	Ditto ...	High up in large trees.	Throughout the plains	Hansi; eggs.
949	The bar-headed Goose	Anser indicus ...	None ...	Unknown ...	The Thibetan lakes ...	Season ends.
954	The brahminy Duck	Casarca rutila ...	Ditto ...	In holes in cliffs ...	The upper Himalayas	Ditto.
958	The Mallard	Anas boschas ...	A shallow pad	In rushes by or in water.	The western Himalayas	Kashmir; eggs.
969	The white-eyed Duck	Aythya nyroca ...	Ditto ...	Ditto ...	Ditto ...	Ditto.

974	The crested Grebe	Podiceps cristatus ...	A large mass of weeds.	Among reeds or rushes in water.	The western Himalayas	Kashmir; eggs.
975	The little "	" philippensis...	Ditto ...	Ditto ...	Throughout India ...	Kashmir, Nilgiris; eggs.
983	The gull-billed Tern	Gelochelidon anglicus	None ...	On the sand on river islands	The western Punjab ...	Wazeerabad; eggs.
991	The black-naped Ternlet	Onochoprion melanauchen.	Ditto ...	On bare rocky islands.	The Andamans and Nicobars.	Season begins.
1005	The common Cormorant	Graculus carbo ...	A loose platform.	On rocks by rivers (or trees).	Upper India locally ...	(Requires confirmation.)

JUNE.

THE breeding season is now just past its height. In all parts of the country the shrikes, the paradise flycatcher, the common bulbuls, weaver birds and sparrows, the black-bellied finch lark, doves, the common sandgrouse, and the little grebe are breeding every where; and throughout the plains the *purple coot* and *waterhens* are pairing and building.

In the HIMALAYAS, a few of the hawks and one of the swallows are still laying. The goatsuckers, bee eater, and roller all have eggs. Also the little kingfishers and broadbills in the low valleys. The Marshall's barbet begins to lay. All the cuckoos and honeysuckers have eggs, and in the far west nuthatches' and tree creepers' eggs may still be found. Most of the minivets, drongos, flycatchers, wrens, thrushes of all kinds, blackbirds, most of the babblers, laughing thrushes, bulbuls, orioles, robins, chats, reed warblers, hill warblers, tree warblers (except the abrornis group, which are early breeders), white throats, forktails, wagtails, pipits, all the hill tits (*Leiotrichinæ*), the carrion crow, the jays and magpies, the mynahs, munias, sparrows, buntings, skylark, pigeons, doves, a few of the pheasants, partridges, grouse and quail (these latter only at the higher elevations), sandpipers, coots, rails, bittern, and some ducks are laying throughout the month. Towards the end of it the *red-winged wall creeper*, *striated jay thrush*, *white-throated bulbul*, *fulvous-breasted* and *large hill warblers*, *tree sparrows*, most of the *finches*, and the *ruddy rail* are pairing and building. The "sacfa" or *Hodgson's partridge* also pairs at the end of this month, in the alpine Himalayas.

In the PUNJAB, the crested honey buzzard, and possibly also some of the eagles and kites have eggs. All the bee eaters are laying. The roller, white-breasted kingfisher, koel, concal, sirkeer, the white-eared bulbul, golden oriole, treepie, mynahs, bush larks, finch larks, black partridge, bustard, plovers, stilts, white-necked storks, and king curlew are all breeding. While the *egrets*, *pond herons*, *cattle herons*, *bitterns*, *night herons*, and *spoonbills* are beginning to pair and build.

In the NORTH-WEST PROVINCES, the true eagles, buzzards, kites, and screech owl, are still breeding. The mosque swallow has eggs also. The goatsuckers and rollers, the little kingfisher, the common gold

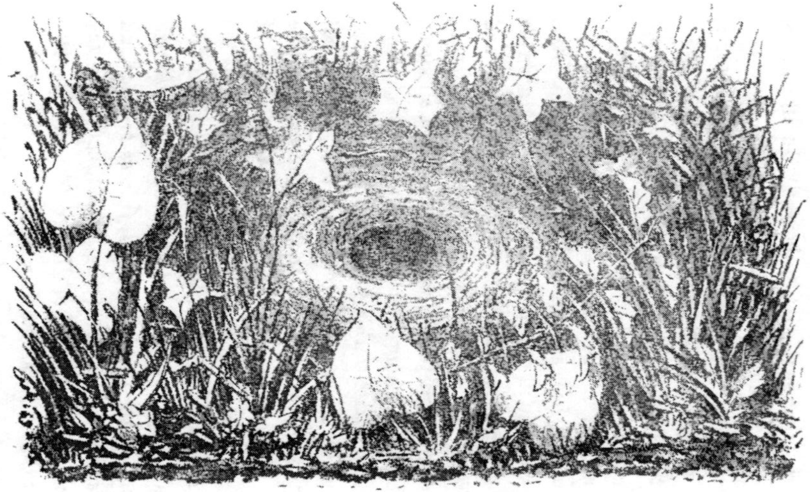

MARSHALL, DEL.

NEST OF THE WHITE-BROWED WARBLER.

(Abrornis, albosuperciliaris.)

back woodpecker (second brood), the koel and concal, the purple honey-sucker, the drongo shrike, white-browed fantail, yellow-eyed babbler, rufous-bellied wren babbler, the Bengal and large grey babblers, the bulbuls, and orioles are breeding. Eggs of the brown-backed robin may still be found. Stewart's wren warbler has begun to lay, so has the earth brown wren warbler and the Indian white-eyed tit and the common crow. The treepie, mynahs, black and chestnut bunting, bush larks, green pigeons, partridges, plovers, white-necked storks, shell ibis, white ibis, black-backed geese, and whistling teal all have eggs during the month. While towards the end of it the *grey-capped wren warbler*, *pheasant-tailed jacana*, *egrets*, *pond herons*, *cattle herons*, some *bitterns*, *night herons*, *spoonbills*, *cotton teal*, and *snake birds* commence to pair and build.

In Bengal, the palm swifts, crested swifts, white-breasted king-fisher, broad-billed rollers, lesser concals, Tickell's flowerpecker, babblers, common bulbuls, common wren warblers, bush larks, florikin, sarus cranes, little pond heron, bitterns, black-backed geese, whistling teal, and pink-headed ducks have eggs. Besides, many other species which breed at this time in the North-West Provinces and Central India. At the end of the month, the *blue-breasted quail*, *bronze-winged jacana*, *watercock*, *ruddy rail*, and *great heron* begin to pair and build.

In Central India, the shikra, the dusky crag martin, most of the nightjars, cuckoo shrikes, small minivets, blue redbreasts, rufous-bellied wren babblers, black-headed orioles, robins, chats, Hodgson's wren warbler, rufous-fronted wren warbler, treepies, brahminy mynahs, bush larks, crown crest larks, plovers, brown rails, herons, and white ibis are the characteristic birds that breed. While *Jerdon's green bulbul*, the *black-backed green bulbul*, the *allied wren warbler*, the *Indian titlark*, the *green amadavat*, the *bronze-winged jacana*, the *white-breasted water-hen*, the *egrets*, *pond herons*, *cattle herons*, and *bitterns* begin pairing and building at the close of the mouth.

In Southern India, the lesser kestril is breeding in the Nilgiris. Also the house swallow and the hill swiftlet, the orange minivet, the white-bellied drongo, the black-naped azure flycatcher, the white-spotted fantail, the blue redbreast, the yellow-eyed babbler, quaker thrushes, white-throated wren babbler, laughing thrush, rufous-tailed and jungle babblers, most of the bulbuls, the ashy and fuscous wren warblers, the rufous grass warbler, the Indian amadavat, the sky lark, the woodpigeon, the peafowl, the red spur fowl, and courier plovers have eggs wherever the birds are found, and the *rufous-bellied munia* is building at the end of the month.

The sea terns and gulls lay throughout this month on the rocky islands in the bay of Bengal, Indian ocean, Red sea, and Persian gulf.

JUNE.

Nos. in Jerdon.	English Names.	Scientific Names.	Shape of Nest.	Site of Nest.	Geographical Range in Breeding Season.	Particulars for the Month.
17	The Kestril	Tinnunculus alaudarius	A large platform.	On ledges of cliffs	The Himalayas, Nilgiris, and Suleimans.	Kashmir, 15th; Kangra, 5th; eggs.
18	The lesser "	Erythropus cenchris ...	Ditto ...	Ditto ...	The Nilgiris ...	Very little known.
23	The Shikra	Micronisus badius ...	A loose cup	High up in lofty trees.	Throughout India ...	Central Provinces; eggs.
24	The sparrow Hawk	Accipiter nisus ...	A small platform.	In trees in wooded valleys.	The western Himalayas	Kashmir, 2nd; eggs.
	The dove "	" melaschistus	Ditto ...	On ledges of cliffs	The Himalayas only ...	Simla, 5th; eggs.
28	The spotted Eagle	Aquila nævia ...	A large platform.	In high trees near top.	Continental India (locally.)	Saharunpur, 3rd, 11th; eggs
29	The Indian tawny "	" vindhyana ...	Ditto ...	Ditto ...	The plains of upper India.	Saharunpur, 3rd; eggs.
30	The long-legged "	" hastata ...	Ditto ...	Ditto ...	Continental India (locally.	Saharunpur, 5th; eggs.
	The changeable hawk "	Spizaetus caligatus ...	Ditto ...	Ditto ...	Bengal and sub-Himalayas.	Season nearly over,
48	The white-eyed Buzzard	Poliornis teesa ...	A small platform.	In forks of trees	Plains of central India	Saharunpur, 9th; eggs.
57	The crested honey "	Pernis cristata ...	Irregular platform.	Ditto ...	Throughout India (locally.)	Saharunpur, 1st, 17th; eggs
59	The black-winged Kite	Elanus melanopterus	A shallow compact cup.	Ditto ...	Ditto ...	The Dehra Doon.
60	The Indian screech Owl	Strix indica ...	None ...	In holes in trees or buildings.	Throughout the plains	Agra, 10th; eggs.
	The barefoot scops "	Ephialtes spilocephala	Ditto ...	In holes in trees ...	The Himalayas ...	Murree, 1st; eggs.
83	The Nilgiri house Swallow	Hirundo domicola ...	A semi-circular saucer.	On buildings or in caves.	The Nilgiris and Tenasserim.	Conoor; season ends.
85	The great Indian mosque "	" daurica ...	Tubular, retort-shaped.	Ditto ...	The Himalayas ...	Throughout the month.
	The " "	" erythropygia	Ditto ...	Ditto ...	Throughout India proper.	Saharunpur, 5th; eggs.

Nos. in Jerdon.	English Names.	Scientific Names.	Shape of Nest.	Site of Nest.	Geographical Range in Breeding Season.	Particulars for the Month.
90	The dusky crag Martin	Cotyle concolor ...	A semi-circular cup.	On buildings or in caves.	Throughout India (locally).	Bundelkhund; eggs.
102	The palm Swift	Cypselus battassiensis	A tiny watch pocket.	On leaves of the toddy palm.	Throughout the plains (locally).	Bengal; eggs.
103	The southern hill Swiftlet	Collocalia unicolor ...	Small semi-circular saucer.	In caves or on rocks	The Nilgiris and Assamboo hills	Nilgiris; season ends.
104	The Indian crested Swift	Dendrochelidon coronatus.	A tiny half saucer.	On dead boughs of high trees.	Forests in India proper.	Darjeeling Terai, 1st; eggs.
108	The Nilgiri Nightjar	Caprimulgus kelaarti	None ...	On the ground often near bushes.	Peninsular India ...	Raipur (C. P.); eggs.
109	The large Bengal ,,	,, albonotatus.	Ditto ...	Ditto ...	Wooded tracts in upper India.	Kumaon, 7th; eggs.
112	The common Indian ,,	, asiaticus	Ditto ...	Ditto ...	Throughout upper India.	Throughout the month.
114	Franklin's ,,	,, monticolus.	Ditto ...	Ditto ...	In all wooded hilly tracts.	Ditto.
	Unwin's ,,	,, unwini	Ditto ...	Ditto ...	The extreme west Himalayas.	Murree, 16th; eggs,
117	The common Bee eater	Merops viridis ...	Ditto ...	In deep holes in banks or plains.	Throughout India proper.	Season nearly over.
118	The blue-tailed ,,	,, philippensis ...	Ditto ...	Ditto ..	Ditto ...	Lahore; eggs.
120	The Egyptian ,,	,, ægyptius ...	Ditto ...	Ditto ...	Plains of the Punjab ...	Delhi; eggs.
121	The European ,,	,, apiaster ...	Ditto ...	Ditto ...	The western Himalayas	Kashmir, 12th; eggs.
123	The common Roller	Coracias indica ...	Ditto ...	In holes in trees or buildings.	Throughout India proper.	Hansi, Meerut; eggs.
125	The European ,,	,, garrula ...	Ditto ...	Ditto ...	The western Himalayas	Kashmir, 10th; eggs.
126	The broad-billed ,,	Eurystomus orientalis	Ditto ...	In holes in lofty trees.	Eastern sub-Himalayas	(Requires confirmation.)
129	The white-breasted Kingfisher	Halcyon smyrnensis ...	Ditto ...	In holes in river banks or wells.	Throughout India proper.	Hansi, 28th; eggs.
134	The little Indian ,,	Alcedo bengalensis ...	Ditto ...	In holes in banks near water.	Ditto ...	Doon, 14th; Kashmir; eggs.
138	The yellow-throated Broadbill	Psarisomus dalhousiæ	Large, rough, pear-shaped	Pendent from twigs in high trees.	The eastern Himalayas	Kumaon, 16th; eggs (extracted).

140	The great Indian Hornbill	Homraius bicornis ..	None ...	In holes in lofty decayed trees.	Eastern sub-Himalayas	Season nearly over.
144	The northern grey "	Meniceros bicornis ...	Ditto ...	In holes in decayed trees.	Throughout the plains	Ditto.
154	The Himalayan pied Woodpecker	Picus himalayanus ...	Ditto ...	In artificial holes in trees.	The Himalayas to Sikkim.	Simla; eggs; season ends.
156	The lesser black "	" cathpharius ...	Ditto ...	Ditto ...	The eastern Himalayas	Nepal, eggs; ditto.
157	The Indian spotted "	" macei ...	Ditto ...	Ditto ...	Himalayas and eastern Bengal.	Murree, 2nd; eggs; do.
172	The black-naped green "	Gecinus occipitalis ...	Ditto ...	Ditto ...	The Himalayas only ...	Kashmir, 30th; eggs.
180	The common gold back "	Brachypternus aurantius.	Ditto ...	Ditto ...	Throughout the plains	Saharunpur, 7th; eggs.
191	The Marshall's Barbet	Megalæma marshallorum.	Ditto ...	Ditto ...	The Himalayas only ...	Kashmir, 22nd; Kumaon. 23rd; eggs.
192	Hodson's green "	" hodgsoni	Ditto ...	Ditto ...	The outer Himalayas	Nepal; season ends.
199	The common Cuckoo	Cuculus canorus ...	(Habits parasitic).	Lays in bushchats' or pipits' nests.	The Himalayas ...	Kotegurh, 11th; eggs; season ends.
201	The hoary-headed "	" poliocephalus	Ditto ...	Lays in warblers' nests.	The western Himalayas	Kashmir, 2nd; eggs; season ends.
204	The hill "	" striatus	Ditto ...	Lays in laughing thrushes' nests.	The Himalayas ...	Kashmir, 17th; eggs; season ends.
207	The large hawk "	Hierococcyx sparverioides.	Ditto (?) ...	Ditto ...	The Himalayas and Nilgiris.	Nepal; season ends.
212	The pied crested "	Coccystes melanoleucus	Ditto ...	Lays in babblers' nests.	Troughout India ...	Season commences.
214	The Koil	Eudynamis orientalis	Ditto ...	Lays in crows' nests	Throughout the plains	Throughout the month.
217	The common Concal	Centropus rufipennis	Large, rough, domed.	In clumps of grass or thorny thickets	Throughout India proper.	Cawnpur, 25th; Hansi; eggs.
218	The lesser "	" viridis ...	Ditto ...	Ditto ...	Eastern Bengal ...	Dacca; eggs.
220	The Bengal Sirkeer	Taccocua sirkee ...	A rough shallow cup.	In low trees or thick bushes.	Plains of upper India	Hansi; eggs.
225	The Himalayan red Honeysucker	Œthopyga miles ...	Pear-shaped, side entrance.	Hanging from tips of branches.	The eastern Himalayas	Nepal; season ends.
229	The maroon-backed "	" nipalensis	Ditto ...	Ditto ...	The eastern Himalayas and Khasia hills.	Ditto.
231	The black-breasted "	" saturata ...	Ditto ...	Ditto ...	Ditto ...	Ditto.
234	The purple "	Arachnechthra asiatica	Ditto ...	Ditto ...	Throughout India ...	Aligurh, 12th; Kashmir; eggs.
238	Tickell's Flowerpecker	Dicæum minimum ...	Ditto ...	Ditto ...	Bombay central and N. E. India.	Calcutta, 26th; eggs.
	Hodgson's Treecreeper	Certhia hodgsoni ...	A rough cup	In crevices on high trees.	The western Himalayas	Kashmir, 5th; eggs.

Nos. in Jerdon.	English Names.	Scientific Names.	Shape of Nest.	Site of Nest.	Geographical Range in Breeding Season.	Particulars for the Month.
249	The white-cheeked Nuthatch	Sitta leucopsis ...	A shallow pad	In natural hollows in trees.	The western Himalayas	Kashmir, 5th; eggs.
256	The Indian grey Shrike	Lanius lahtora ...	A thick massive cup.	In small trees or thorny bushes.	Throughout the dry plains.	Aligurh, 17th; Agra; eggs.
257	The rufous-backed „	„ erythronotus ...	Ditto ...	Ditto ...	Throughout India ...	Throughout the month.
	The pale „ „ „	„ caniceps ...	Ditto ...	Ditto ...	The hilly parts of India	Doon, 21st; Nilgiris; eggs.
258	The grey-backed „	„ tephronotus ...	Ditto ...	Ditto ...	The eastern Himalayas	Kumaon, 30th; Sikkim; eggs.
259	The black cap „	„ nigriceps ...	Ditto ...	Ditto ...	Hill ranges of eastern India.	Ditto.
260	The bay-backed „	„ vittatus ...	A neat cup	Ditto ...	Throughout India ...	Throughout the month.
268	The pied cuckoo „	Volvocivora sykesii ...	A small saucer.	In horizontal forks of trees.	In forests throughout India.	Bundelkhund; eggs.
269	The dark-grey „ „	„ melaschistus	Ditto ...	Ditto ...	The Himalayas ...	Nepal, Murree; eggs.
270	The large-grey „ „	Graucalus macei ...	A broad saucer.	At tops of lofty trees.	Throughout India proper.	Central Provinces; eggs.
271	The large Minivet	Pericrocotus speciosus	A small deep cup.	High trees near tips of boughs.	The Himalayas ...	The Doon, 6th, 17th; eggs.
272	The orange „	„ flammeus	Ditto ...	Ditto ...	The hills of south India	Nilgiris, 24th; eggs.
273	The short-billed „	„ brevirostris	Ditto ...	Ditto ...	The Himalayas ...	Season nearly over.
275	The rosy „	„ roseus ...	Ditto ...	Ditto ...	Ditto ...	Murree, 12th; eggs.
276	The small „	„ peregrinus	Ditto ...	Ditto ...	Throughout India proper.	Jhansi, Saugor; eggs.
278	The common drongo Shrike	Dicrurus albirictus ...	A loose saucer.	In horizontal forks of trees.	Throughout India ...	N. W. P.; eggs; Kumaon; young.
	Walden's „ „	„ waldeni ...	A neat saucer.	Ditto ...	The Himalayas ...	Kumaon, 2nd; Kashmir 10th; eggs.
281	The white-bellied „ „	„ cœrulescens ...	A loose saucer.	Ditto ...	The hilly regions of India.	Season commences.
282	The bronzed „ „	Chaptia ænea ...	A broad saucer.	Ditto ...	In forests throughout India.	Nepal, 6th; eggs.
288	The oar-tailed „ „	Bhringa remifer ...	Ditto ...	Ditto ...	The eastern Himalayas	Sikkim; eggs.
286	The hair-crested „ „	Chibia hottentota ...	Ditto ...	Ditto ...	Ditto ...	Season nearly over.

288	The paradise Flycatcher	Tchitria paradisei ...	A small delicate cup.	In trees on thin branches.	Moist forests throughout India.	Throughout the month.
290	The black-naped azure „	Myiagra azurea ...	A deep compact cup.	Ditto ...	Ditto ...	Nilgiris, 10th, 24th; eggs.
291	The white-throated Fantail	Leucocerca fuscoventris	A tiny inverted cone.	Ditto (or bushes)	Ditto (continental India.)	Kashmir, 27th; Kumaon, 5th; eggs.
292	The white-browed „	„ aureola ...	A tiny cup	Ditto ...	Throughout continental India.	Aligurh, 15th; Murree; eggs.
293	The white-spotted „	„ pectoralis...	A tiny inverted cone.	Ditto ...	The hills of south India	Nilgiris; eggs.
294	The yellow-bellied „	Chelidorhynx hypoxantha.	A deep neat cup.	Ditto ...	The sub-Himalayas ...	Kumaon, Nepal.
295	The grey-headed Flycatcher	Cryptolopha cinereocapilla.	A watch pocket.	Against mossy trunks of trees.	Himalayas, Nilgiris, and Wynaad.	Kumaon, 26th, 29th; eggs.
296	The sooty „	Hemichelidon fuliginosa.	A compact pad	Ditto (or on stumps)	The western Himalayas	Kashmir, 5th; eggs.
301	The verditer „	Eumyias melanops ...	A thick cup	In mossy banks or under bridges.	The Himalayas ...	Kashmir, 7th; Kumaon, eggs.
304	The blue-throated Redbreast	Cyornis rubeculoides...	Ditto (small)	Holes in banks or decayed trees.	Ditto ...	Masuri, 13th; eggs.
305	The southern blue „	„ banyumas ...	Ditto ...	Ditto ...	Southern India ...	Nilgiris; eggs.
306	Tickell's „ „	„ tickelliæ ...	Ditto ...	Ditto ...	Central and southern India	Hoshungabad, 24th; eggs.
310	The white-browed blue Flycatcher	Muscicapula superciliaris.	Ditto ...	In holes or cracks in trees.	The Himalayas ...	Kashmir, 14th; Kumaon, 24th; eggs.
315	Macgregor's fairy „	Niltava macgregoriæ ...	A large thick cup.	In clefts on rocks or under stumps.	The eastern Himalayas	Season nearly over.
316	The large „ „	„ grandis ...	A large thick pad.	Ditto ...	Ditto ...	Ditto.
320	The slaty „	Siphia leucomelanura	A massive little cup.	On the ground at foot of trees.	The western Himalayas	Kashmir, 6th; eggs.
321	The rufous-breasted „	„ superciliaris...	A deep cup	Ditto ...	The Himalayas ...	Nepal; season ends.
324	The grey robin „	„ hyperythra ...	A large deep cup.	In forks in low bushes.	Ditto ...	Ditto.
	The white-tailed „ „	Erythrosterna parva ...	(Unknown)	(Unknown)	The western Himalayas	Kashmir.
333	The Nepal Wren	Troglodytes nipalensis	Neat globular, domed.	Low down in creepers on trees.	The Himalayas ...	Kashmir; eggs.
	The Kashmir Flycatcher	„ neglectus	Ditto ...	Ditto ...	Ditto ...	Ditto.
348	The yellow-billed whistling Thrush	Myiophonus temminckii.	A massive saucer.	On ledges of banks near water.	Ditto ...	Kashmir 1st; Masuri, 16th; eggs.

Nos. in Jerdon.	English Names.	Scientific Names.	Shape of Nest.	Site of Nest.	Geographical Range in Breeding Season.	Particulars for the Month.
344	The Nepal ground Thrush	Hydrornis nipalensis...	Large, globular, domed.	In banks often under a bush.	The eastern Himalayas	Sikkim ; season ends.
351	The blue rock ,,	Petrocossyphus cyaneus.	Cup-shaped.	In holes in banks or walls.	The western ,,	Murree, 4th ; eggs.
353	The blue-headed chat ,,	Orocetes cinclorhynchus.	A neat cup	In banks or at roots of trees.	The Himalayas ...	Kashmir, 18th ; eggs ; Kumaon, 4th ; young.
355	The rusty-throated bush ,,	Geocichla citrina ...	A broad cup	In forks of small trees.	Ditto ...	Masuri, Murree ; eggs.
356	The dusky ,, ,,	,, unicolor ...	Ditto ...	In thick forks or on stumps.	Ditto ...	Kashmir, 18th ; Kumaon. 6th ; eggs.
357	Ward's pied Blackbird	Turdulus wardii ...	Ditto ...	Ditto ,,	Ditto ...	Masuri ; eggs.
361	The grey-winged ,,	Merula boulboul ...	Ditto ...	Ditto ...	Ditto ...	Kashmir, 6th ; Kumaon, 10th ; eggs.
363	The grey-headed Ouzel	,, castanea ...	Ditto ...	In banks sometimes on stumps.	Ditto ...	Kashmir, 8th ; eggs.
368	The Indian missel Thrush	Turdus hodgsoni ...	Ditto ...	In thick forks of trees.	Ditto ...	Kooloo, 22nd ; eggs.
371	The small-billed mountain ,,	Oreocincla dauma ...	Ditto ...	Ditto ...	Ditto ...	Kashmir, 6th ; eggs.
385	The yellow-eyed Babbler	Pyctorhis sinensis ...	A deep neat cup.	On stalks of herbs or bushes.	Throughout India proper. ...	Doon, Agra, Nilgiris ; eggs.
388	The Nepal quaker Thrush	Alcippe nipalensis ...	A deep massive cup.	In low thick bushes	The eastern Himalayas	Sikkim ; eggs.
389	The Nilgiri ,, ,,	,, poiocephala ...	Ditto ...	In thick bushes or saplings.	The hills of south India	Kotagiri, 5th ; eggs.
390	The black-headed ,, ,,	,, atriceps ...	Ditto ...	Low down in grass or reeds.	Ditto ...	Kotagiri, 17th ; eggs.
391	The black-headed wren Babbler	Stachyris nigriceps ...	Ditto ...	In banks near roots of shrubs.	The eastern Himalayas	Sikkim, 17th ; eggs.
392	The red-billed ,, ,,	,, pyrrhops ...	Ditto ...	Near the ground in low bushes.	Western Himalayas to Nepal.	Kashmir ; eggs.
393	The red-headed ,, ,,	,, ruficeps ...	Ditto ...	In bamboo clumps chiefly.	The eastern Himalayas	Nepal ; eggs.
397	The rufous-bellied ,, ,,	Dumetia hyperythra ..	Neat, globular, domed.	In the roots of bamboo clumps.	Central and upper India	Chunar, 26th ; eggs.

398	The white-throated wren Babbler	Dumetia albogularis ...	Neat, globular, domed.	In low bushes ...	Southern India ...	Kotagiri, 9th, 17th ; eggs.
	The Nepal spotted " "	Pellorneum nipalensis	Ditto ...	Low down in bushes or grass.	The eastern Himalayas	Nepal, Sikkim ; eggs.
405	The rusty-cheeked scimitar "	Pomatorhinus erythrogenys.	Large, globular, domed.	On the ground in bush or tuft,	The Himalayas ...	Nepal, 6th, 8th ; Sikkim, 17th ; eggs.
406	The slender-billed " "	Xiphoramphus superciliaris.	Ditto ...	Low down in grass or bushes.	The eastern Himalayas	Nepal, 12th ; eggs.
407	The white-crested laughing Thrush	Garrulax leucolophus	A broad shallow cup.	In thick bushes or low trees.	Himalayas east of Sutlej	The Doon, 28th ; eggs.
408	The grey-sided " "	" cœrulatus ...	A large deep cup.	In saplings or small trees.	The eastern Himalayas	Sikkim, 17th ; eggs.
411	The white-throated " "	" albogularis...	A broad shallow cup.	In thick bushes or low trees.	The Himalayas ...	Kashmir, 6th ; Kumaon, 4th ; eggs.
412	The black-gorgetted " "	" pectoralis ...	Ditto ...	In bamboo clumps	The eastern Himalayas	Sikkim ; eggs.
413	The necklaced " "	" moniliger ...	A large deep cup	In thick bushes or low trees.	Ditto ...	Sikkim, 6th ; eggs.
415	The red headed " "	Trochalopteron erythrocephalum.	Ditto ...	In small trees or bushes.	The western Himalayas	Throughout the month.
416	The yellow-winged " "	" chrysopterum	Ditto ...	Ditto ...	The eastern "	Nepal, Sikkim ; eggs.
417	The plain-coloured " "	" subunicolor...	Ditto ...	Ditto ...	Ditto ...	Ditto.
418	The variegated " "	" variegatum ...	Ditto ...	Ditto ...	The western Himalayas	Murree, 15th ; Simla, 25th ; eggs.
420	The blue winged " "	" squamatum...	Ditto ...	Ditto ...	The eastern "	Sikkim, 10th ; eggs.
421	The red-throated " "	" rufogulare ...	Ditto ...	In thick bushes or trees.	Ditto ...	Simla, Mussoorie.
423	The Nilgiri " "	" cacchinans ...	Ditto ...	In trees or small bushes.	The Nilgiris ...	Season nearly over.
425	The streaked " "	" lineatum ...	Cup-shaped	In low bushes or banks.	The Himalayas ...	Throughout the month.
426	The bristly " "	" imbricatum...	Ditto ...	On the ground under bushes.	The eastern Himalayas	Nepal, 1st ; eggs.
428	The hoary Barwing	Actinodura nipalensis	A shallow cup	In holes in rocks or banks.	Ditto ...	Nepal, Sikkim ; eggs.
429	The black-headed Sibia	Sibia capistrata ...	A neat deep cup.	In outer twigs of trees or bushes.	The Himalayas ...	Kumaon, 29th ; Murree, 5th ; eggs.
	The Assam "	" gracilis ...	Ditto ...	At tops of tall trees	Assam ...	Sikkim, 17th ; eggs.

Nos in Jerdon.	English Names.	Scientific Names.	Shape of Nest.	Site of Nest.	Geographical Range in Breeding Season.	Particulars for the Month.
430	The magpie Sibia	Sibia picaoides ...	A neat dee p cup.	At tops of tall trees	The eastern Himalayas	Darjeeling, 17th ; eggs.
432	The Bengal Babbler	Malacocircus canorus	A loose straggling cup.	In thick bushes or saplings.	Plains of continental India.	Cawnpur, 18th ; Calcutta, 23rd ; eggs.
433	The white-headed „	„ griseus ...	Ditto ...	In thorny trees or hedges.	Plains of south India	Season nearly over.
434	The jungle „	„ malabaricus	Ditto ...	In thick thorny bushes or trees.	The hills of south India.	Nilgiris ; eggs.
435	The rufous-tailed „	„ somervilli	Ditto ...	Ditto ...	The western Ghats ...	Season nearly over.
436	The large grey „	„ malcolmi ...	Cup-shaped	In thorny trees (acacia).	Througout the plains ...	Meerut, 14th ; Cawnpur, 20th ; eggs.
438	The striated bush „	Chattarhœa caudata ...	Ditto ...	In clumps of grass or bushes.	Ditto ...	Saharunpur, Oude ; eggs.
444	The Himalayan black Bulbul	Hypsepetes psaroides	A neat cup	In forks of bushes or trees.	The Himalayas ...	Kumaon, 8th ; Kashmir, 16th ; eggs.
445	The Nilgiri „ „	„ nilgiriensis	A rough shallow cup	In bushes or clumps of parasites.	The Nilgiris ...	Season nearly over.
447	The rufous-bellied „	„ macclellandi	A neat shallow saucer	Hung from forks in thick foliage.	The eastern Himalayas	Ditto.
452	The white-browed bush „	Ixos luteolus ...	A loose straggling cup.	In outer twigs of bushes or trees.	Southern and eastern India.	Bombay, 11th ; eggs.
458	The white-cheeked crested „	Otocompsa leucogenys	A neat cup	In bushes or low trees.	The Himalayas ...	Throughout the month.
459	The white-eared „	„ leucotis	Ditto ...	In dense thorny bushes.	Western continental India.	Sind ; eggs.
	The southern red whiskered „	„ fuscicaudata	Ditto ...	In isolated bushes.	The hills of south India	Season nearly over.
461	The common Bengal „	Pycnonotus pygœus ...	A small slender cup.	In small trees or bushes.	Himalayas and eastern Bengal.	Throughout the month.
462	The common Madras „	„ pusillus ...	Ditto ...	Ditto ...	Throughout the plains	Ditto.
470	The Indian golden Oriole	Oriolus kundoo ...	A neat deep cup.	Hung from slender forks in trees.	Throughout India ...	Ditto.
472	The black-headed „	„ melanocephalus	Ditto ...	Ditto ...	Eastern continental India.	Allahabad, Raipur (C. P.) ; eggs.

475	The magpie Robin	Copsychus saularis ...	A shallow saucer.	In holes in trees or walls.	Throughout India ...	The Himalayas; eggs.
480	The brown-backed "	Thamnobia cambaiensis	A small cup	In holes in banks or buildings.	Plains of upper India	Throughout the month.
481	The black Bushchat	Pratincola caprata ...	A shallow pad	On the ground by clod or tuft.	Himalayas to central India.	Sambhur, 23rd; eggs.
483	The common Indian "	" indica ...	A small cup	In holes in banks or walls.	Himalayas and north-western Punjab.	Throughout the month.
486	The iron grey "	" ferrea ...	Ditto ...	Ditto ...	The Himalayas ...	Ditto.
494	The brown Rockchat	Cercomela fusca ...	A shallow pad	Ditto ...	Dry parts of continental India	Saugor, Rajputana; eggs.
505	The phumbous water Robin	Rutacilla fuliginosa ...	A small cup	In clefts or rocks by rivers.	The Himalayas ...	Kashmir, Kangra; eggs.
508	The white-breasted blue Woodchat.	Ianthia rufilata ...	Ditto ...	In banks or under logs.	The western Himalayas	Kashmir, 2nd; eggs.
513	The white-tailed Rubythroat	Calliope pectoralis ...	A shallow saucer.	In crevices of rocks	The eastern "	Sikkim; eggs.
515	The large reed Warbler	Acrocephalus brunnescens.	A very deep cup.	In reeds growing in water.	The western "	Kashmir, 12th; eggs.
516	The lesser " "	" dumetorum	Globular, domed.	In thick bushes or brambles.	The Himalayas ...	Kashmir, Kangra; eggs.
517	The paddy-field "	" agricolus ..	A very deep cup.	In brambles or thick herbage.	The western Himalayas	Kashmir, 16th; eggs.
526	The strong-footed hill "	Horornis fortipes ...	A small massive cup.	In low thick brushwood.	The eastern "	Sikkim, 12th; eggs.
530	The Indian Tailorbird	Orthotomus longicauda	Deep cup.	Among leaves sewn together.	Throughout India ...	Sikkim, Nilgiris; eggs.
534	The ashy wren Warbler	Prinia socialis ..	A cup sewn in leaves.	Hanging in low bushes.	Southern India ...	Kotagiri; eggs.
535	Stewart's " "	" stewarti ...	Nearly globular.	Ditto (or grass or herbs).	Upper India ...	Cawnpur, 27th; Doon; eggs.
538	Hodgson's " "	" hodgsoni ...	A cup sewn to a leaf.	Hanging in low bushes.	Central India ...	Season begins.
539	The rufous grass "	Cisticola schœnicola ...	A deep narrow purse.	In tufts of fine grass in swamps.	Throughout the plains	South India only.
	The fuscous wren "	Drymoipus fuscus ...	Deep, neat, domed.	In small bushes or grass.	The Terai, Deccan, and Nilgiris.	Nilgiris; eggs.
	The earth brown " "	" terricolor...	Deep, often-domed.	Ditto ...	Plains of continental India.	Calcutta, 24th; Cawnpur, 27th; eggs.
547	The brown hill "	Suya criniger ...	Deep, flimsy-domed.	In low bushes on hill sides.	The Himalayas	Kangra, Doon; eggs.
548	The dusky " "	" fuliginosa ...	Deep neat, domed.	Ditto ...	The eastern Himalayas	Sikkim; eggs.

Nos. in Jerdon.	English Names.	Scientific Names.	Shape of Nest.	Site of Nest.	Geographical Ranges in Breeding Season.	Particulars for the Month.
549	The black-throated hill Warbler	Suya atrogularis ...	Deep, neat, domed.	In small bushes or grass.	The eastern Himalayas	Kumaon, Sikkim; eggs.
551	The rufous-fronted wren „	Franklinia buchanani	Deep, ragged, often-domed	In bushes or low scrub.	Western continental India.	Aligurh, 30th; Chunar; eggs.
552	The aberrant tree „	Neornis flavolivacea ...	A neat shallow cup.	In bushes or low trees.	The eastern Himalayas	Nepal; eggs.
	Tytler's „ „	Phylloscopus tytleri ...	A deep thick cup.	At tips of boughs of high firs.	The western „	Kashmir, 4th; eggs.
562	The large-crowned „	Reguloides occipitalis	A loose cup.	In holes in stumps or banks.	Ditto ...	Murree, 17th; eggs.
565	The crowned „	„ superciliosus	Large, rough, globular.	On the ground in mossy banks.	Ditto ...	Kashmir, 5th; eggs.
566	The Dalmatian „	„ proregulus	Neat, compact, domed.	At tips of boughs of high firs.	Ditto ...	Kashmir, 2nd; eggs.
	The grey-faced „	Abrornis chloronotus ...	Purse-shaped (?)	Hung from twigs in bushes.	The eastern Himalayas	(Requires confirmation)
	The chestnut-headed „	„ castaneiceps...	Ditto (?)...	In thick bushes or mossy banks.	Ditto ...	Nepal; eggs.
580	The Indian golden-crested Wren	Regulus himalayensis	A deep pouch	Hung from outer twigs in firs.	The Himalayas ...	Sutlej valley, 8th; young.
582	The Indian Whitethroat	Sylvia affinis ...	A shallow cup	In low bushes or thickets.	The western Himalayas	Kashmir; eggs.
584	The western spotted Forktail	Henicurus maculatus	A massive cup	On banks or rocks by water.	Ditto ...	Kangra; eggs.
586	The slaty back „	„ schistaceus	Ditto ...	Ditto ...	The eastern Himalayas	Sikkim; eggs.
	The eastern spotted „	„ guttatus ...	Ditto ...	Ditto ...	Ditto ...	Sikkim, 1st; eggs.
590	The whitefaced Wagtail	Motacilla luzionensis...	A shallow pad	Under stones or wood in river beds	The western Himalayas	Kashmir, 1st; eggs.
592	The grey and yellow „	„ melanope ...	Ditto ...	Ditto ..	Ditto ...	Kashmir, 3rd; eggs.
596	The Indian Pipit	Anthus arboreus ...	A shallow cup	On the ground on grassy slopes.	The alpine Himalayas	Kooloo, 3rd; eggs.
597	The tree „	„ maculatus ..	Ditto ...	Ditto ...	Ditto ...	Kotegurh, Kumaon; eggs.
605	The ruddy „	„ roseus ...	Ditto ...	Ditto ...	Ditto ...	Gurhwal, 1st; eggs.
604	The brown rock „	Agrodroma griseorufescens.	A shallow saucer.	On the ground by clod or tuft.	The western Himalayas	Kangra, 1st; Kashmir, 10th; eggs.

606	The upland Pipit	Heterura sylvana ...	A shallow saucer.	On the ground by clod or tuft.	The western Himalayas (extending to Nepal).	Season nearly over.
607	The purple thrush Tit	Cochoa purpurea ...	A large deep cup.	In small tress or bushes.	The eastern Himalayas	Kumaon; eggs.
608	The green " "	" viridis ...	Ditto ...	Ditto ...	Ditto ...	Sikkim; eggs.
609	The red-winged shrike "	Pteruthius erythropterus.	A rather deep cup.	At tops of high trees.	The western Himalayas	Murree, 10th; eggs.
614	The red-billed hill "	Leiothrix luteus ...	A substantial cup.	In thick bushes ...	The eastern "	Nepal, Sikkim; eggs.
615	The silver-eared " "	" argentarius ...	Ditto ...	Ditto ...	Ditto ...	Ditto
616	The stripe-throated " "	Siva strigula ...	Ditto ...	In slender forks of small trees.	Ditto ...	Ditto.
617	The blue-winged " "	" cyanouroptera ...	Ditto ...	Ditto ...	Ditto ...	Ditto.
618	The red-tailed " "	Minla ignotincta ...	Ditto ...	Ditto ...	Ditto ...	Ditto.
619	The chestnut-headed " "	" castaneiceps ...	A broad shallow cup.	In forks in thick bushes.	Ditto ...	Ditto.
621	The golden-breasted " "	Proparus chrysœus ...	Oval, domed	In bamboo clump	Ditto ...	Ditto.
623	The yellow-naped " "	Ixulus flavicollis ...	Ditto ...	On the ground in tufts of grass.	Ditto ...	Nepal, 7th; eggs.
624	The rusty-headed " "	" occipitalis ...	A shallow cup	In forks in small trees.	Ditto ...	Sikkim, 17th; eggs.
626	The stripe throat crested " "	Yuhina gularis ...	Large, globular, domed.	Wedged in forks in trees or rocks.	Ditto ...	Sikkim, 19th; eggs.
628	The black-chinned " "	" nigrimentum	A neat shallow cup.	On thick forks in large trees.	Ditto ...	Sikkim, 17th; eggs.
631	The Indian white-eyed "	Zosterops palpebrosus	A tiny regular cup.	Hung from twigs in trees or bushes.	Throughout India ...	Murree, 16th; Cawnpur, 17th; eggs.
638	The crested black "	Lophophanes melanolophus.	A shallow pad	In holes in walls or trees.	The Himalayas ...	Kashmir; eggs.
644	The mountain "	Parus monticolus ...	A rough mass of feathers.	Ditto ...	Ditto ...	Simla, 20th; eggs; season ends.
654	The rufous-breasted Accentor	Accentor strophiatus	A deep cup	On the ground in tufts of grass.	The eastern Himalayas	Nepal, Sikkim; eggs.
	Jerdon's "	" jerdoni ...	Ditto ...	On lower boughs of pines.	The western "	Kashmir, 6th; eggs.

Nos in Jerdon.	English Names.	Scientific Names.	Shape of Nest.	Site of Nest.	Geographical Range in Breeding Season.	Particulars for the Month.
659	The Indian carrion Crow	Corvus corone ...	A large compact cup.	High up in forks of trees.	The western Himalayas	Kashmir, 2nd ; eggs.
663	The common ,,	,, impudicus ...	Ditto ...	Ditto ...	Throughout India proper.	Cawnpur, 18th ; Meerut. 14th ; eggs.
665	The Jackdaw	,, monedula ...	A small platform.	In holes in buildings or trees.	The western Himalayas	Kashmir ; eggs.
669	The Himalayan Jay	Garrulus bispecularis	A neat compact cup.	On thick boughs of large trees.	The Himalayas ...	Kumaon, 2nd ; eggs.
670	The black-throated ,	, lanceolatus	A loose shallow cup.	In small trees or saplings.	Ditto (from Nepal west).	Throughout the month.
671	The red-billed blue ,,	Urocissa occipitalis ...	Ditto ...	In trees usually small ones.	Ditto (from Nepal to Sutlej).	Season nearly over.
672	The yellow-billed ,, ,	,, flavirostris ...	Ditto ...	In trees or saplings	East and extreme west Himalayas.	Kashmir, 1st ; Sikkim ; eggs.
674	The Indian Treepie	Dendrocitta rufa ...	Ditto ...	In trees near the top	Throughout continental India.	Throughout the month.
676	The Himalayan ,,	,, himalayensis	Ditto ...	In small trees or bushes.	The Himalayas ...	Nepal, 6th ; Sikkim ; eggs.
682	The bright Starling	Sturnus nitens ...	None ...	In holes in trees or buildings.	The north-west Punjab	Kashmir ; season ends.
683	The pied Mynah	Sturnopastor contra ...	Large, globular, domed.	In trees at ends of boughs.	Continental India ...	Throughout the month.
684	The common ,,	Acridotheres tristis ...	None ...	In holes in trees or buildings.*	Throughout India ...	Cawnpur, 17th, 27th ; eggs.
685	The bank ,,	,, ginginianus	Ditto ...	Deep holes in banks or wells.	Plains of continental India.	Aligurh, 18th ; eggs.
686	The jungle ,,	,, fuscus ...	Ditto ...	In holes in trees or buildings.	In wooded hilly tracts	Kashmir, 29th ; Kumaon, 7th ; eggs.
687	The brahminy ,,	Temenuchus pagodarum	Ditto ...	Holes in decayed trees.	Throughout India proper.	Aligurh, 4th ; Saugor ; eggs.
688	The grey-headed ,,	,, malabaricus	Ditto ...	Ditto ...	The eastern Himalayas	Sikkim ; eggs.
694	The common Weaver bird	Ploceus baya ...	A pendent retort.	Hung from tips of boughs.	Throughout India proper.	Throughout the month.

* Sometimes in deserted nests of crows or even in cup-shaped nests of its own building.

698	The chestnut-bellied Munia	Munia rubroniger ...	Large, oval, domed.	In bamboos, reeds, or grass.	Eastern continental India.	Nepal ; season begins.
702	Hodgson's "	" acuticauda ...	Ditto ...	In bamboos, palms, or bushes.	Ditto ...	Sikkim, 20th ; eggs.
704	The Indian Amadavat	Estrelda amandava ...	Ditto ...	In thick bushes near water.	Locally throughout India.	Nilgiris ; eggs.
706	The Indian house Sparrow	Passer indicus ...	A globular mass.	In and about houses	Throughout India ...	Throughout the month.
708	The cinnamon-headed "	" cinnamomeus...	Ditto ...	In holes in trees or houses.	The Himalayas ...	Kashmir, 15th ; Simla, 15th ; eggs.
710	The tree "	" montanus ...	Ditto ...	Ditto ...	The eastern Himalayas	Second brood begins.
713	The meadow Bunting	Emberiza cia ...	A shallow cup	On the ground by clod or tuft.	The western "	Kashmir, 3rd ; Simla, 16th ; eggs.
718	The white-capped "	" stewarti ...	Cup-shaped	Low down in bushes or grass.	Ditto ...	Murree ; eggs.
719	The grey-headed "	" fucata ...	A shallow cup	On the ground by bush or grass.	Ditto ...	Kotegurh, 25th ; eggs.
724	The crested black and chestnut "	Melophus melanicterus	A neat shallow cup.	In holes in banks or walls.	Locally in continental India.	Kashmir, 21st ; Doon, 6th ; eggs.
725	The black and yellow Grosbeak	Hesperiphona icterioides.	Cup-shaped	Near tops of trees or saplings.	The western Himalayas	Kashmir ; eggs.
754	The Bengal bush Lark	Mirafra assamica ...	A shallow cup, domed.	On the ground by tufts of grass.	Eastern continental India.	Saharunpur, 8th, 30th ; eggs.
756	The red-winged " "	" erythroptera	A shallow pad	Ditto ...	Continental India ...	Throughout the month.
757	The singing " "	" cantillans ..	Ditto (often domed.)	Ditto ...	Ditto (but locally)	Lahore, Hansi ; eggs.
759	The desert finch "	Ammomanes lusitanica	A shallow pad	Ditto, by rock or stone.	The western Punjab ...	Nowshera ; season ends.
760	The black-bellied " "	Pyrrhalauda grisea ...	A tiny shallow pad.	Ditto, by clod or tuft.	Throughout the plains	Throughout the month.
765	The northern crown-crest "	Spizalauda deva ...	A shallow cup	Ditto ...	Western continental India.	Jhansi, Saugor ; eggs.
766	The Himalayan sky "	Alauda dulcivox ...	A shallow saucer.	Ditto, on grassy slopes.	The western Himalayas	Kashmir ; eggs.
	The Nilgiri " "	" australis ...	Ditto ...	Ditto by bush or tuft.	The hills of south India	Nilgiris ; eggs.
772	The Bengal green Pigeon	Crocopus phœnicopterus.	A small platform.	On outer forks of large trees.	Eastern sub-Himalayas	Saharunpur, 12th ; eggs.
773	The southern " "	" chlorigastra	Ditto ...	In small trees or bushes.	Throughout the plains	Agra, 2nd ; Muttra, 12th ; eggs.

Nos. in Jerdon.	English Names.	Scientific Names.	Shape of Nest.	Site of Nest.	Geographical Range in Breeding Season.	Particulars for the Month.
778	The kokla green Pigeon	Sphenocercus sphenurus	A small platform.	On outer boughs of trees.	The Himalayas ...	Kashmir, 18th, Kumaon, 30th ; eggs.
781	The bronze-backed ,,	Carpophaga insignis ...	Ditto ...	Ditto ...	The eastern Himalayas	Nepal ; eggs.
	The imperial ,,					
783	The speckled wood ,,	Alsocomus hodgsoni ...	Ditto ...	Unknown ...	The Himalayas ...	Kashmir, Kumaon.
784	The Himalayan ,, ,,	Palumbus casiotis ...	Ditto ...	In thorny bushes or small trees.	The western Himalayas	Kashmir, 20th ; eggs.
786	The Nilgiri ,, ,,	,, elphinstonii	Ditto ...	On thick boughs in forest trees.	The Nilgiris ...	Ootocamund ; eggs.
788	The Indian blue rock ,,	Columba intermedia ...	Ditto ...	On ledges of buildings chiefly.	Throughout India proper.	Saharunpur, 12th ; eggs.
791	The bar-tailed tree Dove	Macropygia tusalia ...	A tiny platform.	In outer forks of low trees.	The eastern Himalayas	Nepal, Sikkim ; eggs.
792	Hodgson's turtle ,,	Turtur pulchrata ...	Ditto ...	On lower boughs of large trees.	The Himalayas ...	Throughout the month.
794	The brown ,, ,,	,, cambaiensis ...	Ditto ...	In low trees or bushes.	Throughout the plains	Ditto.
795	The spotted ,,	,, suratensis ...	Ditto ...	Ditto ...	In all wooded parts ...	Kumaon, 8th ; eggs.
796	The Indian ring ,,	,, risorius .	Ditto ...	Ditto ...	Throughout the plains	Kumaon, 10th ; eggs.
797	The ruddy ,, ,,	,, humilis ...	Ditto ...	Ditto ...	Ditto (but local)	Cawnpur, 17th ; eggs.
798	The emerald ,	Chalcophaps indicus...	A shallow saucer.	In low thick trees or shrubs.	In all dense forests ...	Kumaon ; eggs.
802	The common Sandgrouse	Ptsrocles exustus ...	None ...	On the bare ground	Western continental India.	Throughout the month.
803	The Peacock	Pavo cristatus ...	A few dry leaves.	On the ground in brushwood.	Throughout India ...	Nilgiris ; eggs.
811	The black-backed kalij Pheasant	Gallophasis melanotus	A shallow pad	On the ground in ringal or bracken.	The eastern Himalayas	Sikkim ; eggs.
814	The red Spurfowl	Galloperdix spadiceus	A few dry leaves.	On the ground in dense thickets.	South India to Bundelkhund.	Nilgiris ; eggs.
816	The snow Pheasant	Tetraogallus himalayensis.	Ditto ...	On the ground by rock or bush.	The alpine Himalayas	Throughout the month.

817	The snow Partridge	Lerwa nivicola ...	A few dry leaves.	(Unknown,) probably among rock.)	The alpine Himalayas	Throughout the month.
818	The black „	Francolinus vulgaris ...	Ditto ...	On the ground in grass or crops.	Throughout upper India.	Ditto.
820	The chukor „	Caccabis chukor ...	Ditto ...	On the ground on grassy slopes.	Himalayas, Salt range, and Suleimans.	Season nearly over.
822	The grey „	Ortygornis ponticeriana	Ditto ...	On the ground in grass or bushes.	The plains of India proper.	Aligurh, 12th ; eggs,
824	The peora „	Arboricola torqueola ...	Ditto ...	On the ground in dense cover.	The Himalayas ...	Throughout the month.
833	The Himalayan bustard Quail	Turnix plumbipes ...	Ditto ...	On the ground in grass or bush.	The outer Himalayas ...	Sikkim ; eggs.
836	The Indian Bustard	Eupodotis edwardsii ...	None ...	On the ground in scanty grass.	Western continental India.	Sirsa ; eggs.
838	The Florikin	Sypheotides bengalensis	Ditto ...	On the ground in thick grass.	Eastern Bengal and the Terais.	Throughout the month.
840	The Indian courier Plover	Cursorius coromandelicus.	Ditto ...	On the ground in fallow land.	All dry plains (except the Punjab.)	Etawah, Sholapur ; eggs.
	The cream-coloured „ „	„ gallicus ...	Ditto ...	Ditto ...	The Punjab only.	Throughout the month.
846	The greater shore „	Ægialites leschenaulti	Ditto ...	Ditto by water ...	The Thibetan lakes.	Season ends.
847	Pallas's „ „	„ mongolicus...	Ditto ...	Ditto ...	Ditto ...	Ditto.
855	The red-wattled „	Lobivanellus goensis ...	Ditto ...	On the ground on raised spots.	Throughout India ...	Upper India ; eggs.
859	The stone „	Œdicnemus crepitans ...	Ditto ...	On the ground by bush or tree.	Ditto (but locally)	Saharunpur, 7th, 13th ; eggs.
863	The sarus Crane	Grus antigone ...	Large, truncated cone.	On reedy islands in swamps.	Throughout the plains	Season begins.
893	The common Sandpiper	Actitis hypoleucus ...	None ...	On the ground on river banks.	The western Himalayas	Kashmir ; eggs.
898	The Stilt	Himantopus candidus	Ditto ...	On the ground in Salt works.	Near Delhi and Gurgaon.	Delhi, 5th ; eggs.
903	The common Coot	Fulica atra ...	A large mass of weeds.	Among rice or bushes in water.	Throughout India ...	Kashmir, 12th ; eggs.
908	The brown Rail	Porzana akool ...	A small platform.	In long grass or bushes by water.	Central and upper India.	Jhansi, 10th, 18th ; eggs.
910	Baillon's Crake	„ pygmœa ...	A massive cup.	In reeds or rice in water.	Himalayas and upper India.	Kashmir, Simla ; eggs.
920	The white-necked Stork	Melanopelargus episcopus.	A loose platform.	Near tops of large trees.	Throughout India proper.	Hansi, Saharunpur ; eggs.
923	The common Heron	Ardea cinerea ...	Ditto ...	On large trees (gregarious.)	Throughout India locally.	Saugor ; eggs.

Nos. in Jerdon.	English Names.	Scientific Names.	Shape of Nest.	Site of Nest.	Geographical Range in Breeding Season.	Particulars for the Month.
924	The purple Heron	Ardea purpurea ...	A loose platform.	In thick beds of reeds in water.	Throughout India proper.	Saugor; eggs.
930	The little pond ,,	Ardeola grayi ...	Ditto ...	In forks of trees ...	Ditto ...	Upper India, season begins.
933	The chestnut Bittern	Ardetta cinnamomea...	Ditto ...	In reeds or thickets in water.	Continental India. ...	Tipperah, 6th; eggs.
934	The yellow ,,	,, sinensis ..	Ditto ...	Ditto ...	Eastern Bengal ...	Tipperah, 20th; eggs.
935	The little ,,	,, minuta ...	Ditto ...	Ditto ...	The Himalayas ...	Kashmir, 12th; eggs.
940	The shell Ibis	Anastomus oscitans ...	Ditto ...	On tops of high trees.	Locally throughout India.	Oudh, 28th; eggs
941	The white ,,	Threskiornis melanocephalus.	Ditto ...	Ditto ...	Ditto ...	Etawah, 20th; Jhansi; eggs.
942	The king Curlew	Geronticus papillosus	Ditto ...	High up in large trees.	Throughout the plains	Hansi, 12th, 18th; eggs.
950	The black-backed Goose	Sarkidiornis melanotus	A few leaves	In holes in decayed trees	Ditto ...	Saharunpur, 30th; eggs.
952	The whistling Teal	Dendrocygna arcuata	A loose platform.	In low trees or saplings by water.	Ditto ...	Fatehgurh, 20th; eggs.
958	The Mallard	Anas boschas ...	A shallow pad	In rushes or grass by water.	The western Himalayas	Kashmir, 12th; eggs.
960	The pink-headed Duck	,, caryophyllacea...	Ditto ...	Ditto ...	Lower and eastern Bengal.	Purneah; eggs.
969	The white-eyed ,,	Aythya nyroca ...	Ditto ...	Ditto ...	The western Himalayas	Kashmir, 8th, 9th; eggs.
975	The little Grebe	Podiceps philippensis	A large mass of weeds.	In rushes or low trees over water.	Throughout India ...	Etawah, 8th; Nilgiris, eggs.
984	The whiskered Tern	Hydrochelidon indicus	A slight platform.	On lily or lotus leaves in water.	Himalayas and upper India.	Kashmir, 8th; eggs.
989	The large sea ,,	Sterna bergii ...	None	The bare ground on rocky islands.	The gulf of Oman ...	Astola; eggs.
990	The small ,, ,,	,, bengalensis ...	Ditto ...	Ditto ...	Ditto ...	Ditto.
	The Kentish ,,	,, cantiaca ...	Ditto ...	Ditto ...	Ditto ...	Ditto.
991	The little black-naped ,,	Onochoprion melanauchen.	Ditto ...	Ditto ...	The Andamans and Nicobars.	Throughout the month.

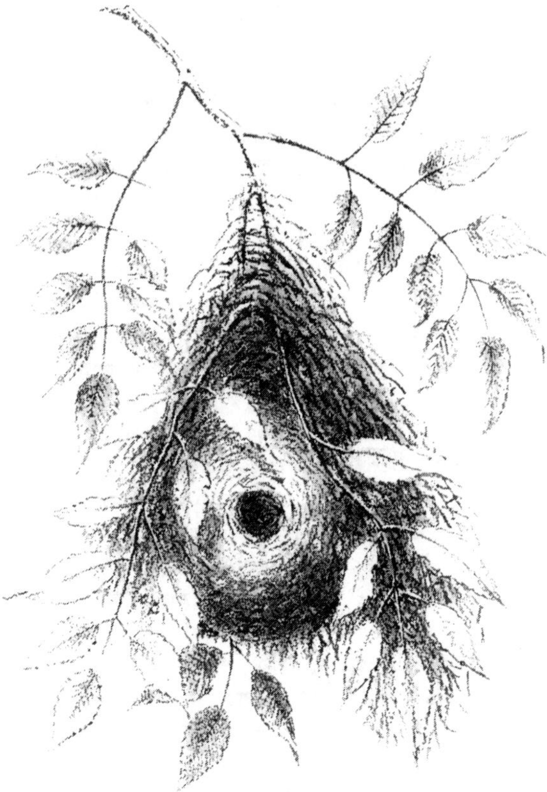

MARSHALL, DEL.

NEST OF THE YELLOW-THROATED BROADBILL.

(Psarisomus dalhousiæ.)

JULY.

THIS is in the plains the principal month for taking the eggs of the water-birds, wren warblers, and munias, while in the Himalayas the finches and buntings are the most numerous breeders. The birds of prey, parrots, hornbills, most of the woodpeckers and the barbets, the nuthatches and creepers, thrushes and blackbirds, and tits of almost all kinds, have ceased to lay. The shrikes, small minivets, the turtle doves, ringdoves are still breeding everywhere. And throughout the plains the eggs of the common drongo, tailor bird, rufous grass warbler, peafowl, bustard quail, red-wattled plovers, purple coots, common coots, and water-hens, may be taken.

In the HIMALAYAS, the eggs of the mosque swallow, the swift, the roller, the Marshall's barbet, the common and large hawk cuckoos, paradise flycatcher, grey-headed and verditer flycatchers, the grey-winged blackbird, striated jay thrush, Nepal quaker thrush, red-billed wren babbler, several of the laughing thrushes, some of the bulbuls, bushchats, hill warblers, tree warblers and pipits, the rufous-breasted accentor, blue magpie, mynahs, munias, sparrows, bartailed tree doves, emerald doves, kalij pheasants, Hodgson's partridges, chukor, peora partridge, bustard quail, rails, and bitterns may still be found, but the season is practically over, except in the more elevated ranges and towards the far west. Eggs of buntings and finches are found throughout the ranges. The *golden woodchat* begins to pair and build during this month.

In the PUNJAB, the crested honey buzzard is still laying. The mosque and cliff swallows have their second brood. The white-breasted kingfisher and common gold back woodpecker breed throughout the month. Also the koel, coucal and sirkeer, the white-eared bulbul, the golden oriole, brown-backed robin, Stewart's wren warbler, and all other wren warblers that occur there, the common crow, mynahs, pin-tailed munias, bushlarks and black-bellied finchlarks, the common sandgrouse, the black partridge, bustard, courier plover, red-wattled plover, white-necked stork, common heron, egrets, pond herons, cattle herons, green bitterns, night herons, and spoonbills have eggs. By the end of the month the *black-winged kites*, the *large button quail*, and *Blyth's water hen* (very rare) are beginning to pair and build.

In the NORTH-WEST PROVINCES, the birds of prey have al lceased to lay. Eggs of all the resident swallows may be found, and the palm swift has its second brood. The cuckoos, coucals and sirkeers are laying. The large grey cuckoo shrike, the fantail, the yellow-eyed babbler, the rufous-bellied wren babbler, all other babblers, except the reed babbler, the golden oriole, the wren warblers, white-eyed tits, tree pies, mynahs, weaver bird, pin-tailed munia, bushlarks, finch larks, stone plover, still have eggs; while those of the sarus crane, pheasant-tailed jacana, Baillon's crane, white-necked stork, herons, and egrets of all kinds, spoonbills, Ibis's geese, teal, and snakebirds are found throughout the month. The *marsh terns* also breed in this month, and the *great rufous wren warbler*, *striated weaver birds*, *cinnamon bitterns*, and *spotted billed ducks* commence to pair and build.

In BENGAL, the palm swift has its second brood. The broad-billed roller is believed to be breeding, but its eggs have not been taken. The coucal, tailor-bird, white-breasted kingfisher, common babbler, yellow-bellied wren warbler, white-winged green bulbul, chestnut-bellied munia and spotted munia, and the bustard quail lay in the neighbourhood of Calcutta. The Bengal grass warbler in the eastern districts, the blue-breasted quail and florikin in the Terai districts. The bronzed-winged jacana, the water cock, Baillon's crane, the great heron, the black bittern and chestnut bittern, the pink-headed duck, and probably most of the other resident water birds lay everywhere throughout the month.

In CENTRAL INDIA, the swallows, dusky crag martins, nightjars, koels, coucals, cuckoo shrikes, fantails, ground thrushes, wren babblers, green bulbuls, robins, rockchats, almost all the wren warblers, titlarks, treepies, mynahs, munias, amadavats, crested buntings, bushlarks, crown crest larks, painted partridges, bustard, jacanas, rails, herons, egrets, and white ibis, are laying still, while *Sykes's warbler*, the *lesser button quail*, and the *larger whistling teal* begin to pair and build.

In SOUTHERN INDIA, the orange minivet, the black-naped azure flycatcher, the white-spotted fantail, the yellow-eyed babbler, black-headed quaker thrush, most of the wren warblers, the white-eyed tit, the jungle mynah, and most of the munias, appear to be the principal breeders during this month. Towards the end of it *Jerdon's wren warbler*, the *Malabar crested lark*, and the *rain quail* commence to pair and build.

JULY.

Nos. in Jerdon.	English Names.	Scientific Names.	Shape of Nest.	Site of Nest.	Geographical Range in Breeding Season.	Particulars for the Month.
57	The crested honey Buzzard	Pernis cristata ...	Irregular platform.	In forks half way up trees.	Throughout India (locally).	Hansi, 5th 10th; eggs.
84	The wire-tailed Swallow	Hirundo ruficeps ...	A semi-circular saucer.	On bridges or rocks by water.	Ditto ...	Aligurh, 27th; Sambhur, 13th; eggs.
85	The great Indian mosque "	" daurica ...	Tubular, retort-shaped	In buildings or in caves.	The Himalayas ...	Second brood begins.
	The " "	" erythropygia	Ditto ...	Ditto ...	Throughout India proper.	Upper India; eggs.
86	The Indian cliff "	" fluvicola ...	Retort-shaped	On cliffs by water or buildings.	Northern and central India.	Second brood begins.
90	The dusky crag Martin	Cotyle concolor ...	Semi-circular cup.	In buildings or in caves.	Throughout India (locally).	Central India; do.
92	The house "	Chelidon urbica ...	Ditto ...	Against rocks or on cliffs.	Southern India ...	Mysore; eggs.
100	The common Indian Swift	Cypselus abyssinicus ...	Semi-globular	Under bridges or eaves of houses.	Throughout India ...	Himalayas; eggs.
102	The palm "	" batassiensis ...	A tiny watch pocket	On leaves of the toddy palm.	Throughout the plains (locally).	Agra, Bengal; eggs.
108	The Nilgiri Nightjar	Caprimulgus kelaarti	None ...	On the ground often by a bush.	Peninsular India ...	Central Provinces; eggs.
112	The common Indian "	" asiaticus	Ditto ...	Ditto ...	Throughout upper India.	Ditto.
114	Franklin's "	" monticolus	Ditto ...	Ditto ...	In all wooded hilly tracts.	Season ends.
125	The European Roller	Coracias garrula ...	Ditto ...	In holes in trees or buildings.	The western Himalayas	Kashmir; do.
126	The broad-billed "	Eurystomus orientalis	Ditto ...	In holes in lofty trees.	Eastern sub-Himalayas	(Requires confirmation).
129	The white-breasted Kingfisher	Halcyon smyrnensis	Ditto ...	Holes in river banks or wells.	Throughout India proper.	Calcutta, 1st; Hansi, 4th, 18th; eggs.
180	The common gold-back Woodpecker	Brachypternus aurantius.	Ditto ...	In artificial holes in trees.	Throughout the plains	Hansi, 17th; eggs.
191	The Marshall's Barbet	Megalæma marshallorum.	Ditto ...	Ditto ...	The Himalayas ...	Season nearly over.

Nos. in Jerdon.	English Names.	Scientific Names.	Shape of Nest.	Site of Nest.	Geographical Range in Breeding Season.	Particulars for the Month.
199	The common Cuckoo	Cuculus canorus ...	(Parasitic habits.)	Eggs laid in bush-chats' or pipits' nests	The Himalayas ...	Kangra, 4th; eggs; season nearly over.
207	The large hawk "	Hierococcyx sparverioides.	Ditto (?)...	Eggs laid in laughing thrushs' nests.	Ditto (and Nilgiris) ...	Nepal; season ends.
212	The pied-crested "	Coccystes melanoleucus	Ditto ...	Eggs laid in babblers' nests.	Throughout India ...	Cawnpur, 13th; eggs (extracted).
214	The Koel	Endynamis orientalis	Ditto ...	Eggs laid in crows' nests.	Throughout the plains	Throughout the month.
217	The common Coucal	Centropus rufipennis	Large, rough, domed.	In clumps of grass or thorny thickets.	Throughont India proper.	Ditto.
220	The Bengal Sirkeer	Taccocua sirkee ...	A rough shallow cup.	In low trees or thick bushes.	The plains of upper India.	Ditto.
234	The purple Honeysucker	Arachnechthra asiatica	Pear-shaped, side entrance.	Hanging from tips of branches.	Throughout India ...	Hansi; eggs; season ends.
247	The red-winged Wallcreeper	Tichodroma muriaria	A rough cup.	In clefts of rocks...	The Himalayas only...	Simla.
256	The Indian grey Shrike	Lanius lahtora ...	A thick massive cup.	In small trees or bushes.	Throughout the dry plains.	Aligurh, 12th; Saugor; eggs.
257	The rufous-backed "	" erythronotus...	Ditto ...	Ditto ...	Throughout India ...	Throughout the month.
	The pale " " "	" caniceps ...	Ditto ...	Ditto ...	The hilly regions of India.	Season nearly over.
258	The grey-backed "	" tephronotus ...	Ditto ...	Ditto ...	The Himalayas ...	Kumaon, 1st; Murree, 5th; eggs.
259	The black cap "	" nigriceps ...	Ditto ...	Ditto ...	Eastern continental India.	Kumaon, 1st; eggs.
260	The bay-backed "	" vittatus ...	A neat cup	Ditto ...	Throughout India ...	Throughout the month.
268	The pied cuckoo "	Volvocivora sykesii ...	A small saucer.	Wedged in outer forks of trees.	In forests throughout India.	Bundelkhund, 26th; eggs.
270	The large grey " "	Graucalus macei ...	A broad saucer.	Ditto (near top) ...	Locally in India proper.	Throughout the month.
272	The orange Minivet	Pericrocotus flammeus	A small deep cup.	In high trees near tips of branches.	The hills of South India	Kotagiri; eggs.
276	The small "	" peregrinus	Ditto ...	Ditto ...	Throughout India proper.	Throughout the month.

278	The common drongo Shrike	Dicrurus albirictus ...	A loose saucer.	In trees in horizontal forks.	Throughout India ...	In the plains ; eggs.
288	The paradise Flycatcher	Tchitrea paradisii ...	A small delicate cup.	On thin branches in trees.	Ditto (in moist forests.)	Murree ; eggs ; season ends.
290	The black-naped azure "	Myiagra azurea ...	A deep compact cup.	Ditto ...	Ditto ditto...	Nilgiris ; eggs.
291	The white-throated Fantail	Leucocerca fuscoventris	A tiny inverted cone.	Ditto (or bushes)	Forests in continental India.	Season nearly over.
292	The white-browed "	" aureola ...	A tiny cup	Ditto ...	Throughout continental India.	Throughout the month.
293	The white-spotted "	" pectoralis ...	A tiny inverted cone.	Ditto ...	The hills of south India.	Season nearly over.
295	The grey-headed Flycatcher	Cryptolopha cinereocapilla.	A watch pocket.	Againt mossy trunks of trees.	The Himalayas, Nilgiris, and Wynaad.	Kumaon, 3rd ; eggs.
301	The verditer "	Eumyias melanops ...	A thick cup	In mossy banks or under bridges.	The Himalayas only ...	Kashmir, 11th ; eggs ; season ends.
345	The Indian ground Thrush	Pitta bengalensis ...	Large, globular, domed.	Near the ground in brushwood.	The Central Provinces and sub-Himalayas.	Raipur (C. P.) ; eggs.
361	The grey-winged Blackbird	Merula boulboul ...	A broad cup	On thick boughs or stumps.	The Himalayas only ...	Kashmir, Kumaon ; eggs.
382	The striated jay Thrush	Grammatoptila striata	A large shallow cup.	On lower boughs of large trees.	The eastern Himalayas	Darjeeling ; eggs.
385	The yellow-eyed Babbler	Pyctorhis sinensis ...	A deep neat cup.	On stalks of herbs or bushes.	Throughout India proper.	Throughout the month.
388	The Nepal quaker Thrush	Alcippe nipalensis ...	A deep massive cup.	In low thick bushes	The eastern Himalayas	Darjeeling ; eggs.
390	The black-headed " "	" atriceps ...	Ditto ..	Low down in grass or reeds.	The hills of south India	Nilgiris, Conoor ; eggs.
392	The red-billed wren Warbler	Stachyris pyrrhops ...	Ditto ...	Low down in small bushes.	The western Himalayas to Nepal.	Mussoorie, 30th ; Murree ; eggs.
397	The rufous-bellied " "	Dumetia hyperythra...	Neat, globular domed.	In the roots of bamboos.	Central and upper India	Throughout the month.
	The Nepal spotted " "	Pellorneum nipalensis	Ditto ...	On the ground in grass or bush.	The eastern Himalayas	Darjeeling ; eggs.
407	The white crested laughing Thrush	Garrulax leucolophus	A broad shallow cup.	In thick bushes or low trees.	The eastern Himalayas to Sutlej.	Doon, 2nd ; Darjeeling ; eggs.
412	The black-gorgetted " "	" pectoralis ...	Ditto ...	In bamboo clumps	The eastern Himalayas	Sikkim ; eggs.
415	The redheaded " ,	Trochalopteron erythrocephalum.	A large deep cup.	In small trees or bushes.	The western Himalayas	Kumaon, 10th ; eggs.
418	The variegated " "	" variegatum.	Ditto ...	Ditto ...	Ditto ...	Murree, 5th, 10th ; eggs.

Nos. in Jerdon.	English Names.	Scientific Names.	Shape of Nest.	Site of Nest.	Geographical Range in Breeding Season.	Particulars for the Month.
421	The red-throated laughing Thrush	Trochalopteron rufogulare.	A large deep cup.	In small trees or bushes.	The eastern Himalayas to Sutlej.	Sikkim; eggs.
425	The streaked „ „	„ lineatum	Cup-shaped	In low bushes or mossy banks.	The Himalayas only ...	Masuri, 25th, 26th; Murree; eggs.
429	The black-headed Sibia	Sibia capistrata ...	A neat deep cup.	In outer twigs of trees or bushes.	Ditto ...	Kumaon, 3rd; Murree; eggs.
432	The Bengal Babbler	Malacocircus canorus	A loose straggling cup.	In thick bushes or small trees.	Plains of continental India.	Calcutta, 6th; Agra 21st; eggs.
426	The large grey „	„ malcolmi	Cup-shaped	In thorny trees (acacia).	Throughout the plains	Aligurh, 25th; eggs.
438	The striated bush „	Chattarhœa caudata ...	Ditto ...	In low bushes or grass.	Ditto ...	Agra; eggs.
451	The white-throated Bulbul	Criniger flaveolus ...	A compact saucer.	In small trees or bushes.	The eastern Himalayas	Darjeeling; eggs.
458	The white-cheeked crested „	Otocompsa leucogenys	A neat cup	Ditto ...	The Himalayas only ...	Murree; eggs.
459	The white-eared „	„ leucotis ...	Ditto ...	In dense thorny bushes.	Western continental India.	Hansi; eggs.
462	The common Madras „	Pycnonotus pusillus ...	A small slender cup.	In small trees or bushes.	Throughout the plains	Season nearly over.
463	Jerdon's green „	Phyllornis jerdoni ...	A small shallow cup.	In trees near tips of branches.	Central and southern India.	Raipur (C. P.); eggs.
467	The black-backed „	Iora zeylanica ...	A tiny cup	In trees near tips of boughs.	Southern and central India.	Mirzapur, Raipur; eggs.
468	The white-winged green „	„ typhia ...	Ditto ..	Ditto ...	Plains of upper India	Calcutta, 13th; eggs.
470	The Indian golden Oriole	Oriolus kundoo ...	A neat deep cup.	Hung from slender forks in trees.	Throughout India ...	Hansi, 14th; Fatehgurh, 9th; eggs.
475	The magpie Robin	Copsychus saularis ...	A shallow saucer.	In holes in trees or walls.	Ditto ...	Season nearly over.
480	The brown-backed „	Thamnobia cambaiensis	A small cup	In holes in banks or buildings.	Plains of upper India	Saugor, Delhi; eggs.
483	The common Indian Bushchat	Pratincola indica ...	Ditto ...	In holes in banks or walls.	The Himalayas and N. W. Punjab.	Simla, Murree; eggs.
486	The iron-grey „	„ ferrea ...	Ditto ...	Ditto ...	The Himalayas only	Murree; eggs.
494	The brown Rockchat	Cercomela fusca ...	A shallow pad	Ditto ...	Western continental India.	Saugor; eggs.

	The brown-breasted hill Warbler	Dumeticola brunneipectus.	Oval, domed	Low down in clumps of reeds.	The Himalayas.	Nepal; eggs.
523	The fulvous-breasted „ „	Hororis fulviventer	A small massive cup.	On the ground in mossy banks.	The eastern Himalayas	Darjeeling; eggs.
526	The strong-footed „ „	„ fortipes ...	Ditto ...	In thick brushwood or low jungle.	Ditto ...	Ditto.
529	The large „ „	Horeites major ...	Ditto ...	Low down in thorny bushes.	Ditto ...	Native Sikkim; eggs.
530	The Indian Tailorbird	Orthotomus longicauda	Deepcup sewn in leaves.	In creepers or herbage.	Throughout India ...	Throughout the plains.
532	The yellow-bellied wren Warbler	Prinia flaviventris ...	Oval, often domed.	Sewn to twigs or leaves in shrubs.	Eastern Bengal ...	Calcutta, 30th; eggs.
534	The ashy „ „	„ socialis ...	A cup sewn in leaves	Hanging in low bushes.	Southern India	In the plains; eggs.
535	Stewart's „ „	„ stewarti ...	Nearly globular.	In low bushes often sewn to leaves.	Upper India ...	Agra, 17th, 30th; eggs.
537	The grey-capped „ „	„ cinereocapilla ...	A cup sewn in leaves.	In creepers or low bushes.	The sub-Himalayas ...	The Doon, 22nd; eggs.
538	Hodgson's „ „	„ hodgsoni ...	Ditto ..	In low bushes or herbage.	Central India ...	Raipur (C. P.), 1st, 12th, 13th; eggs.
539	The rufous grass „	Cisticola schœnicola ...	A deep narrow purse.	In tufts of fine grass in swamps.	Throughout the plains..	Throughout the month.
542	The Bengal „ „	Graminicola bengalensis.	A deep compact cup.	Fixed between reeds in swamps.	Eastern Bengal ...	Dacca; eggs.
543	The common wren „	Drymoipus inornatus	Deep, neat, often domed.	Attached to twigs or leaves in shrubs.	Bombay presidency ...	Season commences.
	The earth-brown „ „	„ terricolor ...	Ditto ...	In long grass or small bushes.	Plains of continental India.	Throughout the month.
544	The long-tailed „ „	„ longicaudatus	Ditto ...	Ditto ..	Central and southern India.	(Requires confirmation).
	The great „ „	„ insignis ...	Ditto ...	Low down in thick bushes.	Central India.	Seoni, 29th; eggs.
546	The allied „ „	„ neglectus ...	Ditto ...	In forks of thorny bushes.	Ditto ...	Raipur; eggs.
	The fuscous „ „	„ fuscus ...	Ditto ...	In long grass or small bushes.	The Terai, Deccan, and Nilgiris.	Nilgiris; season ends.
551	The rufous-fronted „ „	Franklinia buchanani	Deep ragged, often domed.	In bushes or low scrub jungle.	Western continental India.	Chunar, Hansi; eggs.

Nos. in Jerdon.	English Names.	Scientific Names.	Shape of Nest.	Site of Nest.	Geographical Range in Breeding Season.	Particulars for the Month.
552	The aberrant tree Warbler	Neornis flavolivacea ...	A neat shallow cup.	In bushes or low trees.	The eastern Himalayas	Darjeeling, 10th; eggs.
563	The large crowned „	Reguloides occipitalis	A loose cup	In holes in stumps or bushes.	The western „	Murree, 10th; eggs; season ends.
586	The slaty-backed Forktail	Henicurus schistaceus	A massive cup	On banks or rocks by water.	The eastern „	Native Sikkim; eggs.
600	The Indian Titlark	Corydalla rufula ...	A shallow saucer.	On the ground by clod or tuft.	Throughout India ...	Saugor, 16th; eggs.
604	The brown rock Pipit	Agrodroma griseorufescens.	Ditto ...	Ditto ...	The western Himalayas	Murree; season ends.
606	The upland „	Heterura sylvana ...	Ditto ...	Ditto ...	Ditto (extending to Nepal).	Simla; ditto.
614	The red-billed hill Tit	Leiothrix luteus ...	A substantial cup.	In forks of thick bushes.	The eastern Himalayas	Nepal; eggs.
631	The Indian white-eyed „	Zosterops palpebrosus	A tiny regular cup.	Hung from twigs in trees or bushes.	Throughout India ...	Poona, 21st; Cawnpur; eggs.
654	The rufous-breasted Accentor	Accentor strophiatus...	A deep cup	On the ground in tufts of grass.	The eastern Himalayas	Nepal; eggs.
663	The common Crow	Corvus impudicus ...	A large compact cup.	High up in forks of trees.	Throughout the plains	Season nearly over.
672	The yellow-billed blue Jay	Urocissa flavirostris ...	A loose shallow cup.	In forks of trees or saplings.	The east and extreme west Himalayas.	Murree; eggs.
674	The Indian Treepie	Dendrocitta rufa ...	Ditto ...	In trees near the top.	Throughout continental India.	Saugor, Fatehgurh; eggs.
676	The Himalayan „	„ himalayensis.	Ditto ...	In small trees or bushes.	The Himalayas only ...	Sikkim, 30th; eggs.
683	The pied Mynah	Sturnopastor contra ...	Large, globular, domed.	In trees at ends of boughes.	Throughout continental India,	Jhansi; eggs.
684	The common „	Acridotheres tristis ...	None ...	In holes in trees or buildings.*	Throughout India ...	Aligurh, 20th; Sambhur, 15th; eggs.
685	The bank „	„ ginginianus	Ditto ...	In deep holes in banks or wells.	Continental India ...	Aligurh, 8th; eggs.
686	The jungle „	„ fuscus ...	Ditto ...	In holes in trees or buildings,	In all wooded hilly tracts.	Murree, Conoor; eggs.

* Or in old crows' nests or similar nests even of its own construction.

687	The brahminy Mynah	Temenuchus pagodarum	None ...	I holes in decayed parts of trees.	Throughout India proper.	Hansi, Saugor; eggs.
694	The common Weaver bird	Ploceus baya ...	A pendent retort.	Hung from tips of boughs of trees.	Ditto ...	Mynpuri, 20th; eggs.
697	The black-headed Munia	Munia malacca ...	Large, oval, domed.	On sugarcane or reeds in water.	Southern and central India.	Central Provinces, 25th; eggs.
698	The chestnut-bellied „	„ rubroniger ...	Ditto ...	In bamboos, reeds, or grass.	Eastern continental India.	Calcutta, 5th, 27th; C. P. 30th; Nepal; eggs.
699	The spotted „	„ undulata ...	Ditto ...	Usually in thick thorny bushes.	In all moist wooded tracts.	Throughout the month.
700	The rufous-bellied „	„ pectoralis ...	Ditto ...	In bushes or eaves of thatches.	The Nilgiris ...	Kotagiri; eggs.
701	The white-backed „	„ striata ...	Ditto ...	Usually in thick thorny bushes.	Peninsular and eastern India.	Ditto.
702	Hodgson's „	„ acuticauda ...	Ditto ...	In palms, bamboos, or small trees.	Bengal and eastern Himalayas.	Nepal, Sikkim; eggs.
703	The pin-tailed „	„ malabarica ...	Ditto ...	In thick bushes or eaves of thatches.	Throughout India proper.	Second brood begins.
704	The Indian Amadavat	Estrelda amandava ...	Ditto ...	In thick bushes near water.	Locally throughout India.	Ditto.
705	The green „	„ formosa ...	Ditto ...	On stalks of sugarcane.	Central India.	Central Provinces, 16th; eggs.
710	The tree Sparrow	Passer montanus ...	A globular mass	In holes in trees (or houses).	The eastern Himalayas	Darjeeling, 24th; eggs.
711	The yellow-throated „	„ flavicollis ...	Ditto ...	In holes in decayed trees.	Generally throughout India.	Murree; eggs.
713	The meadow Bunting	Emberiza cia ...	A shallow cup	On the ground by stone or tuft.	The western Himalayas	Simla; eggs.
718	The white-cap „	„ stewarti ...	Cup-shaped	Low down in bushes or grass.	Ditto ...	Murree, 4th; eggs.
719	The grey-headed „	„ fucata ...	A shallow cup	On the ground in bush or grass.	Ditto ...	Koteguhr; eggs.
724	The black and chestnut crested Bunting.	Melophus melanicterus	A neat shallow cup.	In holes in banks or walls.	In continental India (locally)	Jhansi, Aboo, 18th; eggs.
732	The orange Bulfinch	Pyrrhula aurantiaca ...	(Unknown)	(Unknown) ...	The western Himalayas	Kashmir.
737	The Circassian rose Finch	Carpodacus rubicilla...	Cup-shaped	On the ground in a furze bush.	The western alpine Himalayas.	West Thibet, 7th; eggs.
748	The red-browed „	Callacanthis burtoni ...	A large cup	In pine forests on outer boughs.	The western Himalayas	Kashmir.
750	The Indian Siskin	Chrysomitris spinoides	A neat massive cup.	On boughs often against the trunk.	Ditto ...	Simla, Nepal; eggs.

Nos. in Jerdon	English Names.	Scientific Names.	Shape of Nest.	Site of Nest.	Geographical Range in Breeding Season.	Particulars for the Month.
756	The red-winged bush Lark	Mirafra erythroptera	A shallow pad	On the ground by tuft of grass.	Continental India in the plains.	Throughout the month.
757	The singing " "	" cantillans ...	Ditto (often domed).	Ditto ...	Ditto (locally) ...	Hansi; eggs.
760	The black-bellied finch "	Pyrrhalauda grisea ...	A tiny shallow pad.	On the ground by clod or tuft.	Throughout the plains	Etawah, 28th; eggs.
765	The northern crown-crest "	Spizalauda deva ...	A shallow cup	Ditto ...	Western continental India.	Throughout the month.
791	The bar-tailed tree Dove	Macropygia tusalia ...	A tiny platform	In outer forks of low trees.	The eastern Himalayas	Darjeeling; eggs.
792	Hodgson's turtle "	Turtur pulchrata ...	Ditto ...	On lower boughs of large trees.	The Himalayas only ...	Season nearly over.
794	The brown " "	" cambaiensis ...	Ditto ...	In low trees or bushes.	Throughout the plains	Throughout the month.
796	The Indian ring "	" risorius ...	Ditto ...	Ditto ...	Ditto ...	Ditto.
798	The emerald "	Chalcophaps indicus ...	A shallow saucer.	In thick shrubs or low trees.	In all densely wooded tracts	Kumaon, 2nd; eggs.
802	The common Sandgrouse	Pterocles exustus ...	None ...	On the bare ground	Western continental India.	Sirsa, 1st, 23rd; eggs.
803	The Peacock	Pavo cristatus ...	A few dry leaves.	On the ground in brushwood.	Throughout India.	Saharunpur, 27th; Nilgiris; eggs.
811	The black-backed kalij Pheasant	Gallophasis melanotus	A shallow pad	On the ground in ringal or fern.	The eastern Himalayas	Darjeeling; eggs.
	Hodgson's Partridge	Perdix hodgsoniæ ...	A few dry leaves.	On the ground in grass and scrub.	The alpine Himalayas	Pangong (17,000ft.), 12th; eggs.
818	The black "	Francolinus vulgaris ...	Ditto ...	On the ground in grass or crops.	Upper India (locally)	Season nearly over.
819	The painted "	" pictus ...	Ditto ...	Ditto ...	Central India to Jumna	Jhansi; eggs.
820	The chukor "	Caccabis chukor ...	Ditto ...	On the ground in grassy slopes.	Himalayas, Salt range, and trans-Indus hills.	Thibet, 29th; eggs.
824	The peora "	Arboricola torqueola ...	Ditto ...	On the ground in dense cover.	The Himalayas ...	Simla, 1st; eggs.
831	The blue-breasted Quail	Excalfatoria sinensis ...	Ditto ...	On the ground in grass and scrub.	The eastern sub-Himalayas.	Purneah, the Doon; eggs.
832	The bustard "	Turnix taigoor ...	Ditto ...	Ditto ...	In all wooded tracts ...	Throughout the month.

833	The Himalayan bustard Quail	Turnix plumbipes ...	A few dry leaves.	On the ground in grass or scrub	The outer Himalayas	The Doon, 30th; eggs.
836	The Indian Bustard	Eupodotis edwardsii...	None ...	On the ground in scanty grass.	Western continental India.	Throughout the month.
838	The Florikin	Sypheotides bengalensis	Ditto ...	On the ground in long grass.	The Terais and eastern Bengal.	Ditto.
840	The Indian courier Plover	Cursorius coromandelicus.	Ditto ...	On the ground on fallow-land.	All dry plains, except the Punjab.	Season ends.
	The cream coloured „ „	„ gallicus ...	Ditto ...	Ditto ...	The Punjab only ...	Throughout the month.
855	The red wattled „	Lobivanellus goensis...	Ditto ...	On the ground on raised spots.	Throughout India ...	Ditto.
859	The stone „	Œdicnemus crepitans	Ditto ...	On the ground by bush or trees.	Ditto (but locally)	Saharunpur; eggs.
863	The sarus Crane	Grus antigone ...	Large, truncated cone.	On islands in shallow jheels.	Throughout the plains	Aligurh, 25th; eggs.
900	The bronze-winged Jacana	Metopidus indicus ...	A small pad of rushes.	Floating among water plants.	In all moist rainy tracts	Throughout the month.
901	The pheasant-tailed „	Hydrophasianus sinensis.	Ditto ...	Ditto ...	Throughout India.	Cawnpur, 8th; Aligurh, 30th; eggs.
902	The purple Coot	Porphyrio poliocephalus.	A large mass of weeds.	In thick grass or rushes by tanks.	Throughout the plains	Throughout the month.
903	The common „	Fulica atra ...	Ditto ...	Ditto ...	Throughout India ...	Ditto. ...
904	The water Cock	Gallicrex cristatus ...	Ditto ...	On floating weeds or beds of rushes.	In all moist rainy tracts	Lower Bengal; eggs.
905	The „ Hen	Gallinula chloropus ...	Ditto ...	Ditto (or on boughs overhanging water)	Throughout India ...	Throughout the month.
907	The white-breasted „ „	Porzana phœnicura ...	A rough platform.	In bamboos, thickets, or reeds.	Ditto (locally) ...	Raipur (C. P.); eggs.
908	The brown Rail	„ akool ...	A small platform.	In long grass or rushes.	In central and upper India.	Jhansi; eggs.
910	Baillon's Crake	„ pygmœa ...	A massive cup	In beds of rushes or rice in water.	Himalayas and upper India.	Throughout the month.
911	The ruddy Rail	„ fusca ...	Ditto ...	In beds of rushes or rice in water.	In moist tracts throughout India.	Ditto.
920	The white-necked Stork	Melanopelargus episcopus.	A loose platform.	Near tops of large trees.	Throughout India proper.	Jhansi, 5th; Saharunpur, 25th; eggs.
922	The great Heron	Ardea sumatrana ...	Ditto ...	On high trees in swamps.	The eastern sub-Himalayas.	Darjeeling, Terai; eggs.
923	The common „	„ cinerea ...	Ditto ...	On large trees near water.	Throughout India locally.	Etawah; eggs.
924	The purple „	„ purpurea ...	Ditto ...	In tall reeds or in bushes.	Throughout India proper.	Saugor, Etawah, 31st; eggs.

Nos. in Jerdon.	English Names.	Scientific Names.	Shape of Nest.	Site of Nest.	Geographical Range in Breeding Season.	Particulars for the Month.
925	The white Heron	Herodias alba ...	A loose platform.	Near tops of trees	Throughout the plains	Upper India.
926	The little white "	" egrettoides ...	Ditto ...	Ditto ...	Ditto ...	Ditto.
927	The little Egret	" garzetta ...	Ditto ...	Ditto ...	Ditto ...	Ditto.
929	The cattle "	Buphus coromandus ...	Ditto ...	Ditto ...	Ditto ...	Ditto.
930	The little pond Heron	Ardeola grayi ...	Ditto ...	In forks of trees.	Ditto ...	Ditto.
931	The little green Bittern	Butorides javanicus ...	Ditto ...	In trees or thickets by water.	Ditto (locally) ...	Delhi, 21st ; eggs.
932	The black "	Ardetta flavicollis ...	Ditto ...	In bushes or reeds in water.	Eastern Bengal ...	Purneah ; eggs.
933	The chestnut "	" cinnamomea...	Ditto ...	In reeds or canebrakes in water.	The Himalayas and upper India.	Kashmir, 11th ; Calcutta, 6th, 27th ; eggs.
937	The night Heron	Nycticorax griseus ...	Ditto ...	In high trees (sometimes in reeds.)	Throughout India ...	The Doab ; eggs.
939	The Spoonbill	Platalea leucorodia ...	Ditto ...	On high trees near tanks.	Ditto ...	Ditto.
940	The shell Ibis	Anastomus oscitans ...	Ditto ...	Ditto ...	Ditto (locally) ...	Upper India.
941	The white "	Threskiornis melanocephalus.	Ditto ...	Ditto ...	Ditto ...	Jhansi, Etawah ; eggs.
942	The king Curlew	Geronticus papillosus	Ditto ...	High up in large trees.	Throughout the plains	Aligurh, 30th ; eggs.
950	The black-backed Goose	Sarkidiornis melanotus	A few leaves	In hollows in decayed trees.	Ditto ...	Saharaunpur, 20th ; eggs.
951	The cotton Teal	Nettapus coromandelianus.	Ditto ...	Ditto ...	Ditto ...	Upper India.
952	The whistling "	Dendrocygna arcuata	A loose platform.	In small trees in or by water.	Ditto ...	Aligurh, 25th ; Saharunpur, 27th ; eggs.
960	The pink-headed Duck	Anas caryophyllacea ...	A shallow pad	In rushes or grass in tanks.	In lower and eastern Bengal.	Purneah ; eggs.
975	The little Grebe	Podiceps philippensis	A large mass of weeds.	In rushes or on low boughs in water.	Throughout India ...	Calcutta, 5th; Jhansi; eggs
984	The whiskered Tern	Hydrochelidon indicus	A slight platform.	On floating lily or lotus leaves.	In Kashmir and upper India.	Oudh, 7th; Kashmir, 26th; eggs.
991	The little black-naped "	Onochoprion melanauchen.	None	On the ground on rocky islands.	Andamans and Nicobars	Throughout the month.
1008	The Indian Snake bird	Plotus melanogaster ...	A rough platform.	On trees standing in water.	Throughout the plains	Etawah ; eggs.

MARSHALL. DEL.

NEST OF THE WHISTLING TEAL.

(Dendrocygna arcuata.)

AUGUST.

In this month the water-birds and small wren warblers are the principal breeders throughout the plains. The eggs of the rufous grass warbler, the white-eyed tit, the pin-tailed munia, the jungle bush quail, the bustard quail, and the little grebe may be taken.

In the Himalayas, the season is now nearly over. Eggs of the mosque swallow, the small minivet, the grey-winged blackbird, the red-headed and streaked laughing thrushes, the golden woodchat, the brown-breasted hill warbler, the red-billed hill tit, the yellow-billed blue jay, the chestnut-bellied and spotted munias, the meadow bunting, the Indian siskin, Hodgson's turtle dove, and the black partridge may still be found, though only a few stragglers are laying. Probably at the higher elevations many of the *finches* breed in this month, but their nests have not as yet been found.

In the Punjab, the black-winged kite is breeding, also the wire-tailed and mosque swallows; eggs of the sirkeer, the bay-backed shrike, the white-eyed bulbul, the striated reed babbler (second brood). The rufous-fronted wren warbler, the large button quail, the big bustard, Blythe's water hen, and most of the resident water-birds may still be taken. The *streaked wren warbler* is building for its second brood.

In the North-West Provinces, the wire-tailed and mosque swallows, the common swifts, the pied crested cuckoos, coucals, sirkeers rufous-backed and bay-backed shrikes, large grey cuckoo shrikes, white-browed fantails, babblers, reed babblers, wren warblers, mynahs, striated and common weaver birds, black-bellied finch larks, peafowl and almost all the resident water-birds, waders and swimmers, except the terns and plovers, have eggs throughout the month; while the *grass babbler*, *streaked wren warbler*, *black-throated weaver bird*, *painted snipe*, and *black-necked stork* commence building towards the end of the month.

In Bengal, the characteristic breeders are the yellow-bellied wren warbler, the tailor bird, the Bengal grass warbler, the chestnut-bellied munia, the peafowl, jacanas, rails and coots and bitterns, which almost all have eggs, besides,. many of those which breed at this season in other parts. The *grass babbler* and *black-throated weaver bird* begin to build in this month.

In CENTRAL INDIA, eggs of the cliff swallow, Nilgiri nightjar, purple honey sucker, blackcap shrike, pied cuckoo shrike, large grey cuckoo shrike, small minivet, white-browed fantail, ground thrush, rufous-bellied wren warbler, green bulbuls, ioras, the great and allied wren warblers, Sykes' warbler, the chestnut-bellied and spotted munias, the Indian amadavat, the crested bunting, the painted partridge, the lesser button quail, jacanas, coots, rails, king curlew, large whistling teal, and lesser cormorant may be taken during the month. The *likh florikin* and the *painted snipe* commence pairing and building towards the end of the month.

In SOUTHERN INDIA, the honey suckers have eggs, also the ashy wren warbler, the common wren warbler, the brahminy mynah, the spotted white-backed and pin-tailed munias, the Indian amadavat, the crown-crest lark, the rain quail, bush quail, and bustard quail: probably the eggs of many other species also may be found. The *white-browed bush bulbul* and the *Nilgiri skylark* are building towards the end of the month for their second brood.

AUGUST.

Nos. in Jerdon.	English Names.	Scientific Names.	Shape of Nest.	Site of Nest.	Geographical-Range in Breeding Season.	Particulars for the Month.
59	The black-winged Kite	Elanus melanopterus	A shallow compact cup.	In forks of trees.	Locally througbout the plains.	Sambhur, 14th ; eggs.
84	The wire-tailed Swallow	Hirundo ruficeps ...	A semi-circular saucer.	On bridges or rocks by water.	Ditto	Agra, 18th ; Hansi ; eggs
85	The great Indian mosque „	„ daurica ...	Tubular, retort-shaped.	In buildings or in caves.	The Himalayas ...	Season nearly over.
	The „ „	„ erythropygia	Ditto ...	Ditto ...	Throughout India proper.	Upper India ; eggs.
86	The Indian cliff „	„ fluvicola ...	Retort-shaped.	On buildings or on cliffs by water.	Central and northern India.	Jhansi ; eggs.
100	The common Indian Swift	Cypselus abyssinicus...	Semi-globular	Against buildings.	Throughout India ...	Saharunpur, 17th ; eggs.
108	The Nilgiri Nightjar	Caprimulgus kelaarti	None ...	On the ground often by a bush.	Southern to central India	Raipur (C. P.); eggs.
114	Franklin's „	„ monticolus	Ditto ...	Ditto ...	In all wooded hill ranges	Season ends.
212	The pied-crested Cuckoo	Coccystes melanoleucus	(Parasitic habits).	Eggs laid in babblers' nests.	Throughout India ...	Throughout the month.
217	The common Coucal	Centropus rufipennis	Large, rough, domed.	In long grass, thickets, or thorny trees.	Throughout India proper.	Aligurh, 29th, 30th ; eggs.
220	The Bengal Sirkeer	Taccocua sirkee ...	A rough shallow cup.	In low trees or thick bushes.	The plains of upper India.	Hansi ; eggs.
232	The amethyst-rumped Honey-sucker.	Leptocoma zeylanica...	Pear-shaped, side entrance	Hanging from tips of branches.	Bengal and peninsular India.	Salem ; eggs.
233	The tiny „ „	„ minima ...	Ditto ...	Ditto ...	The Nilgiris ...	Season begins.
234	The purple „ „	Arachnechthra asiatica	Ditto ...	Ditto ...	Throughout India ...	Central India ; eggs.
257	The rufous-backed Shrike	Lanius erythronotus...	A thick massive cup.	In forks of trees or thorny bushes.	Ditto ...	Agra, 21st ; eggs.
259	The black-cap „	„ nigriceps	Ditto ...	Ditto ...	Hills of eastern and central India.	Season ends.
260	The bay-backed „	„ vittatus ...	A neat cup	Ditto ...	Throughout India ...	Throughout the month.
268	The pied cuckoo „	Volvocivora sykesii ...	A small saucer.	In thin horizontal forks of trees.	Forests of south and central India.	Bundelkhund ; eggs.

Nos. in Jerdon	English Names.	Scientific Names.	Shape of Nest.	Site of Nest.	Geographical Range in Breeding Season.	Particulars for the Month.
270	The large grey cuckoo Shrike	Graucalus macei ...	A broad saucer.	At tops of lofty trees	Locally in India proper	Throughout the month.
276	The small Minivet	Pericrocotus peregrinus	A small deep cup.	In high trees near tips of boughs.	Throughout India proper.	Kashmir, 1st; Aligurh, 27th; eggs.
292	The white-browed Fantail	Leucocerca aureola ...	A tiny cup	On thin boughs in trees or bushes.	Throughout continental India.	Agra, 1st; Saugor; eggs.
345	The Indian ground Thrush	Pitta bengalensis ...	Large, globular, domed.	On or near the ground in brush wood.	Central Provinces and sub Himalayas.	Raipur (C. P.); eggs.
361	The grey-winged Blackbird	Merula boulboul ...	A broad cup	On stumps or thick boughs of trees.	The Himalayas.	Kumaon, 8th; eggs.
385	The yellow-eyed Babbler	Pyctorhis sinensis ...	A deep neat cup.	On stalks of herbs or low bushes.	Throughout India proper.	Throughout the month.
396	The red-capped wren ,,	Timalia pileata ...	Rough, globular, domed.	In thickets, bushes, or grass.	North-Eastern India.	Calcutta, 12th; eggs.
397	The rufous-bellied ,, ,,	Dumetia hyperythra...	Neat, globular, domed.	In the roots of bamboo clumps.	Central and upper India	Hoshungabad, 6th; eggs.
415	The red-headed laughing Thrush	Trochalopteron erythrocephalum.	A large deep cup.	In small trees or bushes.	The western Himalayas	Kumaon, 16th; eggs.
425	The streaked ,, ,,	,, lineatum.	Cup-shaped	In low bushes or mossy banks.	The Himalayas ...	Mussoorie, 16th; Simla, 16th; eggs.
436	The large grey Babbler	Malacocercus malcolmi	Ditto ...	In thorny trees or bushes.	Throughout the plains	Aligurh, 25th; eggs.
438	The striated bush ,,	Chattarhœa caudata ...	Ditto ...	In low bushes or clumps of grass.	Ditto	Throughout the month.
439	The striated reed ,,	,, earlii ...	Ditto ...	In reeds or clumps of grass.	Eastern continental India.	Second brood begins.
459	The white-eared Bulbul	Otocompsa leucotis ...	A neat cup	In dense thorny bushes.	Western continental India.	Hansi; eggs.
462	The common Madras ,,	Pycnonotus pusillus ...	A small slender cup.	In small trees or bushes.	Throughout the plains	Season ends.
463	Jerdon's green ,,	Phyllornis jerdoni ...	A small shallow cup.	In high trees near tips of boughs.	Central and southern India.	Raipur (C. P.); eggs.
467	The black and yellow ,,	Iora zeylanica ...	A tiny cup	In trees near tips of boughs.	Southern and central India.	Ditto.
470	The Indian golden Oriole	Oriolus kundoo ...	A neat deep cup.	In high trees hung in outer forks.	Throughout India ...	Season ends.

511	The golden Woodchat	Tarsiger chrysæus ...	A compact saucer.	In banks at roots of trees.	The eastern Himalayas	Nepal; eggs.
	The brown-breasted hill Warbler.	Dumeticola brunneipectus.	Oval, domed	Near the ground in beds of reeds.	The alpine „	Nepal, 2nd; eggs.
530	The Indian Tailor bird	Orthotomus longicauda	Deep cup sewn in leaves.	In bushes or creepers	Throughout India ...	Calcutta, 10th; eggs; season ends.
532	The yellow-bellied wren Warbler	Prinia flaviventris ...	Oval, often domed.	Attached to leaves in shrubs.	Eastern Bengal ...	Calcutta, 4th; eggs.
534	The ashy „ „	„ socialis ...	A cup sewn in leaves.	Hung in low bushes or herbs.	Southern India ...	Conoor; eggs.
535	Stewart's „ „	„ stewarti ...	Nearly globular.	Ditto ...	Upper India ...	Agra, 8th; Fatehgurh, 17th; eggs.
539	The rufous grass „	Cisticola schœnicola ...	A deep narrow purse.	In tufts of grass in dry jheels.	Throughout the plains	Throughout the month.
542	The Bengal „ „	Graminicola bengalensis.	A deep compact cup.	Among reeds in damp places.	Eastern Bengal ...	Dacca; eggs.
543	The common wren „	Drymoipus inornatus...	Deep, neat, often domed	Attached to leaves in shrubs.	Bombay coast ...	Bombay, 22nd, 28th; eggs.
	The earth brown „ „	„ terricolor ...	Ditto ...	In small bushes or long grass.	Western continental India.	Aligurh, 29th, 30th; eggs.
544	The long-tailed „ „	„ longicaudatus	Ditto ...	Ditto ...	Central and southern India.	(Requires confirmation.)
	Jerdon's „ „	„ jerdoni ...	Ditto ...	Ditto ...	The Nilgiris.	Throughout the month.
	The great rufous „ „	„ rufescens ...	Ditto ...	Low down in thorny bushes.	Continental India ...	Seetapur (Oudh); eggs.
	The great „ „	„ insignis ...	Ditto ...	Low down in thick bushes.	Central India ...	Seoni (C. P.); eggs.
546	The allied „ „	„ neglectus ...	Ditto ...	In forks of thorny bushes.	Ditto ...	Jhansi, 21st; eggs.
551	The rufous-fronted „ „	Franklinia buchanani	Deep, ragged, often domed	In bushes or low scrub.	Western continental India.	Hansi; eggs.
553	Sykes's „	Hyppolais rama ...	Ditto ...	Low down in thorny bushes.	Ditto ...	Jhansi, 12th; eggs.
614	The red-billed hill Tit	Leiothrix luteus ...	A substantial cup.	In forks of thick bushes.	The eastern Himalayas	Nepal, 12th; eggs.
631	The Indian white-eyed „	Zosterops palpebrosus	A tiny regular cup.	Hung from twigs in trees or bushes.	Throughout India ...	In the plains; eggs.
672	The yellow-billed blue Jay	Urocissa flavirostris ...	A loose shallow cup.	In forks of trees or saplings,	East and extreme west Himalayas.	Murree, 15th; eggs.
683	The pied Mynah	Sturnopastor contra ...	Large, globular, domed.	In trees at ends of boughs.	Continental India ...	Season nearly over.

Nos. in Jardon.	English Names.	Scientific Names.	Shape of Nest.	Site of Nest.	Geographical Range in Breeding Season.	Particulars for the Month.
684	The common Mynah	Acridotheres tristis ...	None ...	In holes in trees or buildings.	Throughout India ...	Aligurh, 7th; eggs.
687	The brahminy „	Temenuchus pagodarum	Ditto ...	In holes in decayed trees.	Throughout India proper	Shevaroy hills; eggs.
694	The common Weaver bird	Ploceus baya ...	A pendent retort.	Hung from tips of boughs of trees.	Ditto ...	Aligurh, 30th; Calcutta; eggs.
695	The striated „ „	„ manyar ...	Retort fixed to reeds.	Hung from reeds or grass by water.	Ditto (locally) ...	Etawah, 28th; eggs.
698	The chestnut-bellied Munia	Munia rubroniger ...	Large, oval, domed.	In bamboos, reeds, or grass.	Eastern continental India	Calcutta, 21st; Nepal and C. P.; eggs.
699	The spotted „	„ undulata ...	Ditto ...	Usually in thick thorny shrub.	In all moist wooded tracts.	Throughout the month.
701	The white-backed „	„ striata ...	Ditto ...	Ditto ...	Peninsular and eastern India.	Nilgiris; eggs.
703	The pin tailed „	„ malabarica ...	Ditto ...	Ditto (or eaves of houses)	Throughout India proper.	Throughout the month.
704	The Indian Amadavat	Estrelda amandava ...	Ditto ...	In thick bushes near water.	Ditto (locally) ...	Ditto.
713	The meadow Bunting	Emberiza cia ...	A shallow cup	On the ground by stone or tuft.	The western Himalayas	Simla, 4th; eggs.
724	The black and chestnut-crested Bunting.	Melophus melanicterus	A neat shallow cup.	In holes in banks or walls.	Western continental India.	Jhansi, 14th; Aboo; eggs.
750	The Indian Siskin	Chrysomitris spinoides	A neat massive cup.	On boughs often against the trunk.	The Himalayas only ...	Simla; eggs.
756	The red-winged bush Lark	Mirafra erythroptera	A shallow pad	On the ground by tufts of grass	Plains of continental India.	Season ends.
760	The black-bellied finch „	Pyrrhalauda grisea ...	A tiny shallow pad.	On the ground by clod or sprig.	Throughout the plains	Etawah, 21st; eggs.
765	The northern crown crest „	Spizalauda deva ...	A shallow saucer.	Ditto ...	Western continental India.	Throughout the month.
768	The Malabar crested „	Alauda malabarica ...	Ditto ...	Ditto ...	Southern India ...	Mysore, Nilgiris; eggs.
792	Hodgson's turtle Dove	Turtur pulchrata ...	A tiny platform.	On lower boughs of large trees.	The Himalayas only ...	Simla, eggs; season ends.
794	The brown „ „	„ cambaiensis ...	Ditto ...	In low trees or bushes.	Throughout the plains	Agra, 2nd; eggs.

796	The Indian ring Dove	Turtur risorius ...	A tiny platform.	In low trees or bushes	Throughout the plains	Throughout the month.
803	The Peacock	Pavo cristatus ...	A few dry leaves.	On the ground in brushwood.	Throughout India proper.	Upper India; eggs.
818	The black Partridge	Francolinus vulgaris ...	Ditto ...	On the ground in grass or crops.	In upper India (locally).	Kashmir, 5th; eggs.
819	The painted „	„ pictus ...	Ditto ...	Ditto ...	Central India ...	Throughout the month.
826	The jungle bush Quail	Perdicula cambaiensis	Ditto ...	On the ground in long grass.	Throughout India ...	Ditto.
830	The rain „	Coturnix coromandeliana	Ditto ...	On the ground in grass or crops.	Southern and central India.	Ditto.
832	The bustard „	Turnix taigoor ...	Ditto ...	On the ground in grass or scrub.	In all wooded tracts ...	Ditto.
834	The large button „	„ tanki ...	Ditto ...	On the ground in crops or grass.	Throughout India proper.	Sialkot, 26th; eggs.
835	The lesser „ „	„ dussumieri ...	Ditto ...	Ditto ...	Ditto ...	The Deccan, 17th; eggs.
836	The Indian Bustard	Eupodotis edwardsii	None ...	On the ground in scanty grass.	Western continental India.	Sirsa; eggs.
855	The red-wattled Plover	Lobivanellus goensis	Ditto ...	On the ground on raised spots	Throughout India ...	Season nearly over.
859	The stone „	Œdicnemus crepitans	Ditto ...	On the ground often under trees.	Ditto (locally) ...	Ditto.
863	The sarus Crane	Grus antigone ...	Large, truncated cone.	On islands among rushes in tanks.	Throughout the plains	Aligurh, 20th; eggs.
900	The bronze-winged Jacana	Metopidus indicus ...	A small pad of rushes.	Among lilys or rushes in water.	The moist parts of India	Bengal, Bundelkhund; eggs.
901	The pheasant-tailed „	Hydrophasianus sinensis	Ditto ...	Ditto ...	Throughout India ...	Aligurh, 3rd; Saugor; eggs.
902	The purple Coot	Porphyrio poliocephalus	A large mass of reeds.	In grass or wild rice in tanks.	Throughout the plains	Etawah, 23rd; Saugor; eggs.
903	The common „	Fulica atra ...	Ditto ...	Ditto ...	Throughout India ...	Etawah, Ahmednuggur, 21st; eggs.
904	The water Cock	Gallicrex cristatus ...	Ditto ...	On floating weeds or beds of rushes.	In moist parts of India.	Eastern Bengal; eggs.
905	The „ Hen	Gallinula chloropus ...	Ditto ...	In rushes or boughs overhanging water.	Throughout India ...	Etawah, 18th; eggs.
906	Blyth's „ „	„ burnesii ...	Ditto ...	Ditto ...	North-west India (rare)	Salt range; eggs.
907	The white-breasted „ „	Porzana phœnicura ...	A rough platform.	In bamboos, thickets, or reeds.	Throughout India (locally)	Saugor, 11th; Oudh; eggs.
908	The brown Rail	„ akool ...	A small platform.	In rushes or thickets on islands.	Central and upper India.	Jhansi, 7th; eggs.
910	Baillon's Crake	„ pygmœa ...	A massive cup	In rushes or rice in water.	Himalayas and upper India.	Etawah, 16th; eggs.

Nos. in Jerdon.	English Names.	Scientific Names.	Shape of Nest.	Site of Nest.	Geographical Range in Breeding Season.	Particulars of the Month.
911	The ruddy Rail	Porzana fusca ...	A massive cup	In rushes or rice in water.	In moist parts of India.	Eastern Bengal; eggs.
920	The white-necked Stork	Melanopelargus episcopus.	A loose platform.	Near tops of large trees.	Throughout India proper.	Aligurh, 15th, 30th; eggs.
922	The great Heron	Ardea sumatrana ...	Ditto ...	On high trees in swamps.	The eastern sub-Himalayas.	(Requires confirmation.)
923	The common "	" cinerea ...	Ditto ...	In large trees high up.	Throughout India (locally.)	Etawah, 1st; eggs.
924	The purple "	" purpurea ...	Ditto ...	In thick beds of reeds.	Throughout India proper.	Etawah, 23rd; eggs.
925	The white "	Herodias alba ...	Ditto ...	Near tops of trees	Throughout the plains	Season nearly over.
926	The little " "	" egrettoides...	Ditto ...	Ditto ...	Ditto ...	Aligurh, 18th; eggs.
927	The little Egret	" garzetta ...	Ditto ...	Ditto ...	Ditto ...	Aligurh, 29th; eggs.
929	The cattle "	Buphus coromandus...	Ditto ...	Ditto ...	Ditto ...	Season nearly over.
930	The little pond Heron	Ardeola grayi ...	Ditto ...	In forks of trees ..	Ditto ...	Ditto
931	The little green Bittern	Butorides javanicus ...	Ditto ...	In trees or thickets by water.	Locally throughout India.	Aligurh, 15th; eggs.
933	The chestnut "	Ardetta cinnamomea...	Ditto ...	In reeds or cane brakes in water.	Himalayas and continental India.	Calcutta, 6th; Etawah, 24th; eggs.
937	The night Heron	Nycticorax griseus ...	Ditto ...	In high trees (sometimes in reeds).	Throughout India ...	Etawah, 21st; eggs.
939	The Spoonbill	Platalea leucorodia ...	Ditto ...	On high trees near water.	Ditto ...	Etawah, 8th; eggs.
940	The shell Ibis	Anastomus oscitans ...	Ditto ...	Ditto ...	Ditto (locally) ...	Etawah, 28th; eggs.
941	The white "	Threskiornis melanocephalus.	Ditto ...	Ditto ...	Ditto ...	Etawah, 20th; eggs.
942	The king Curlew	Gerenticus papillosus	Ditto ...	High up in large trees.	Throughout the plains	Jhansi, 27th; eggs.
950	The black-backed Goose	Sarkidiornis melanotus	A few leaves	In holes in decayed trees.	Ditto ...	Etawah, 1st; eggs.
951	The cotton Teal	Nettapus coromandelianus.	Ditto ...	Ditto (or walls)	Ditto ...	Jhansi, Etawah, Budaon; eggs.
952	The whistling "	Dendrocygna arcuata	A loose platform.	In small trees by or in water.	Ditto ...	Season nearly over.
953	The large " "	" major ...	Some grass and twigs.	In holes in decayed trees.	In all moist districts...	Saugor, 15th; eggs.

959	The spotted-billed Duck	Anas poecilorhyncha ...	A shallow pad	In rushes or grass by water.	Throughout the plains	Etawah, 1st; Aligurh, 31st; eggs.
975	The little Grebe	Podiceps philippensis	A large mass of weeds.	In rushes or boughs over water.	Throughout India ...	Throughout the month.
984	The whiskered Tern	Hydrochelidon indicus	A slight platform.	On floating lily or lotus leaves.	Western Himalayas and upper India.	Etawah, 14th; eggs.
1006	The lesser Cormorant	Graculus fuscicollis ...	A rough platform.	On low trees in water.	Central and eastern India.	Jhansi; eggs.
1007	The little ,,	,, javanicus ...	Ditto ...	Ditto ...	Throughout India ...	Etawah, 28th; eggs.
1008	The Indian Snakebird	Plotus melanogaster ..	Ditto ...	Ditto ...	Throughout the plains	Etawah, 9th; eggs.

SEPTEMBER.

In this month the water-birds form the bulk of the breeders, and with them the season practically ends in upper India. Most of the wren warblers and the rufous grass warbler and pin-tailed munias too are breeding everywhere in the plains, and a few stragglers of other families and genera.

In the Himalayas, eggs of the streaked laughing thrush have been taken, but no others are recorded, and the season may be looked on as practically over.

In the Punjab, eggs of the common sandgrouse, the grey partridge, and probably also those of the likh florikin may be taken. The pelican ibis too begins to lay in the eastern part of the province.

In the North-West Provinces, eggs of the common coucal, the yellow-eyed babbler, the grass babbler, the common bulbul, all the wren warblers and weaver birds, the red-winged bush lark, common sandgrouse, the peafowl, painted snipe, black-necked and white-necked storks, purple herons, chestnut bitterns, spoonbills, king curlew and little grebes, and possibly of several other kinds may be found; but the breeding season is now perceptibly on the decline.

In Bengal, the amethyst-rumped honeysucker, the grass babblers, the black-throated weaver birds, chestnut-bellied munias, bustard, quail, and painted snipe have eggs, while the *grass owls* begin pairing towards the end of the month.

In Central India, the common bulbul, the allied wren warbler, the common sandgrouse, the painted partridge, the likh florikin, the painted snipe, the bronze-winged jacana, and the lesser cormorant are known to have eggs.

In South India, eggs of the tiny honeysucker, the white-browed bush bulbul, the ashy wren warbler, the common wren warbler, the pin-tailed munia, the Malabar-crested lark, the turtle and ring doves, the red-billed bush quail, the rain quail, the likh florikin have been taken, and probably many other kinds lay. Towards the end of the month the *white-headed babbler*, the *jungle babbler*, *Adams's wren warbler*, and the *grey jungle fowl* commence to pair and build.

MARSHALL, DEL.

BREEDING PLACE OF THE LITTLE CORMORANTS.

SEPTEMBER.

Nos. in Jerdon.	English Names.	Scientific Names.	Shape of Nest.	Site of Nest.	Geographical Range in Breeding Season.	Particulars of the Month.
84	The wire-tailed Swallow	Hirundo ruficeps ...	A semi-circular saucer.	On bridges or rocks by water.	Locally throughout India.	Season nearly over.
86	The Indian cliff „	„ fluvicola ...	Retort-shaped	On cliffs by water or buildings.	Central and northern India.	Season ends.
90	The dusky crag Martin	Cotyle concolor ...	Semi-circular cup.	Against buildings or rocks.	Locally throughout India.	Delhi; eggs.
217	The common Coucal	Centropus rufipennis	Large, rough, domed.	In clumps of grass or thorny thickets.	Throughout India proper.	Etawah, 5th; eggs.
232	The amethyst-rumped Honeysucker	Leptocoma zeylanica	Pear-shaped, side entrance.	Hanging from tips of branches.	In lower Bengal and peninsular India.	Calcutta, 25th; season ends.
233	The tiny „	„ minima...	Ditto ...	Ditto ...	The Nilgiris ...	Throughout the month.
260	The bay-backed Shrike	Lanius vittatus ...	A neat cup.	In forks of trees or thorny bushes.	Throughout India ...	Season ends.
385	The yellow-eyed Babbler	Pyctorhis sinensis ...	A deep neat cup.	On stalks of herbs or bushes.	Throughout India proper.	Agra, 25th; eggs.
425	The streaked laughing Thrush	Trochalopteron lineatum	Cup-shaped.	In low bushes or mossy banks.	The Himalayas only ...	Simla, 6th; eggs.
436	The large grey Babbler	Malacocercus malcomi	Ditto ...	In thorny trees or bushes.	Throughout the plains	Season nearly over.
438	The striated bush „	Chattarhœa caudata ...	Ditto ...	In low bushes or clumps of grass.	Ditto ...	Ditto.
439	The „ reed „	„ earlii ...	Ditto ...	In reeds or clumps of grass.	Locally in continental India.	Ditto.
441	The grass „	Chætornis striatus ...	(Unknown)	(Probably) in reeds or grass.	Eastern continental India.	Etawah, 13th; eggs (extracted).
452	The white-browed bush Bulbul	Ixos luteolus ...	A loose straggling cup.	In outer twigs of bushes.	Southern and eastern India.	Bombay, 14th; eggs.
462	The common Madras „	Pycnonotus pusillus ...	A small slender cup.	In small trees or bushes.	Throughout the plains	Aligurh, 1st, 8th; Madras; eggs.
534	The ashy wren Warbler	Prinia socialis ...	A cup sewn in leaves.	Hanging in bushes or creepers.	Southern India ...	Nilgiris, Conoor; eggs.
539	The rufous grass „	Cisticola schœnicola ...	A deep narrow purse.	In tufts of grass in dry jheels.	Throughout the plains	Throughout the month.

Nos. in Jerdon.	English Names.	Scientific Names.	Shape of Nest.	Site of Nest.	Geographical Range in Breeding Season.	Particulars for the Month.
543	The common wren Warbler	Drymoipus inornatus ...	Deep, neat, often domed.	Attached to leaves or twigs of shrubs.	The Bombay presidency	Bombay; eggs.
	The earth brown „ „	„ terricolor ...	Ditto ...	In small bushes or long grass.	Western continental India.	Aligurh, 4th; eggs.
544	The long-tailed „ ,	, longicaudatus	Ditto ...	Ditto ...	Central and southern India.	(Requires confirmation).
546	The allied „ „	„ neglectus ...	Ditto ...	Low down in thorny bushes	Central India ...	Jhansi, 1st; eggs.
550	The streaked „ „	Burnesia lepida ...	Large, globular, domed.	In clumps of grass near rivers.	Northern India ...	Fatehgurh, Delhi; eggs.
551	The rufous-fronted „ „	Franklinia buchanani	Deep, ragged, often domed.	In bushes or low scrub jungle.	Western continental India.	Hansi, Delhi; eggs.
631	The Indian white-eyed Tit	Zosterops palpebrosus	A tiny regular cup.	Hung from twigs in trees or bushes.	Throughout India ...	The plains; season ends.
694	The common Weaver bird	Ploceus baya ...	A pendent retort.	Hung from tips of boughs in trees.	Throughout India proper.	Aligurh, 1st; eggs.
695	The striated „ „	„ manyar ...	Retort fixed to reeds.	Hung from reeds or grass by water.	Ditto (locally)	Etawah, Aligurh, 4th; eggs
696	The black-throated „ „	„ bengalensis ...	Retort with no tube.	In low bushes in grass jungle.	Eastern continental India.	Etawah, 15th; Calcutta; eggs.
698	The chestnut-bellied Munia	Munia rubroniger ...	Large, oval, domed.	In bamboos, reeds, or grass.	Ditto ...	Calcutta, 28th; eggs.
703	The pin-tailed „	„ malabarica ...	Ditto ...	In thick bushes or eaves of houses.	Throughout India proper.	Throughout the month.
756	The red-winged bush Lark	Mirafra erythroptera ..	A shallow pad	On the ground by tufts of grass.	Plains of continental India.	Aligurh, 4th, 5th; eggs.
768	The Malabar-crested „	Alauda malabarica ...	Ditto ...	On the ground by clod or tuft.	Southern India ...	Nilgiris; season ends.
794	The brown turtle Dove	Turtur cambaiensis ...	A tiny platform.	In low trees or bushes.	Throughout the plains	Aligurh, 31st; eggs.
796	The Indian ring „	„ risorius ...	Ditto ...	Ditto ...	Ditto ...	Aligurh, 3rd, 16th; eggs.
802	The common Sandgrouse	Pterocles exustus ...	None ...	On the bare ground	Western continental India.	Through the month.
803	The Peacock	Pavo cristatus ...	A few dry leaves.	On the ground in brushwood.	Throughout India ...	Aligurh, 5th; Agra; eggs.

819	The painted Partridge	Francolinus pictus ...	A few dry leaves.	On the ground in grass or crops.	Central India ...	Jhansi, the Berars; eggs.
822	The grey „	Ortygornis ponticeriana	Ditto ...	On the ground in grass or bushes.	Plains of India proper	The Punjab; eggs.
826	The jungle bush Quail	Perdicula cambaiensis	Ditto ...	On the ground in long grass.	Locally throughout India.	(Requires confirmation.)
828	The red-billed „ „	„ erythrorhyncha	Ditto ...	On the ground under shelter.	The Nilgiris ...	Kotagiri; eggs.
830	The rain „	Coturnix coromandeliana	Ditto ...	On the ground in crops or grass.	Southern and central India.	Throughout the month.
832	The bustard „	Turnix taigoor ...	Ditto ...	On the ground in grass or scrub.	In all wooded tracts ...	Calcutta, 25th; eggs.
839	The likh Florikin	Sypheotides auritus ...	None ...	On the ground by clumps of grass.	Western peninsular India.	Sholapur, 15th; eggs.
873	The painted Snipe	Rhynchœa bengalensis	A large pad	On the ground in rushes or rice.	In all moist tracts ...	Throughout the month.
900	The bronze-winged Jacana	Metopidus indicus ...	A small pad of rushes.	Floating among rushes or weeds	Ditto ...	Central provinces; eggs.
917	The black-necked Stork	Mycteria australis ...	A large platform.	At tops of large trees.	Throughout the plains	Aligurh, 11th; eggs.
920	The white-necked „	Melanopelargus episcopus.	A loose platform.	Ditto ...	Throughout India proper.	Aligurh, 2nd; eggs.
924	The purple Heron	Ardea purpurea ...	Ditto ...	In thick beds of reeds.	Ditto ...	Etawah, 9th; eggs.
927	The little Egret	Herodias garzetta ...	Ditto ...	Near tops of trees	Throughout the plains	Season ends.
933	The chestnut Bittern	Ardetta cinnamomea...	Ditto ...	In reeds or thickets in water.	Himalayas and continental India.	Etawah, 4th; eggs.
938	The pelican Ibis	Tantalus leucocephalus	Ditto ...	On high trees near water.	Throughout India (very local).	Muttra, 20th; eggs.
939	The Spoonbill	Platalea leucorodia ...	Ditto ...	Ditto ...	Throughout India proper.	Aligurh, 3rd; eggs.
941	The king Curlew	Geronticus papillosus	Ditto ...	High up in large trees.	Throughout the plains	Aligurh, 17th; eggs.
950	The black-backed Goose	Sarkidiornis melanotus	A few leaves	In holes in decayed trees.	Ditto ...	Season ends.
959	The spotted-billed Duck	Anas pœcilorhynchus...	A shallow pad	In sedge or grass by water.	Ditto ...	Season nearly over.
975	The little Grebe	Podiceps philippensis	A large mass of weeds.	In rushes or boughs over water.	Throughout India ...	Cawnpur; eggs.
1006	The lesser Cormorant	Graculus fuscicollis ...	A rough platform.	On low trees in or by water.	Central and eastern India.	Jhansi; eggs
1007	The little „	„ javanicus ...	Ditto ...	Ditto ...	Throughout India ...	Season nearly over.

OCTOBER.

The breeding season of the water-birds is now over, except in the range of the north-east monsoon where it has not begun. The large birds of prey have not commenced to lay to any extent, and only a few stragglers of various families breed during this month. The eggs of the river tern have once been found in large numbers in this month, but this is probably a most unusual circumstance.

In the HIMALAYAS, as far as is known, not a single species lays in this month. There is no record of an egg of any kind having been taken.

In the PUNJAB, eggs of the rufous grass warbler, the streaked wren warbler, the pin-tailed munia, the common sandgrouse, the grey partridge, the black-necked stork, and the pelican ibis have been taken. The likh florikin certainly breeds there in this month, but further particulars are required. Towards the end of the month the *long-billed vulture* and the *striated bunting* begin to pair and build.

In the NORTH-WEST PROVINCES, eggs of the white-backed vulture, the ring-tailed fishing eagle, the large grey babbler, the streaked wren warbler, the pin-tailed munia, the common sandgrouse, and the pea fowl may be taken. Some of the *Indian hoopoes* too begin to pair and build.

In BENGAL, the grass owl is known to lay. Also the ring and turtle doves, black-necked storks, and some other species; and the *common kites*, the *common sand martins*, and the *adjutants* begin to build.

In CENTRAL INDIA, eggs of the rain quail and likh florikin have been taken; and by the end of the month the *painted sandgrouse* begin to pair.

In SOUTH INDIA, eggs of the white-headed and jungle babblers, Adams's wren warbler, the common wren warbler, the black-headed munia, the Malabar-crested lark, the turtle doves, the grey jungle fowl, the red-billed bush quail, the rain quail, the likh florikin, and the black-necked stork have been taken. The *king curlew* builds towards the end of the month.

MARSHALL, DEL.

NEST OF THE YELLOW-BELLIED FANTAIL.

(Chelidorhynx hypoxantha.)

OCTOBER.

Nos. in Jerdon.	English Names.	Scientific Names.	Shape of Nest.	Site of Nest.	Geographical Range in Breeding Season.	Particulars for the Month.
5	The white-backed Vulture	Gyps bengalensis ...	A large platform.	Near tops of large trees.	Throughout continental India.	Fatehgurh, 15th; eggs.
42	The ring-tailed fishing Eagle	Haliaetus leucoryphus	Ditto ...	On high trees near water.	Throughout northern India.	Aligurh, 29th; eggs.
61	The grass Owl	Scelostrix caudida ...	None ...	On the ground in long grass.	Northern Bengal ...	Tirhoot, 26th, 27th; eggs.
90	The dusky crag Martin	Cotyle concolor ...	Semi-circular cup.	On buildings or in caves.	Throughout India locally.	Delhi; eggs,
232	The amethyst-rumped Honeysucker	Leptocoma zeylanica ...	Pear-shaped, side entrance	Hanging from tips of branches.	Lower Bengal and peninsular India.	Season nearly over.
233	The tiny „	„ minima ...	Ditto ...	Ditto ...	The Nilgiris ...	Season ends.
260	The bay-backed Shrike	Lanius vittatus ...	A neat cup	In forks of trees or bushes.	Throughout India ...	Ditto.
433	The white-headed Babbler	Malacocercus griseus ...	A loose straggling cup.	In low trees or thorny hedges.	The plains of south India.	Madras, Mysore; eggs.
434	The jungle „	„ malabaricus	Ditto ...	Ditto ...	The hills of south India	The Nilgiris; eggs.
436	The large grey „	„ malcolmi	Cup-shaped	In thorny trees or bushes.	Throughout the plains	Muttra; eggs.
438	The striated bush „	Chattarhœa caudata...	Ditto ...	In low bushes or clumps of grass.	Ditto ...	Season nearly over.
533	Adams's wren Warbler	Prinia adamsi ...	Oval, often domed.	Suspended from leaves of cereals.	Peninsular India. ...	Ahmednugger; eggs.
539	The rufous grass „	Cisticola schœnicola ...	A deep narrow purse.	In tufts of grass in beds of jheels.	Throughout the plains	Delhi; eggs; season ends.
543	The common wren „	Drymoipus inornatus...	Deep, neat, often domed	Attached to twigs or leaves in shrubs.	The Bombay presidency	Bombay, 13th; eggs.
550	The striated „ „	Burnesia lepida ...	Large, globular, domed	In clumps of grass near rivers.	Northern India ...	Delhi, Fatehgurh; eggs.
551	The rufous-fronted „ „	Franklinia buchanani	Deep, ragged, often domed	In bushes or low scrub jungle.	Western continental India.	Delhi; eggs.

Nos. in Jerdon.	English Names.	Scientific Names.	Shape of Nest.	Site of Nest.	Geographical Range in Breeding Season.	Particulars for the Month.
697	The black-headed Munia	Munia malacca ...	Large, oval, domed.	In sugar-cane or reeds in water.	Southern and central India.	Coimbatore; eggs.
703	The pin-tailed „	„ malabarica ...	Ditto ...	In thick bushes or eaves of houses.	Throughout India proper.	Oudh, Punjab; eggs,
768	The Malabar-crested Lark	Alauda malabarica ...	A shallow saucer.	On the ground by clod or tuft.	Southern India ...	(Requires confirmation).
794	The brown turtle Dove	Turtur cambaiensis ...	A tiny platform.	In low trees or in bushes.	Throughout the plains	A few stagglers breed.
802	The common Sandgrouse	Pterocles exustus ...	None ...	On the bare ground	Western continental India.	Sirsa, 3rd, 22nd; Etawah, 19th; eggs.
803	The Peacock	Pavo cristatus ...	A few dry leaves.	On the ground in brushwood.	Throughout India ...	Agra, 14th; eggs.
813	The grey jungle Fowl	Gallus sonneratii ...	Ditto ...	On the ground in dense thickets.	Central and southern India.	Nadivatam; eggs.
822	The grey Partridge	Ortygornis ponticeriana	Ditto ...	On the ground in bushes or grass.	Plains of India proper	The Punjab; eggs.
826	The jungle bush Quail	Perdicula cambaiensis	Ditto ...	On the ground in long grass.	Throughout India locally.	(Requires confirmation).
828	The red-billed „ „	„ erythrorhyncha	Ditto ...	On the ground under shelter.	The Nilgiris ...	Kotagiri; eggs.
830	The rain „	Coturnix coromandeliana	Ditto ...	On the ground in crops or grass.	Southern and central India.	Sholapur; season ends.
839	The likh Florikin	Sypheotides auritus ...	None ...	On the ground between tufts of grass.	Western peninsular India.	Sholapur, 5th, 27th; eggs.
917	The black-necked Stork	Mycteria australis ...	A large platform.	At tops of large trees.	Throughout the plains	Throughout the month.
938	The pelican Ibis	Tantalus leucocephalus	A loose platform.	On large trees ...	Throughout India (very local)	Muttra, 20th; eggs.

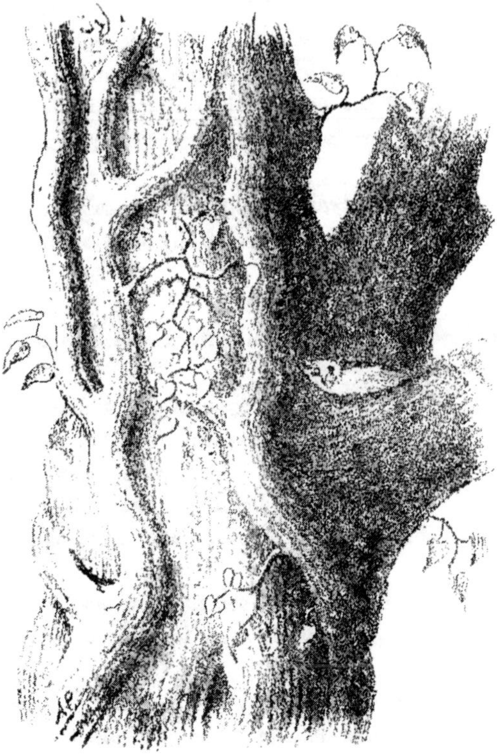

MARSHALL, DEL.

NEST OF THE BROWN FISH OWL.

(Ketupa ceylonensis)

NOVEMBER.

In this month the breeding season is at its lowest ebb. The larger birds of prey are commencing to pair and build, but few of them lay so early. The breeding of the water-birds is almost completely over, and it is only here and there that in particular localities some few species may be found breeding.

In the Himalayas, the *bearded vulture*, and possibly also the *roc vulture*, commence to build, but no eggs of any species have been recorded as taken.

In the Punjab, the striated bunting, the common sandgrouse, and the grey partridge have eggs, while the *raven* begins to build at the latter end of the month.

In the North-West Provinces, eggs of the white-backed vulture, the ring-tailed fishing eagle, the rock-horned owl, the pin-tailed munia, and the black-necked stork may be found, while *Bonelli's eagle* and the *dusky-horned owl* are pairing and building; the latter is, more strictly speaking, selecting than building, for it usually occupies an old kite's or eagle's nest.

In Bengal, eggs of the grass owl, the common sand martin, and the adjutant, may be found, and possibly some few others, but only these are recorded.

In Central India, the Indian tawny eagle, the black-winged kite, the Indian screech owl, the mottled wood owl, and the painted sandgrouse are all laying. The *green amadavat* and *Sykes' turtle dove* are pairing and building.

In Southern India, eggs of the amethyst-rumped honeysucker, the jungle babbler, the Indian amadavat, the grey jungle fowl, and the king curlew have been taken; and by the end of the month the *golden-backed woodpecker*, the *white-necked stork*, and all kinds of *egrets* have begun to pair and build.

NOVEMBER.

Nos. in Jerdon.	English Names.	Scientific Names.	Shape of Nest.	Site of Nest.	Geographical Range in Breeding Season.	Particulars for the Month.
	The long-billed Vulture	Gyps indicus ...	A large platform.	At tops of high trees.	Plains of north India	Delhi, 20th; eggs.
5	The white-backed "	" bengalensis ...	Ditto ...	Ditto ...	Throughout continental India.	Bijnor, 1st, 31st; Meerut; eggs.
7	The bearded "	Gypaetus barbatus ...	Ditto ...	On ledges of cliffs	Himalayas and Suleiman ranges.	Season commences.
29	The Indian tawny Eagle	Aquila vindhyana ...	Ditto ...	In high trees ...	Western continental India.	Bundelkhund; season begins.
42	The ring-tailed fishing "	Haliaetus leucoryphus	Ditto ...	Ditto (near water)	Throughout northern India.	Saharunpur, 11th; eggs.
56	The common Kite	Milvus govinda ...	Irregular platform.	In forks of trees ...	Throughout India ...	Calcutta; season begins.
59	The black-winged "	Elanus melanopterus	A shallow compact cup.	Ditto ...	In wooded parts of India proper.	Central Provinces; eggs.
60	The Indian screech Owl	Strix indica ...	None ...	In holes in trees or buildings.	Throughout the plains	Raipur (C. P.), 25th; eggs.
61	The grass "	Scelostrix caudida ...	Ditto ...	On the ground in long grass.	Northern Bengal ...	Tirhoot; eggs.
65	The mottled wood "	Bulacca sinensis ...	Ditto ...	In holes or hollows in large trees.	Throughout the plains	Raipur (C. P.); eggs.
69	The rock-horned "	Ascalaphia bengalensis	Ditto ...	On ledges of banks.	Throughout India proper.	Meerut, 10th; eggs.
72	The brown fish "	Ketupa ceylonensis ...	Ditto ...	In clefts in rocks or old trees.	Throughout India ...	Calcutta; season begins.
89	The Indian sand Martin	Cotyle sinensis ...	A loose cup	In deep holes in banks of rivers.	Ditto (rare in south)	Calcutta; eggs.
232	The amethyst-rumped Honeysucker	Leptocoma zeylanica	Pear-shapped, side entrance.	Hanging from tips of branches.	Lower Bengal and peninsular India.	Madras; eggs.
434	The jungle Babbler	Malacocercus malabaricus.	A loose straggling cup.	In low trees or thick thorny bushes.	The hills of south India	Nilgiris; eggs.
436	The large grey "	" malcolmi	Cup-shaped	In thorny trees or bushes.	Throughout the plains	A few stragglers breed.

703	The pin-tailed Munia	Munia malabarica ...	Large, oval, domed.	In thick bushes or eaves of houses.	Throughout India proper.	Oudh, 5th ; eggs.
704	The Indian Amadavat	Estrelda amandava ...	Ditto ...	In thick bushes by water.	Throughout India (locally.)	The Nilgiris ; eggs.
	The striolated Bunting	Emberiza striolata ...	A thick cup.	On the ground under a stone.	Western continental India.	Ajmir, 12th ; eggs.
800	The painted Sandgrouse	Pterocles fasciatus ...	None ...	On the ground by bush or tuft.	Rocky parts of central India.	Chanda (C. P.), 28th ; eggs.
802	The common "	" exustus ...	Ditto ...	On the ground unsheltered.	Western continental India.	Sirsa, 24th ; eggs.
813	The grey jungle Fowl	Gallus sonneratii ...	A few dry leaves.	On the ground in dense thickets.	Central and southern India.	The Nilgiris ; eggs.
822	The grey Partridge	Ortygornis ponticeriana	Ditto ...	On the ground in bush or grass.	Open plains of India proper.	The Salt range ; eggs.
826	The jungle bush Quail	Perdicula cambaiensis	Ditto ...	On the ground in long grass.	Locally throughout India.	(Requires confirmation.)
915	The Adjutant	Leptoptilus argala ...	A large platform.	At tops of large trees.	The Sunderbuns and Gorakpur.	Throughout the month.
917	The black-necked Stork	Mycteria australis ...	Ditto ...	Ditto ...	Throughout the plains	Season nearly over.
938	The pelican Ibis	Tantalus leucocephalus	A loose platform.	In forks of high trees.	Throughout India (very local.)	Ditto.
942	The king Curlew	Geronticus papillosus	Ditto ...	High up in large trees.	Throughout the plains	Sholapur, 5th, 20th ; eggs.

DECEMBER.

By this time in Upper India the season for eggs of the large birds of prey has fairly commenced. In the extreme south and east coast, the water-birds that are monsoon breeders, such as egrets, pond herons, curlews, &c., are all breeding; and everywhere throughout the plains, the eggs of the ring-tailed fishing eagle and of the ring dove may be taken.

In the Himalayas, eggs of the bearded vulture have been taken; while the *roc vultures, black eagles, Nepal hawk eagles,* and *Himalayan fishing eagles* are all building.

In the Punjab, the pale long-billed vulture, the white-backed vulture, the ring-tailed fishing eagle, the striated bush babbler, the raven, and the common sandgrouse all have eggs.

In the North-West Provinces, the white-backed vulture, Bonelli's eagle, the ring-tailed fishing eagle and rock-horned owl, the dusky-horned owl, the brown fish owl, the hoopoe, the pin-tailed munia, and the black-necked stork have all got eggs. The *pale long-billed vulture*, the *dusky sand martin*, and the *turtle doves* are building.

In Bengal, the ring-tailed fishing eagle and white-bellied sea eagle, the common kite, the brown fish owl, the Indian sand martin, and the ring doves have all got eggs.

In Central India, eggs of the pale long-billed vulture, the Indian tawny eagle, the ring-tailed fishing eagle, the black-winged kite, the screech owl, the mottled wood owl, the Indian amadavat, the green amadavat, and Sykes's turtle dove have all been taken; and among the birds that commence pairing and building in this month may be mentioned the *shaheen falcon*, the *bar-tailed fishing eagle* (possibly, but this requires confirmation), the *dusky crag martin*, the *white-backed munia*, and the *ruddy turtle dove*.

In Southern India, eggs of the white-bellied sea eagle, the common kite, the southern golden-backed woodpecker, the amethyst-rumped honeysucker, the jungle babbler, the Indian pied wagtail, the Indian amadavat, the black-bellied finch lark, the ring dove, the grey jungle fowl, the white-necked stork, the egrets, pond herons, king curlews, and all of the resident water-birds may be taken; and watch should be kept on the *white scavenger vultures, shaheen falcons, bar-tailed fishing eagles, purple honeysuckers, Nilgiri flowerpeckers, red-billed bush quail,* and *Indian snake birds,* which are known to commence building in the course of the month.

MARSHALL, DEL.

NEST OF THE PURPLE HONEY SUCKER.

(Arachnechthra asiatica.)

Nos. in Jerdon.	English Names.	Scientific Names.	Shape of Nest.	Site of Nest.	Geographical Range in Breeding Season.	Particulars for the Month.
3	The roc Vulture	Gyps himalayensis ...	A large platform.	On ledges of cliffs	The Himalayas only ...	Season commences.
4	The pale long-billed „	„ pallescens ...	Ditto ...	Ditto ...	Western and central India.	Ditto.
	The „ „ „	„ indicus ...	Ditto ...	At tops of high trees.	Plains of north India	Delhi; eggs.
5	The white-backed „	„ bengalensis ...	Ditto ...	Ditto ...	Throughout continental India.	Muttra, 6th; eggs.
7	The bearded „	Gypaetus barbatus ...	Ditto ...	On ledges of cliffs	Himalayas and Suleiman range.	Kangra, 25th; eggs.
29	The Indian tawny Eagle	Aquila vindhyana ...	Ditto ...	In high trees ...	Western continental India.	Bundelkhund, 13th; eggs.
33	Bonelli's „	Nisaetus bonellii ...	Ditto ...	On cliffs or high trees.	Throughout India ...	Etawah, 25th; eggs.
42	The ring-tailed fishing „	Haliaetus leucoryphus	Ditto ...	On high trees near water.	Throughout northern India.	Throughout the month.
43	The white-bellied sea „	„ leucogaster	Ditto ...	On high trees near the coast.	All round the coast ...	Season begins.
56	The common Kite	Milvus govinda ...	Irregular platform.	In forks of trees ...	Throughout India ...	Calcutta, Madras, Nilgiris; eggs.
59	The black-winged „	Elanus melanopterus...	A shallow compact cup.	Ditto ...	The wooded parts of India proper.	Sumbhulpur, 20th; eggs.
60	The Indian screech Owl	Strix indica ...	None ...	In holes in trees or buildings.	Throughout the plains	Raipur (C. P.), 4th; eggs.
65	The mottled wood „	Bulacca sinensis ...	Ditto ...	In holes or hollows in large trees.	Ditto ...	Raipur (C. P.), 5th; eggs.
69	The rock-horned „	Ascalaphia bengalensis	Ditto ...	On ledges of banks	Throughout India ...	Meerut, 15th; eggs.
70	The dusky-horned „	„ coromanda	Ditto ...	In forks of large trees.	Throughout the plains	Muttra, 5th; eggs.
72	The brown fish „	Ketupa ceylonensis ...	Ditto ...	In clefts of rocks or large trees.	Throughout India ...	Etawah, 25th; eggs.
89	The Indian sand Martin	Cotyle sinensis ...	A loose cup	In deep holes in river banks.	Ditto (rare in south)	Calcutta; eggs.

Nos. in Jerdon.	English Names.	Scientific Names.	Shape of Nest.	Site of Nest.	Geographical Range in Breeding Season.	Particulars for the Month.
167	The southern gold-backed Woodpecker.	Chrysocolaptes delesserti.	None ...	In artificial holes in trees.	The hills of south India.	Season begins.
232	The amethyst-rumped Honeysucker.	Leptocoma zeylanica...	Pear-shaped, side entrance.	Hanging from tips of branches.	Lower Bengal and peninsular India.	Madras; eggs.
255	The Indian Hoopoe	Upupa nigripensis ..	None ...	In holes in trees or buildings.	Throughout India ...	Allahabad, 29th; eggs.
434	The jungle Babbler	Malacocercus malabaricus.	A loose straggling cup.	In small trees or thorny hedges.	The hills of south India.	The Nilgiris; eggs.
438	The striated bush "	Chattarhœa caudata ...	Cup-shaped	In low bushes or clumps of grass.	Throughout the plains	Hansi; eggs.
589	The Indian pied Wagtail	Motacilla maderaspatana	A shallow pad	On the ground or buildings by water.	Ditto ...	Madras, 26th; eggs.
657	The Raven	Corvus corax ...	A large compact cup.	In forks of solitary trees.	Western continental India.	Hansi, 19th; eggs.
703	The pin-tailed Munia	Munia malabarica ...	Large, oval, domed.	In thick bushes or eaves of houses.	Throughout India proper.	Mirzapur, Oudh; eggs.
704	The Indian Amadavat	Estrelda amandava ...	Ditto ...	In thick bushes near water.	Ditto (locally)	Raipur, 8th; Kotagiri; eggs.
705	The green "	" formosa ...	Ditto ...	On stalks of sugar-cane.	Central India ...	Saugor; eggs.
760	The black-bellied finch Lark	Pyrrhalauda grisea ...	A tiny shallow pad	On the ground by clod or tuft.	Throughout the plains	Poona, 24th; eggs.
793	Sykes's turtle Dove	Turtur meena ...	A tiny platform.	In low trees in thick foliage.	Peninsular and eastern India.	Raipur; eggs.
796	The Indian ring "	" risorius ...	Ditto ...	In low trees or bushes.	Throughout the plains	Etawah; eggs.
802	The common Sandgrouse	Pterocles exustus ...	None ...	On the bare ground	Western continental India.	Sirsa, 7th, 20th; eggs.
813	The grey jungle Fowl	Gallus sonneratii ...	A few dry leaves.	On the ground in dense thickets.	Central and south India.	The Nilgiris; eggs.
826	The jungle bush Quail	Perdicula cambaiensis	Ditto ...	On the ground in long grsas.	Locally throughout India.	(Requires confirmation).
917	The black-necked Stork	Mycteria australis ...	A large platform.	At tops of large trees.	Throughout the plains	Mynpoorie, 27th; eggs.

920	The white-necked Stork	Melanopelargus episcopus.	A loose platform.	Near tops of large trees.	Throughout India proper.	Sholapur, 18th ; eggs.
925	The white Heron	Herodias alba ...	Ditto ...	In forks of trees by water.	Throughout the plains	South India only.
926	The little white "	" egrettoides ...	Ditto ...	Ditto ...	Ditto ...	Ditto.
927	The little Egret	" garzetta ...	Ditto ...	Ditto ...	Ditto ...	Ditto.
929	The cattle "	Buphus coromandus ...	Ditto ...	Ditto ...	Ditto ...	Ditto.
930	The little pond Heron	Ardeola grayi ...	Ditto ...	Ditto ...	Ditto ...	Ditto.
942	The king Curlew	Gerontious papillosus	Ditto ...	High up on large trees.	Ditto ...	Sholapur, 1st, 9th ; eggs.

ABSTRACT

SHOWING NUMBER OF SPECIES KNOWN TO BUILD IN EACH MONTH.

		All kinds of Birds.	Raptores.			Gemitores	Rasores.	
			Diurnal.	Nocturnal.	Total.	Doves and Pigeons.	Game Birds.	Total.
1	January	56	22	6	28	5	2	7
2	February	89	24	7	31	7	4	11
3	March	186	22	10	32	8	13	21
4	April	299	24	11	35	12	15	27
5	May	394	19	9	28	13	22	35
6	June	316	12	2	14	15	13	28
7	July	193	1	...	1	5	12	17
8	August	124	1	...	1	3	9	12
9	September ...	55	...	...	...	2	8	10
10	October	30	2	1	3	1	8	9
11	November ...	28	5	4	9	...	5	5
12	December	41	10	5	15	2	3	5